The FOX and the HOUND

The BIRTH of AMERICAN SPYING

DONALD E. MARKLE

FALL RIVER PRESS

New York

This book is dedicated to
a very special person—
my wife, Geraldine.
Without her help and support,
this book would never have happened.

FALL RIVER PRESS

New York

An Imprint of Sterling Publishing
1166 Avenue of the Americas
New York, NY 10036

Jacket design by David Ter-Avanesyan
Book design by Philip Buchanan

ISBN 978-1-4351-5903-7

For information about custom editions, special sales, and premium and
corporate purchases, please contact Sterling Special Sales at 800-805-5489
or specialsales@sterlingpublishing.com.

Manufactured in the United States of America

2 4 6 8 10 9 7 5 3 1

www.sterlingpublishing.com

CONTENTS

A Person of Interest in the New England Department
Dr. Benjamin Church Jr.

Contents

A Person of Interest in the Middle Department
Sergeant Daniel Bissell
✦ 73 ✦

A Person of Interest in the New York Department
Christopher Ludwick, Washington's Baker
✦ 88 ✦

A Person of Interest in the Canadian Department
Sarah Kast McGinnis
✦ 102 ✦

A Person of Interest in the Southern Department
James Armistead (Lafayette)—Slave and Spy
✦ 139 ✦

Contents

Contents

A Person of Interest in American Technology
An Unknown Innkeeper
✦ 229 ✦

A Person of Interest in Codes and Ciphers
James Lovell
✦ 245 ✦

ACKNOWLEDGMENTS

This book is a labor of love—the love of a wife who kept me going during some tough times for a writer. About the time I decided to undertake the project, my eyes fell prey to advanced macular degeneration—the last thing a researcher wants to have happen. But with five different lighting systems in the room and three sets of glasses, each for a special purpose, the work continued. Then five years ago I was diagnosed with Follicular Lymphoma cancer that has required three years of chemotherapy, but again with the support of my wife, the work continued.

Secondly, I want to acknowledge the support of my publisher Hippocrene Books, Inc. They have been very patient in waiting for the finished manuscript, and I do thank them for that. In particular Priti Chitnis Gress, the Chief Editor, was a tremendous support throughout the entire project. She made it work.

In addition, there are many organizations that responded to my queries and requests, including The Library of Congress, The National Archives, The New York City Public Library (Map Division), The National Cryptologic Museum, and various local historical societies. All assisted in filling in the gaps along the way.

I would be greatly remiss if I did not mention three individuals whose help and expertise were of great value as the project progressed. First, Mr. Marc Bennett, a graduate of Georgetown University, with a lifetime fascination with the Revolutionary War, who kept me on the straight and narrow. He was a fact checker extraordinaire. Unfortunately, he died of cancer shortly before the publication of this book. The second individual, Mr. Arthur Thimsen, is a superb researcher who readily accepted any challenge I threw at him and always came up with the answer. His outstanding work included the creation of the net diagrams and the excellent research regarding Sgt. Champe. And last but not least, my son Kevin, my computer guru who kept me from loading a shotgun to shoot my computer that seemed to have a mind of its own.

And finally, editors can be helpful or a challenge and I was blessed that my specific editors, Carolyn McBroom and Barbara Keane-Pigeon, are editors extraordinaire for both grammar and content.

Without these individuals this project would not have been completed.

The necessity of procuring good intelligence is apparent & need not be further urged—All that remains for me to add is, that you keep the whole matter as secret as possible. For upon Secrecy, success depends in most Enterprises of the kind, and for want of it, they are generally defeated, however well planned & promising a favorable issue.

—George Washington
July 26, 1777

INTRODUCTION

George Washington's reputation as a world class spymaster is well earned—he was a master of the art. When looking at the Revolutionary War and its geographic spread, however, a question arises. How did George Washington manage the intelligence operations over such a large geographic area? The surprising answer is that he didn't!

When studying the intelligence or spying activities of the American Revolutionary War, modern historians tend to focus solely on General George Washington. There is no doubt that Washington was an extraordinary spymaster and that the networks he established in the New York and Boston areas did excellent work—with the Culper Ring for the New York City area, and the Paul Revere Group in the Boston area. But as the war progressed, and the areas of military action spread over a significant land mass, he could not possibly manage the entire network.

When George Washington was named commander-in-chief of the Continental Army, a structured government did not exist in the Colonies beyond the two Continental Congresses. There wasn't an Executive Branch or Cabinet position, such as the Secretary of War, to assist in organizing the military. With no central government, all the work was done by committees of the Continental Congresses, and there were over 450 such committees.

Washington's early actions help the reader better understand the intelligence activities of the American Revolutionary War. Recognizing the vast size of the Colonies his army was charged with protecting, Washington proposed to the Continental Congress that separate Military Departments be established for specific geographic areas. The Continental Congress accepted these terms and the Colonies were eventually divided into seven separate Military Departments: Middle (or Continental Army), Northern, Highlands, Canadian, Southern, Eastern, and Western Departments, each operating with a high degree of autonomy. Each department would have a separate command structure, and although ultimately under the command of George Washington, each would function independently as required. They were composed of a blend of regular army troops as well as local militias who were commanded by local officers. Intelligence requirements from the higher authorities would be given through the command structure, but in contrast, the intelligence requirements for a specific department were generated within that department. It's important to note that if intelligence related only to a certain department, it would not necessarily be reported to General Washington. If, however, the information related to the overall military efforts it would be forwarded on to Washington's headquarters.

General Washington was concerned with two areas of intelligence requirements. The first requirement was to alert Washington of any actions of the British Army that would impact on the Continental Army. The second requirement was more specific. It kept Washington informed on the actions of the British headquarters in New York City. The first requirement decentralized the intelligence activities of the various departments. Even when components of the Main Army deployed into one of the other military departments (such as the deployment into the Southern Department for the eventual battle of Yorktown), separate intelligence operations were maintained—for that specific department and another independent one for the Main Army's requirements. In addition, in all the departments, civilians operated independently as spies, providing intelligence to both the regular army and the militia. These individuals normally functioned on their own and through their own initiative.

George Washington was dubbed by British General Charles Cornwallis as "The Fox" for his elusive maneuvers and stands apart as a great master of intelligence. However, other individuals involved in the intelligence efforts for both the American and the British sides deserve more recognition than they have received to date. The purpose of this book is to analyze the intelligence (or spying) activities of the American Revolutionary War, department by department. In addition to the general role of intelligence, the predominant individuals, such as Dr. Benjamin Church, James Armistead, and Rev. Johann Heckewelder, known to be active in the area of their department will be profiled. Where possible an attempt will be made to show not only the activity of an agent, but also the impact their work had on a specific battle or event. Two prime examples being the battle of Princeton and the battle of Yorktown.

It is fascinating to look at the intelligence activities of the American Revolutionary War with an eye toward what is happening in the world of intelligence today. The initial foundations of U.S. intelligence commenced with the activities of George Washington and the cast of Revolutionary War spies. Even though the world of intelligence now has developed into a very complex and multi-faceted discipline, the basic tenets established by Washington remain the basis of American intelligence efforts today.

I

Revolutionary War Intelligence Operations

BRITISH VS. COLONIAL

THE AMERICAN COLONIES AND GREAT BRITAIN WERE LIKE DAVID and Goliath in regard to their military effectiveness and intelligence acumen. Due to their location, the British had been involved in the power struggles of Europe for centuries and had developed a substantial army and navy to counter the constant conflicts. Even before the reign of Queen Elizabeth I, British intelligence operations had been one of the best in Europe—and not only for covert operations but for code making and code breaking as well. The American colonies, on the other hand, had not experienced a major war and therefore their capabilities—both for military and intelligence operations—were very limited. But when the need for such a capability emerged many men, such as Benjamin Franklin, James Lovell, Thomas Jefferson, and most importantly, George Washington, rose to the occasion. They quickly grasped the importance of good intelligence in the coming conflict with the British.

When British forces arrived in the Colonies to end the rebellion, they held the Colonists in very low esteem and believed the revolt would be easily quelled. The British looked upon the Colonials as a conglomerate of uneducated people, with little knowledge of such areas as codes and code breaking. When the first British contingent under General Henry Clinton arrived in New York City on July 3, 1776, they did not have any intelligence capability or code breakers with them. They had completely underestimated their enemy. When they captured an encoded message, they had to send it back to England to be broken, which was a very inefficient system.

When the conflict began in 1775 with such battles as Lexington and Concord, the British military employed a traditional system for intelligence operations. All intelligence operations were controlled by the commanding general in a highly centralized organization. In addition, due to their experience as a colonial power, they had learned to depend heavily on the local population, specifically Loyalists, to assist them with intelligence information. They had no firmly established decentralized networks.

The Colonists, on the other hand, began to develop a very different system. Most Revolutionary War enthusiasts are familiar with names such as George Washington, Benjamin Franklin, James Lovell, and Robert Tallmadge, but have never heard of such personalities as Captain Martin Gambill (known as the "Paul Revere of the South") or Emily Geiger of South Carolina, whose Revolutionary War exploits are incorporated into the seal of South Carolina.

The Colonists set up intelligence networks where possible. The more formally organized networks were concentrated primarily in Boston and New York. In the more outlying areas, individuals and families came forward and served as agents in support of the Colonial effort. For the Western and Southern Departments, both of which had large Indian populations, Colonial intelligence requirements were twofold: first, the British military tactics in their areas and second, the Indians and whose side they would support. Many of the Indian tribes sided with the British, assisting them with geographic intelligence, and with British encouragement they conducted frequent raids on local populations. These networks were decentralized, meaning that the various department commanders worked them independently of the central command.

Did the receipt of intelligence make a difference in the American Revolutionary War? It most definitely did. Was it slow and amateurish? Yes, but it functioned out of loyalty to the cause. Did the British underestimate the Colonies' capabilities both militarily and intelligence wise? Yes, they did. The military had to adapt to a new way of fighting that was learned from Indians. This type of fighting consisted of guerilla-style warfare, rather than two forces facing one another and advancing in columns. Timely tactical intelligence, like Indian war cries alerting an enemy, became much more important.

The first part of this book will analyze Colonial intelligence operations, with a discussion of the intelligence of each individual Continental military department, as each department differed greatly in both structure and successes. Later chapters will cover the cryptanalytic efforts and the technology employed by each combatant.

Interestingly, while the value of gathering intelligence was known to many involved in the Revolutionary War, it did not flourish or even really continue after the conflict. Once American independence was achieved, it seemed the Atlantic and Pacific Oceans provided a formidable barrier and no one worried about possible impending conflicts that required intelligence activities. Americans did not identify closely with Europe and they had a different form of government as well as a more independent spirit. They felt they could do without Europe! So for example, twenty-nine years after the Revolutionary War ended, in the War of 1812, the British would come as close as twelve miles to the District of Columbia before the Americans knew they were there.

NATIVE AMERICAN AND AFRICAN AMERICAN CONTRIBUTIONS TO INTELLIGENCE

While there are limited studies of the specific activities of Native Americans and African Americans during the Revolutionary War, individual reports of battles frequently recount their activities. Virtually no first person accounts exist but these two minority groups did play critical roles in the intelligence activities of both sides.

In the case of the American Indians, the British had a distinct advantage when it came to convincing the Indians to work with and for them. The British promised to halt the encroachment of settlers into Indian territory once they had won the war. A tempting offer! Recruitment was done on a tribal basis and not at the individual level for both the British and Americans.

American Indian spies were not used by either side for intelligence gathering in populated areas. An Indian strolling down a city street would hardly go unnoticed and would instead arouse suspicion. An Indian in the wilderness, however, would appear quite natural. They were useful to both sides as scouts and guides in the wilderness. Gathering strategic intelligence, which didn't require an immediate response, was useless. The American Indians' value was limited mainly to tactical purposes such as responding immediately to time-sensitive information. If, for example, the Colonial army was approaching, the Indians would be quick to alert the British military of the advance and often joined in the counter-attack. Despite the value of the American Indians, the language barrier presented a problem, as both sides were dependent upon a few white men who made their living trading with the Indians to serve as interpreters.

The only records that exist regarding the intelligence work of the Indian relate to specific tribes—not individuals. These tribes were active for both sides in the Northern Department, the Southern Department, and most importantly, the Western Department, where those aiding the British were under the control of Colonel Henry Hamilton, the British commander at Fort Detroit. One important case of Indian support for the Americans occurred during George Rogers Clark's expedition through the Illinois territory to capture the fort at Vincennes on the Mississippi River. Along the way, friendly Indians advised Clark about specific routes to take to avoid the British, whereby Clark could and did achieve his desired element of surprise.

While the majority of the Indian activity took place in the Western Department there are examples in all of the other military departments with the exception of the Eastern Department.

———

The British had a recruiting advantage for the black slave population too. They promised the slaves freedom once the war was won. Interestingly, while the British attempted to recruit blacks to work for their intelligence, there is no record of the Americans conducting a concerted effort to recruit blacks for their intelligence work. The slave culture prevailed.

The black population presented a different intelligence potential for both the British and the Americans. Unlike an Indian, it was quite normal to see a person of color on the streets of colonial towns and cities. Their presence would not arouse any suspicion. In addition, blacks were frequently found in military camps as cooks or servants attending to the troops. In contrast to the intelligence derived from Indians, the intelligence derived from blacks could be of both tactical and strategic value. Their unfettered access proved to be a valuable asset to both sides.

As discussed previously, the British promised blacks their freedom after the war was over. The Americans made no such offer. This message was, of course, more effective in the southern areas where slavery existed than it was in the northern states where most of the blacks were already free men. However, a black serving just as a spy for the Americans did so knowing that the offer of freedom after the war did not pertain to them. It was only for those who served in the army.

The activities of both Native Americans and African Americans definitely impacted the outcome of the Revolutionary War. The British exploited both of these groups to their advantage. On the American side, however, the reasons for Indian and black cooperation were more abstract. The intelligence provided by both of these groups was predominately of the day-to-day tactical nature, and not generally of a strategic nature. Nevertheless, both ethnic groups played an integral role in the American Revolutionary War.

American Black Spies

One can find numerous references to blacks providing information to the Continental Army, but these individuals remain anonymous. However, there is one man whose story is known.

JAMES ARMISTEAD (LAFAYETTE)—James was a slave on the plantation of William Armistead, a strong supporter of the revolution. James went to his master and asked permission to enter the Continental Army. His master would not allow that because James would have been freed at war's end. Armistead did agree, however, to allow him to serve as a volunteer servant to his friend General Lafayette of the Continental Army—thereby returning him to slavery when the war was over. Impressed with James Armistead's intelligence, Lafayette soon recruited Armistead to enter the enemy lines posing as an escaped slave to spy for him. Armistead successfully penetrated the enemy line and quickly came to the attention of General Cornwallis, to whom he relayed false information about the Continental Army and Lafayette (which will be more fully discussed in a later chapter).

British Black Spies

Blacks served as spies for the British, not out of loyalty to the Empire but because of the British promise of freedom once the war was over. The following are examples of their intelligence work.

HARRY—Harry was a slave owned by a Mr. Gaillard of South Carolina, who upon hearing of the British offer of freedom, escaped from the plantation and joined them. He became a spy for Lord Rawdon and later worked for Lt. Colonel C. Balfour. Both officers were well pleased with his accomplishments. In November 1782, he was sent out on a mission from Monck's Corner, South Carolina, and soon fell into the hands of troops assigned to Brigadier General Francis Marion—"the Swamp Fox," so nicknamed because of his ability to utilize the swampy areas of South Carolina to his advantage. He was quickly identified as a British spy and executed immediately without a trial. His value as an intelligence agent must have been significant as shown by the letter reporting his death to British authorities. The letter states:

> *I do hereby Certify that a Negro Man named Harry the property of Mr. Gailliard was frequently employed as a Spy by order of Lord Rawdon, in which capacity He was very serviceable; & that after his Lordships departure He was employed in the same manner for the late Commandant Lt. Co. Balfour & enrolled as a Guide in the Qr. Mr. Genl. Department.*
>
> *That being sent out from Monck's Corner for intelligence He was taken Prisoner by Marion's party, by whom He was beheaded & his head set upon a Stake, when Genl. Gould's Army passed the Greenland Swamp.*
>
> *As Witnessed my hand Chas. Town*
> *Novr. 27 1782*
> *J Doyle Majr. V.I.*
> *Jno. McKinnon*
> *Dy. Qr. M: G*

JAMES—James was a slave who belonged to Gilbert Ogden living in the North Castle area of New Jersey. Unknown to his master, James had become an intelligence asset for the British and a successful one at that. In late September 1778, he reported that Washington had moved his troops near Fredericksburgh, and then distributed to Danbury. His report confirmed previously reported intelligence. He was sent back to his master with orders to continue his spying and was given a reward of two guineas for his reporting.

BENJAMIN WHITECUFF—The second son born into a free black family living at Hempstead, Long Island. When the Revolutionary War broke out, his father and brother joined the Continental Army, but Benjamin joined the British forces. For the next two years General

Henry Clinton employed him as a spy. On one occasion, intelligence he gathered prevented a Rebel attack on British soldiers as they marched from Trent Town to New York. For his work during this period, he was rewarded with fifteen guineas and the statement that he was "very assiduous and successful in the part he undertook" by General Clinton.

Whitecuff continued his spying efforts until he was arrested in Cranbury, New Jersey, for being a British spy and hanged without a trial. He dangled from the noose for about three minutes when a British patrol found him and cut him down—miraculously alive. He was taken back to New York where he recovered and soon found himself on a mission to Virginia. But as fate would have it, the mission was not to happen. His ship was attacked and he was once again arrested as a British spy, condemned, and sent to Boston to be hanged. But while aboard the American ship, it was attacked by the *Eagle*, a British privateer, and Whitecuff was rescued and taken to England.

Soon after his arrival in England, he signed on one of His Majesty's brigs and sailed off to the North African coast. Finally in February 1783, he was discharged and settled in Deford, England. That next year, a Loyalist compensation board directed that the black spy "was to receive such aid or relief for his losses and services may be found to deserve." His claim was for thirteen pounds to include his Long Island farm, a yoke of oxen, and a cart. His claim was honored, but nothing is known of his later life.

~~~

CHAPTER

II

Intelligence Organizations
of the Continental Congress

BOTH THE FIRST AND SECOND CONTINENTAL CONGRESSES HAD
a major disadvantage when it came to administering a new government—administrative departments or civil servants didn't exist. In order
to alleviate this problem, the First Continental Congress established the procedure
of creating committees to perform various required functions, some that were very
basic like providing uniforms to the troops and some that were more complicated
like collecting intelligence. The First Continental Congress established hundreds
of these committees on an as-required basis, but there were also standing committees handling the major areas of concern, such as finances and foreign affairs,
most of which later became Cabinet departments.

Intelligence in all its forms was a critical part of the new government, and
the Continental Congress was quick to create several committees that would help
meet the intelligence requirements. Two especially important committees were the
Secret Committee established in September 1775, and the Committee of Secret
Correspondence established in November 1775. In addition to the above standing committees, additional committees, such as the Committee on Spies, were
established for intelligence purposes as the specific needs arose. Each committee
focused on a different set of intelligence operations. The descriptions below provide an understanding of the workings of these committees.

THE COMMITTEES

The Secret Committee

The Secret Committee was established to obtain military supplies covertly. Given a wide range of authority and large sums of money, the committee was responsible for monitoring all secret contracts with foreign suppliers for military supplies. In order to achieve this task the committee employed covert agents overseas—both American and non-American. These agents provided not only intelligence regarding the contracts, but also more general intelligence derived from their contacts abroad. They were able to provide the consensus regarding the revolution. Ships carrying the military supplies to the Colonies on instructions from the Secret Committee used foreign flags to protect them from the British Navy.

The contacts of this committee were providing valuable information about whether a specific country would be inclined to assist the Colonies in their revolution against the British. Often the assistance was retaliation against the British rather than sympathy for the Colonists' cause.

Congressional members of the Secret Committee included John Dickinson (PA), Benjamin Franklin (PA), John Lang (NY), Robert Livingston (NY), Thomas McKean (PA), Robert Morris (PA), Samuel Ward (NY), and Thomas Willing (PA). The Committee remained active throughout the Revolutionary War period.

The Committee of Secret Correspondence

On November 29, 1775, the Second Continental Congress passed the following resolutions thereby creating the Committee of Correspondence:

> *"RESOLVED, That a committee of five would be appointed for the sole purpose of corresponding with our friends in Great Britain, and other parts of the world, and that they lay their correspondence before Congress when directed;*
> *RESOLVED, That this Congress will make provision to defray all such expenses as they may arise by carrying on such correspondence, and for the payment of such agents as the said Committee may send on this service."*

This committee soon became known as the Committee of Secret Correspondence, with the initial congressional members being Benjamin Franklin, Benjamin Harrison (VA), and Thomas Johnson (MD). Later, James Lovell (MA) joined the group as an expert on codes and ciphers. While the functions of the committee did not change, on April 17, 1777, the name was changed to the Committee on Foreign Affairs. Change continued to happen on January 10, 1781, when the functions of the committee were absorbed into the new Department of Foreign Affairs, which was the predecessor of the current Department of State.

During the Revolutionary War, this committee conducted a very wide and diversified range of activities in the arena of intelligence, all of which focused predominately on communications in America and abroad. Human intelligence was the committee's biggest responsibility, handling American agents abroad. Their first agent was Arthur Lee, an American living in England, and the second was Charles Dumas, a Swiss journalist living in The Hague. A courier system was developed to ensure classified correspondence was delivered to the proper addressee. The messages to American diplomats were enciphered in special codes developed at the request of the committee (that will be more fully explained in a later chapter). Along with agents abroad, the committee maintained correspondence with known sympathizers of the cause who lived in Europe.

Perhaps the most powerful responsibility of this committee was in regards to public correspondence. The committee had the power to open and read any private correspondence they deemed important to the cause. This enabled them to maintain a closer watch on the Loyalist population and their support of the Crown.

And finally, they were responsible for the funding and creation of any and all propaganda to be employed both in the Colonies and abroad. Benjamin Franklin, as a member of the committee, used his expertise in the world of propaganda for an elaborate effort in Canada, attempting to have that colony revolt along with the Americans.

The Committee on Secret Correspondence was very powerful. It operated under the watchful eye of the president of the Continental Congress. The actions of the committee were predominately beneficial to the political rather than the military.

The Committee on Spies

While both the Secret Committee and the Committee of Secret Correspondence were established to fill anticipated needs, the Committee on Spies was formed to solve an immediate problem. When Dr. Benjamin Church was arrested, tried, and found guilty of spying for the enemy, the Continental Congress found that there was no official rule for punishing civilian spies. The adopted Articles of War only addressed the penalty for spying/espionage of military personnel, which was death.

To quickly remedy the situation, the Continental Congress established a Committee on Spies on June 5, 1776, "to consider what is proper to be done with persons giving intelligence to the enemy or supplying him with provisions." The committee was to establish penalties for spying/espionage that included both military and civilian perpetrators. The members of the committee were John Adams (MA), Thomas Jefferson (VA), Robert Livingston (NY), Edward Rutledge (SC), and James Wilson (PA).

Based on a report given by the committee to the Continental Congress on August 21, 1776, Congress enacted the following resolution:

> *"That all persons, no members of nor owing allegiance to any of the United States of America, as described in a resolution to the Congress of the 24th of June last, who shall be found lurking as spies or about the fortification or encampments of the armies of the United States, or of any of them, shall suffer death according to the law and usage of nations, by sentence of court martial, or such other punishment as such court martial may direct."*

It was further resolved that the act "be printed at the end of the rules and articles of war." Again on February 27, 1778, by action of the Continental Congress, the act was further revised to include "any inhabitants of these states whose intelligence activities aided the enemy in capturing or killing Patriots." This act (or resolution) remained the law of the land until the Constitution was adopted, which made it the responsibility of Congress to establish penalty for treason as shown in Article III, Section 3 of the Constitution which states:

> *"Treason against the United States shall consist only in levying War against them, or in adhering to their Enemies, giving them Aid and Comfort. No Person shall be convicted of Treason unless on the Testimony of two witnesses to the same overt Act, on Confession in open Court.*
>
> *The Congress shall have Power to declare the Punishment of Treason, but no Act of Treason shall work Corruption of Blood, or Forfeiture except during the Life of the Person tainted."*

This was followed by the fourth of what are called the Alien and Sedition Acts of 1798. The fourth of these laws, titled "Act for Punishment of Certain Crimes Against the United States" also known as "The Sedition Act," contained punishment for what were then called "sedition acts." However these acts were repealed in 1801.

During the American Colonial period the Colonies knew only British laws concerning treason and those were based on the Treason Act of 1351. This act did not differentiate between civilian or military perpetrators—they were treated identically by the monarch. Even when an American colonist was arrested for treason in the Colonies, he was sent to England for trial and punishment—no distinction. Hence when the American Constitution was drawn up and the treason clause inserted, following British tradition no differentiation was made between military or civilian.

It is interesting to note that from 1801 until the Sedition Act of May 18, 1918, there was no stated federal penalty for espionage or treason activities against the United States by civilians. The penalty for treason by a member of the U.S. military was covered under the Articles of War (based on the Articles of War written in England in 1688) until 1951 when the Uniform Code of Military Justice was adopted. The Committee on Spies would have been appalled!

The Committee (later Commission) for Detecting and Defeating Conspiracies

The first organization of a counter-intelligence nature designed to prevent British spying in the Colonies was set up under the Articles of Confederation and called the Committee for Detecting and Defeating Conspiracies. The members were not from the Continental Congress but from specific geographic areas of interest, i.e. New York and Philadelphia where the committee was active.

The work of this committee was to apprehend British spies and couriers, to collect intelligence, and to be watchful over suspected British sympathizers. The committee had the authority to arrest, convict, grant bail and parole, and imprison or deport. To accomplish their mission the committee had a company of militia troops under their command.

During its existence this committee heard over five-hundred cases of disloyalty or subversion. Such as the cases of Enoch Crosby and David Gray, who both served the British as spies. These cases were heard by John Jay, who has become known as the first Chief of Counter-Intelligence in the United States.

The group was particularly active in New York's Hudson River Valley where John Jay had ships anchored to hold the prisoners suspected of espionage activities. One of the committee's intelligence "coups" occurred on February 25, 1777, when an agent reported that General John Burgoyne planned to march via Fort Ticonderoga down the Hudson to New York. The report came to the committee/commission fifteen days before the plan was submitted to King George for his approval.

NEW YORK COMMITTEE FOR DETECTING AND DEFEATING CONSPIRACIES

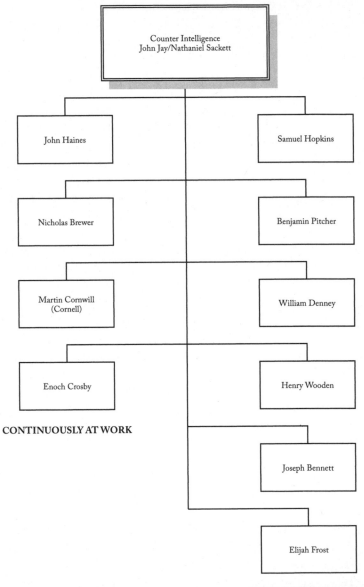

Counter Intelligence
John Jay/Nathaniel Sackett

John Haines

Samuel Hopkins

Nicholas Brewer

Benjamin Pitcher

Martin Cornwill
(Cornell)

William Denney

Enoch Crosby

Henry Wooden

CONTINUOUSLY AT WORK

Joseph Bennett

Elijah Frost

CALLED WHEN NEEDED

Similar groups existed in other cities, such as in Philadelphia when under British control in order to prevent penetration of the colonial networks working in the area.

The work of the Committee was recognized by George Washington, who on March 24, 1776, wrote:

> *There is one evil I dread, and that is their spies. I could wish therefore, the most attentive watch be kept. I wish a dozen or more of honest sensible and intelligent men were employed ... in order to question, cross question ... all such persons as are unknown, and cannot give an account of themselves in a straight and satisfactory manner. I think it is a matter of importance to prevent them obtaining intelligence of our situation.*

The Committees of Safety

Committees of Safety began to form independently in the Colonies as early as 1760. They were generally organized by a specific state to authorize the state militia to monitor the Royal government of that state and to serve as the national authority once the Royal government left. The first Provisional Congress which met in 1775 passed a resolution that the state Committees of Safety would be empowered with executive power when Congress was not in session. While not specifically charged with intelligence matters, they soon became local intelligence collectors, frequently responding to queries from General Washington and other senior members of his staff. All the state Committees of Safety had direct communications with the Committee for Secret Correspondence.

There are many examples of their contribution to the intelligence efforts of the Colonies. As early as 1776 the Committee for Secret Correspondence had the Continental Congress resolve that various Committees of Safety in the individual states would be the sole authority in the matter of intercepting mail. They alone would have the authority to open correspondence or to detain letters from the Postal Service.

Simon Newall and Eleazar Curtis contributed by independently serving as spy catchers. They roamed the countryside of New York impersonating British Loyalists seeking other Loyalists, kept a list of names they uncovered, and turned it into the Committee of Safety. They also discovered that a man named James Drake, the local chairman of the Committee of Safety, was working not only for the Colonies but for the British as well. If someone wanted to go through the American lines, Drake was equally friendly to both sides and could facilitate the move. He was in essence helping Loyalists escape to the British side.

And in 1781 a man by the name of Tench Tilghman met with the Committee of Safety in Annapolis, Maryland, and delivered the news of the British surrender at Yorktown. He then went on to Philadelphia where on October 24, 1781, he delivered the news of the British surrender to the Continental Congress.

The Committee of Three

Once the Congress received valid intelligence that the British were recruiting Hessians, professional military men, to serve with their army in America, the Continental Congress decided to act. They appointed a Committee of Three to "devise a plan for encouraging the Hessians and other foreigners to quit that iniquitous service." The original members of the committee were Thomas Jefferson, Richard Stone, and James Wilson.

The original plan was to offer land grants to the Hessians who deserted. They translated the proposed plan into German and had it distributed covertly among the German troops. Later Benjamin Franklin joined the Committee and helped to write a pamphlet for propaganda use. The pamphlet was disguised as a tobacco packet meant to fall into enemy hands. Later while in France, Franklin confiscated a letter from one of the Hessian commanders in America. The letter disputed the British casualty figures and spoke of the "blood money" the prince received for each Hessian killed. The prince encouraged the Hessian commanders to allow the wounded to die rather than try to save them as cripples unfit for battle. Was this letter legitimate or was it just another bit of Franklin's propaganda?

The work of this committee must have been successful since between 5,000 and 6,000 Hessian troops deserted the British Army. Many received land grants from a Colonial state.

End of the Committee System

With the adoption of the United States Constitution and the creation of governmental departments, the committee system was no longer necessary. Some of the functions were dispersed among the departments while others, such as intelligence, rapidly faded away. The general feeling of America at that time was that our oceans would protect us. Distance was our friend.

All of the above organizations were organized predominantly for governmental aspects of intelligence work. The intelligence organization of the military was not as well structured and depended greatly on the generals in charge. For example, General Nathanael Greene, trained by General Washington, was a very competent general while General Benjamin Lincoln did not understand the importance of the intelligence he received.

SUMMARY

The committee system established by the Continental Congress had served the Congress very well. There was no central government with an established authority—everything had to be accomplished by majority rule which could take considerable time. By delegating the authority for a specific area of interest such as logistics, finance, or intelligence to a committee, missions could be accomplished much more rapidly. In the case of the intelligence committees, security could be maintained. And time was often a factor in the decision-making process. Congress maintained the oversight function; however, in most cases the committees operated very independently in an efficient manner. The country had been blessed with an exceptional group of talented men (such as Jefferson and Franklin) fully capable of serving as committee heads as required.

Once the country had an official government with George Washington as president and the establishment of the Cabinet system, independent committees were no longer required. Departments such as State and Treasury incorporated the committee functions into their directives.

CHAPTER

III

Command Structures of the Opposing Forces

THE BRITISH

THE BRITISH HAD DEVELOPED A HIGHLY CENTRALIZED structure for their army as a result of their long history of involvement in European wars. By tradition, they always had one commander for all their forces, and this was true in the Colonies. After the British retreated from Boston to Halifax, the British troops returned to New York City. There Commander General Thomas Gage established his headquarters. It was a central location, but not necessarily near the battles. While successful in Europe, this commander structure did not serve the British well during the Revolutionary War, where Colonists had learned a new type of warfare from the Indians—less regimented and more like what we call today guerilla warfare.

The British intelligence operations were structured similarly—little freedom of operation on the lower level. For example, if the British obtained a copy of a rebel enciphered document, that document had to be sent to England for decryption. General Gage and his replacement, General Charles Cornwallis, had no capability to perform the task on this side of the Atlantic for the entire period of the war. The following diagram depicts the British intelligence network in the Colonies:

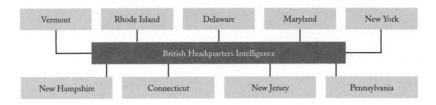

THE AMERICANS

The Continental Congress was quick to realize that the geographic expanse of the Colonies made it nearly impossible for one Continental Army to efficiently operate in all areas. With this knowledge the Continental Congress took two actions. First, on June 14, 1775, the Continental Army was established and second, George Washington was named as commander-in-chief. The next day the Congress addressed the geographic question by creating the Middle Department, usually referred to as the Main Army. When formed, each department had its own Table of Organization and Equipment (TO&E) detailing the number of officers and enlisted men authorized, as well as equipment.

General George Washington assumed two roles in the new structure. He was appointed as the commanding general of the entire Continental Army and also the commanding general of the Main Army. Departments had their own intelligence requirements, spies and spy networks, and in some cases the commander within had private tutelage from General Washington on the subject of intelligence collection and use. For example, General Nathanael Greene used these acquired skills to provide excellent support during Washington's advance against Cornwallis in Virginia.

Early on it became obvious to Washington that he needed assistance in the collection and interpretation of intelligence. He chose to designate one of his personal aides, Joseph Reed, as his intelligence aide. Reed was the first of a long series to fill the role. The list of confidential aides serving Washington in the handling of intelligence includes:

Joseph Reed	July 4, 1775
Thomas Mifflin	July 4, 1775
John Trumbull	July 27, 1775
George Baylor	August 15, 1775
Edmund Randolph	August 15, 1775
Robert H. Harrison	November 5, 1775
Stephen Moylan	March 5, 1776
William Palfrey	March 6, 1776
Caleb Gibbs	May 16, 1776
George Lewis	May 16, 1776
Richard Cary	June 21, 1776
Samuel B. Webb	June 21, 1776
Alexander C. Hanson	June 21, 1776
William Grayson	June 21, 1776
Pierre Penet	October 14, 1776
John Fitzgerald	November 1776
George Johnston	January 20, 1777
John Walker	February 19, 1777
Alexander Hamilton	March 1, 1777
Richard K. Meade	March 12, 1777
Peter P. Thornton	September 6, 1777
John Laurens	September 6, 1777
James McHenry	May 15, 1778
Tench Tilghman*	June 21, 1780
David Humphreys	June 23, 1780
Richard Varick	May 25, 1781
Jonathan Trumbull, Jr.	June 8, 1781
David Cobb	June 15, 1781
Peregrine Fitzhugh	July 2, 1781
William S. Smith	July 6, 1781
Benjamin Walker	January 25, 1782
Hodijah Baylies	May 14, 1782

*Served as a volunteer aide from August 1776

GEORGE WASHINGTON'S INTELLIGENCE AIDES AND NETS

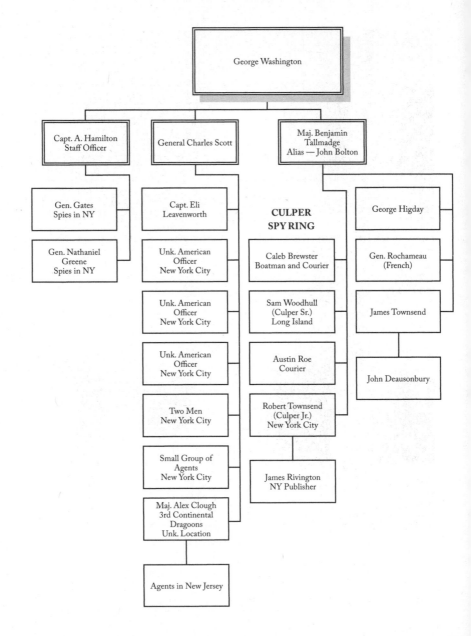

GEORGE WASHINGTON PORTRAIT COMMEMORATING VICTORY AT
THE BATTLE OF PRINCETON ON JANUARY 3, 1777.

GEORGE WASHINGTON'S SPY NETWORKS
Dayton - Mersereau - Hendricks - Vanderhovan - Sackette

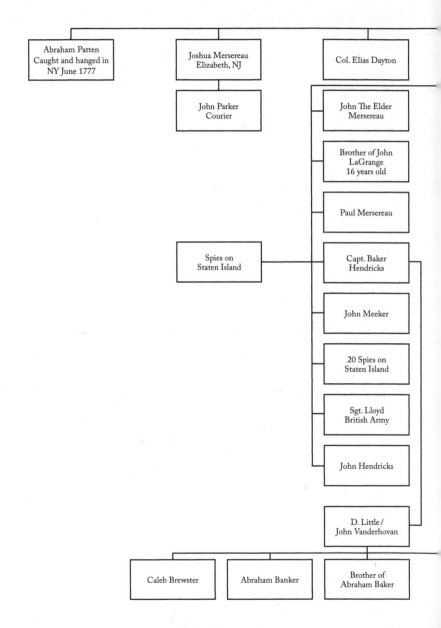

Command Structures of the Opposing Forces

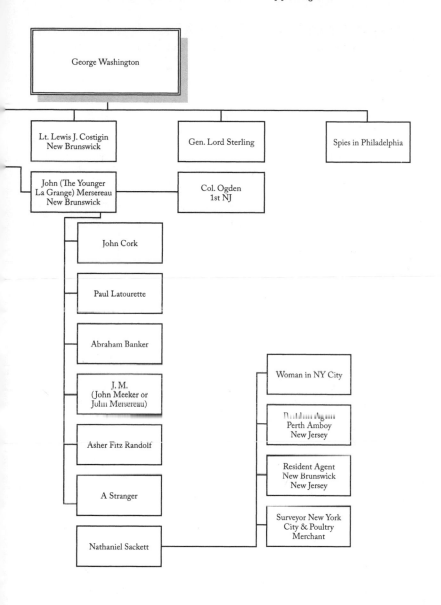

George Washington

Lt. Lewis J. Costigin
New Brunswick

Gen. Lord Sterling

Spies in Philadelphia

John (The Younger
La Grange) Mersereau
New Brunswick

Col. Ogden
1st NJ

John Cork

Paul Latourette

Abraham Banker

J. M.
(John Meeker or
John Mersereau)

Woman in NY City

Resident Agent
Perth Amboy
New Jersey

Asher Fitz Randolf

Resident Agent
New Brunswick
New Jersey

A Stranger

Surveyor New York
City & Poultry
Merchant

Nathaniel Sackett

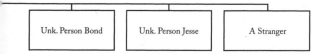

Unk. Person Bond

Unk. Person Jesse

A Stranger

GEORGE WASHINGTON AND HIS GENERALS
Intelligence and Spying Matters

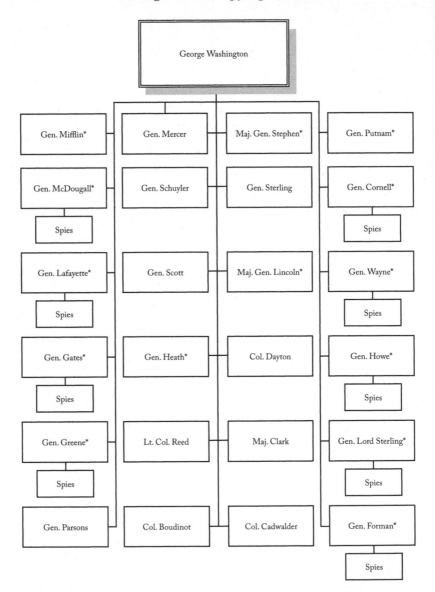

*These generals also ran separate intelligence services.

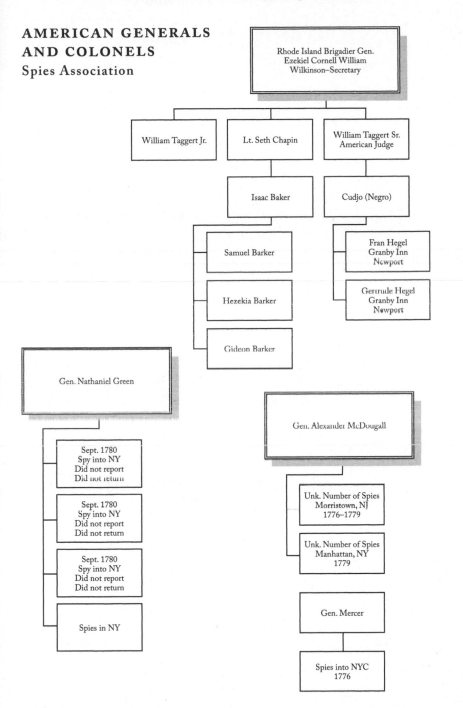

AMERICAN GENERALS AND COLONELS
Spies Association

Rhode Island Brigadier Gen.
Ezekiel Cornell William
Wilkinson–Secretary

William Taggert Jr.

Lt. Seth Chapin

William Taggert Sr.
American Judge

Isaac Baker

Cudjo (Negro)

Samuel Barker

Fran Hegel
Granby Inn
Newport

Hezekia Barker

Gertrude Hegel
Granby Inn
Newport

Gideon Barker

Gen. Nathaniel Green

Gen. Alexander McDougall

Sept. 1780
Spy into NY
Did not report
Did not return

Unk. Number of Spies
Morristown, NJ
1776–1779

Sept. 1780
Spy into NY
Did not report
Did not return

Unk. Number of Spies
Manhattan, NY
1779

Sept. 1780
Spy into NY
Did not report
Did not return

Gen. Mercer

Spies in NY

Spies into NYC
1776

TOP SECRET LIBERTY

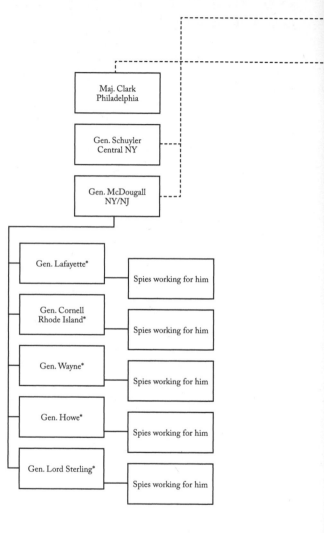

*These generals also ran separate intelligence services.

Command Structures of the Opposing Forces

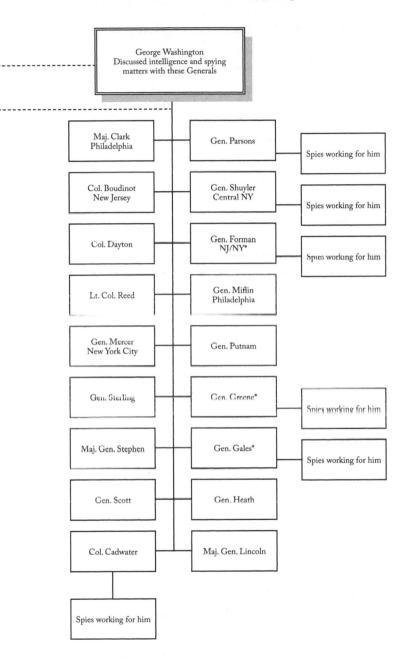

These aides received the intelligence reports, read them, filed them, and as appropriate, informed Washington of the pertinent intelligence. They also on occasion went out on intelligence missions of their own.

In 1777, Major Benjamin Tallmadge was named as Washington's Intelligence Chief. As an additional duty, in 1779 he was responsible for the Culper Ring, a spy network active in New York and Long Island. The other military departments adopted a similar structure for their intelligence operations.

When the Main Army moved from New York to New Jersey, General Washington named General Philip Schuyler, then the commander of the Middle Department (Main Army), to become the new commander of the reorganized Northern Department. Washington assumed command of the Middle Department (Main Army). Since Pennsylvania was in the middle of the Colonies, Washington intended to exercise his overall command from the Pennsylvania location whenever possible. As shown when the Main Army moved into the Southern Department, Washington did not assume command of the department he was in. The area of the Southern Department was extensive so Greene continued in his command role in conjunction with Washington's offensive against Cornwallis. The following diagrams indicate the extent of the Continental Army's intelligence networks.

SUMMARY

Between the two command structures, it's clear that the Americans had an advantage in intelligence over the British. Where the British lacked useful and timely delivery of information, the Americans had efficient intelligence reporting. The major downfall of the British was the centralized system of intelligence, which required all information to be reported to the upper levels of command, often resulting in irrelevant information. When George Washington created a decentralized command structure, he wisely allowed his departmental commanders liberties to conduct intelligence operations independent of the Main Army. He also did not hesitate to remove a departmental commander if he felt that a commander was not capable of the command or was needed for a more critical command elsewhere.

Vestiges of the departmental command structure could be found in the United States Army for many years when armies within the continental limits were specific to an area, i.e. the First Army in New England, Second Army in the mid-Atlantic. And the system expanded as it now contains two armies abroad—the Seventh Army in Europe and the Eighth Army in the Far East—a reflection of America's role on the modern world stage.

IV

Continental Army
Department Structure

MILITARY DEPARTMENTS

THE VARIOUS MILITARY DEPARTMENTS IN THE CONTINENTAL Army were established on a geographic basis. However, the role of one department was unique and must be seen as an independent entity. If and when the need arose, elements of a department were transferred to another for a more coherent structure. Not all of the departments were active throughout the entire war period. Here are the departments in order of establishment.

The Middle Department (also known as the Main Army)

On June 15, 1775, one day after George Washington was named commander of the Continental Army by the Continental Congress, the Middle Department was established. This department, which also incorporated the Main Army, was referred to as the Main Army Department. When Washington and his army entered New Jersey, he reorganized the newly formed Northern Department by moving the states of New Jersey, Pennsylvania, Delaware, and Maryland from the Northern Department to the Middle Department (though later both Maryland and Delaware were transferred to the Southern Department). Since George Washington was the commander of the Middle Department as well as the Continental Army, this department was more commonly referred to as simply the Main Army.

The New York Department

Since most—if not all—of the early military actions took place adjacent to the New York colony, Congress felt compelled to organize the colony for military action. As a result, the New York Department was established on June 25, 1775. In the department's early days, it was meant to serve only matters of intelligence involving New York; but later, when the Middle Department expanded to include multiple states, the New York Department was absorbed as part of the Middle Department—but not for long. On April 14, 1776, the New York Department shifted yet again into the Northern Department. But New York City's eventual occupation by the British in September led to the abolishment of the New York Department.

The Canadian Department

The Canadian Department was established on February 17, 1776, and primarily focused on the military activities associated with the areas of Montreal and Quebec. General Richard Montgomery was the first of six commanders of the department, due to officers with medical issues. The main intelligence emphasis beyond the immediate military actions was to acquire information regarding the possibility of the forming of a British Army in Canada to invade the Colonies. After the disastrous invasion of Canada by Colonial forces in the spring of 1776, the Canadian Department was dissolved in July.

The Southern Department

The Southern Department was established on March 1, 1776, and included the Virginia, North Carolina, South Carolina, and Georgia colonies in addition to the western borders of these states, now known as Kentucky and Tennessee. Later in the war, Maryland and Delaware were transferred from the Middle to the Southern Department. General Charles Lee was the first of five commanders of the department. Taking advantage of the warmer climate, the Southern Department operated on a year-round basis, in contrast to other departments whose operations halted during the winter months, and military activity continued for both sides throughout the year. It's no surprise that militarily, this was the most active of all the departments.

The Eastern Department

Due to New England being the center of the early battles, the Eastern Department existed prior to the establishment of the Continental Congress, and was unofficially known as the New England Department. Its main function was to support the troops involved in the siege of Boston and the colonies of Massachusetts, New Hampshire, Rhode Island, and Connecticut. It was officially declared the Eastern Department by Congress on April 4, 1776. General Artemas Ward was the first of three commanders of the department. The Eastern Department was abolished in November 1779 as all the military action had moved south.

The Northern Department

Originally formed as the New York Department, the Northern Department was created on April 14, 1776, after the British occupied New York City. General Philip Schuyler was the first of its nine commanders. It consisted of the New York, New Jersey, Delaware, Maryland, and Pennsylvania colonies. New York City and Long Island were excluded as these areas were under British control for the majority of the Revolutionary War. Later in 1777, New Jersey, Delaware, Maryland, and Pennsylvania were relocated to the Middle Department.

The Highlands Department

Previously operating under the Northern Department, the Highlands Department became independent on November 12, 1776, upon the request of General Washington. Realizing the importance of the Hudson River, Washington determined that the needs of the Main Army would be better served with a military department designated solely to the Highlands region. Unlike the other departments, Washington kept a close eye on the Highlands, particularly during the period when an invasion from Canada through the Hudson River Valley appeared a strong possibility. General William Heath, one of Washington's most trusted generals, was the first of nineteen commanders of the department.

The Western Department

The Western Department was established on April 10, 1777, and was composed of the frontier territories west and northwest of Virginia and Pennsylvania and included the future states of Ohio, Indiana, Michigan, and Illinois (at that time part of the Province of Quebec). General Edward Hand was the first of four commanders of the department.

INTELLIGENCE GATHERING IN
THE MILITARY DEPARTMENTS

While George Washington is rightly credited with creating an extensive intelligence system, the departments were responsible for carrying out tasks outside of Washington's guidance or instructions. Day-to-day activities were not under Washington's purview and were only pertinent to that individual organization. Unless intelligence was found to be important to the commander-in-chief, the intelligence flow stopped with the department's commander. In reality, the intelligence network of the Continental Army was a loosely formed grouping of intelligence networks, targeting specific geographic areas of interest, and operating as independent organizations. General Washington had confidence in his concept of decentralized intelligence operations, which not only shortened the time of receipt of intelligence to the commander, but also ensured him that the information would be relative to his area of interest. The concept of decentralized command proved valid not only militarily, but for intelligence operations as well.

~~~

The New England Provincial Army

MAJOR EVENTS

1770
Boston Massacre

1773
The Boston Tea Party

1775
Battles of Lexington and Concord
Siege of Boston
Battle of Bunker Hill
Battle of Gloucester
Battle of Stonington

THE EARLIEST MILITARY ACTION THAT SOWED THE SEEDS FOR the American Revolution occurred on March 5, 1770, when Boston citizens stormed the Customs House in protest of British oppression. The mob threw snowballs at the British guards, who opened fire on the protesters, killing five and wounding six others. The event came to be known as the Boston Massacre. Citizens were outraged. Boston supporters as well as Britain supporters recorded the event differently, attempting to influence opinion. The incident can

be attributed as one of the reasons for the growth of state militia groups, as well as the turn of Colonial outlook against Britain.

Although hostile, the Colonists remained relatively quiet until the Boston Tea Party, which took place on December 16, 1773, in a protest of a new tax on tea. Battling British oppression, a group of Colonists boarded a British ship and threw its cargo of tea into Boston Harbor. Needless to say, the action was not well received by the British. The Boston Tea Party provoked the British to pass the Coercive Acts, more commonly referred to as the Intolerable Acts, which were a series of laws that stripped the New England area of its right of self-government.

For the Massachusetts colony, the only Colonial military protecting the citizens from the British was the local militia—all volunteers and untrained. In September 1774, when General Thomas Gage ordered the removal of powder from a storage area in Somerset, it created what came to be known as a "Powder Alarm," and about one-hundred militias marched en masse toward Cambridge to protest. General Gage grew more cautious and wary of these local militia groups—the most famous being the Sons of Liberty. These militia groups were semi-covert, but tolerated by the British until 1775. They were funded strictly by the local populations and therefore limited in their capabilities. Open hostilities began after the English Parliament passed the New England Restraining Act in February 1775, declaring the Massachusetts colony to be in open revolt.

After the battles of Lexington and Concord, the revolution became a reality and the Colonists realized that independent militia groups were no match for the powerful British Army. With this in mind, on April 8, 1775, the Massachusetts Provincial Congress passed a resolution creating what they called a Provincial Army of 13,000 men. The colonies of Massachusetts, Connecticut, New Hampshire, and Rhode Island all were asked to contribute troops to the new army. The troops were expected to volunteer for a one-year enlistment. The Provincial Army's purpose was to consolidate various militia groups under one command structure, which resulted in the first American army to contain troops from more than one state under one command.

This army soon became known colloquially as the New England Army and functioned independently until June 15, 1775, when George Washington was named as the commander-in-chief of the newly formed Continental Army. In July of that year, Washington moved his headquarters to Boston, and he changed the name of the Provincial Army to the Army of New England. The Army of New England, now under the command of General Artemas Ward, remained an independent army operating with the guidance of General Washington until April 4, 1776, when General Washington began to move his troops to New York and it became the Eastern Department.

The new department essentially replaced the Army of New England and had continuing authority over the entire New England area. Though the majority of military activity in the New England area took place prior to the formation of the Eastern Department, it's interesting to note how the military functioned based on individual militia groups compared to the later developed departmental command structure.

INTELLIGENCE ACTIVITIES
IN NEW ENGLAND

In addition to the military aspects of these militias, they also had an intelligence function that was loosely organized with little or no direction from outside. Prior to the establishment of the department structure, each state was responsible for intelligence activities in their own state. The British, on the other hand, came with a centralized intelligence network that was employed throughout the Revolutionary War.

Early British Intelligence

British intelligence operations, like their military command, were always centrally controlled. When General Gage returned to the Colonies in 1774 to become the governor of Massachusetts, he found there was already an intelligence network in place. It was headed by Major Stephen Kemble, who had served as the deputy adjutant general for the British Army in America, and in that capacity was in charge of intelligence work. Kemble functioned in this role from 1772 to 1779 when he was replaced by Major John André. Another interesting fact about Kemble is that his sister, Margaret Kemble, was married to none other than General Gage. Margaret Gage was suspected of supplying information to Dr. Joseph Warren of the Sons of Liberty, and was eventually sent to England for the remainder of the war.

General Gage and Kemble knew that many of the Colonists were Loyalists—some acknowledged and some not—willing to supply information to the British, and they were exploited by the British generals. While identities of the Loyalist informers are relatively obscure, several prominent leaders in the colony are known to have provided intelligence to the British military.

One Colonist who provided intelligence to the British was Dr. Benjamin Church. He was a respected doctor in the Boston area who served as a member of the Provisional Congress on the Committee for Safety (sometimes as chairman) and the Committee of Correspondence. Both committees were involved in intelligence matters for the colony of Massachusetts. In addition, he served as a delegate to the Continental Congress that began to meet in 1774 in Philadelphia, thereby gathering intelligence at the national level.

When Dr. Church began passing information to the British is not certain, but as early as 1774 he was passing intelligence to Thomas Hutchinson, the royal governor of the colony of Massachusetts. The communications were normally by letters written in English, but on two occasions they were in French. The letters were mostly written by Dr. Church and other times by another British spy,

Benjamin Thompson, who was passing on intelligence from Dr. Church. The intelligence letters of late March and early April 1775 are good examples of just how valuable Dr. Church's information was to General Gage. These letters provided Gage with information on the amounts and locations of arms, powder, canons, and provisions stockpiles at Concord as well as information on the sentiments of the Colonists and actions of the Provincial Congress:

MARCH 9 AND 11, 1775: These two letters, written in French, detailed where military supplies were hidden in and around Concord. The reported locations were recorded and given to Lieutenant Colonel Francis Smith, who led the British force to Concord on April 19, 1775. The letters were assumed to have been written by a man named Joseph Hull, who had spent some time in Canada and may have learned some French there.

APRIL 3, 1775: Church alerted Gage to the fact that the Provincial Congress in a proclamation informed the Colonists that, if the British marched out of Boston with artillery and baggage, the populous should be alerted and prepared for battle. With this knowledge, Gage ordered his troops to march without artillery or baggage. When they marched toward Lexington and Concord in late April, his troops deployed following General Gage's orders as not to alarm the citizens. This, however, proved to be a mistake as their lack of artillery was a major factor in their defeat.

APRIL 9, 1775: Church reported that members of the Provincial Congress were proposing to raise a Continental Army; however, Church reports a "spirit of irresolution" in making a decision. The letter goes on to state that the American commitment while thought to be solid was, in fact, full of caution, doubt, and misgivings. Additionally, the men in power were not ready to take immediate action thus allowing Gage some breathing room while he waited for reinforcements.

APRIL 11, 1775: Church reported on the recent developments of the Provincial Congress for a second time. He reported that discussions continued in regard to raising an army to include the number of men required, the possibility of seizing Fort Powell in Maine, a study of provisions on hand, and a plan to send committees to the other New England colonies to discuss the potential of a New England Army. Some members were recommending a recess in order to discuss the matter with their constituents. Church informed Gage he thought he might be able to arrange such a recess. This would allow Gage more time as he awaited orders from England. He then suggested that an early military blow in the Boston area, now or immediately after the arrival of reinforcements from England (if they came within a fortnight), would most certainly cause concern in all the Colonies.

APRIL 15, 1775: Church assured General Gage that the adjournment of the Congress would take place that day and they would not reconvene for two weeks. He provided the proposed manning requirements for the new army. The total would be 18,000, of which 8,000 were from Massachusetts, 5,000 from Connecticut, 3,000 from New Hampshire, and 2,000 from Rhode Island plus 19 companies of artillery. Gage realized that the Colonial army was inevitable, and also that they would be dependent upon the cache of hidden weapons and powder. He had to act quickly to prevent the weapons and powder from falling into the Colonists' hands.

APRIL 18, 1775: Gage is informed that the military provisions at Concord have been distributed throughout the town, in particular in the area around the bridge.

Even before intelligence letters began to flow to General Gage, he had several teams operating in the area to gather data of interest to include: conditions of the roads, terrain features, and other geographic information relevant to the local area. Gage was very specific about what these teams were to ascertain. One team, comprised of Captain John Brown and Ensign Henry de Berniere, received the following written instruction prior to their departure on February 22, 1775. The instructions read:

You will go through the counties of Suffolk and Worcester, taking a sketch of the country as you pass; It is not expected you should make out regular plans or surveys, but make out the roads and distances from town to town and also the situation and nature of the country: all passes must be particularly laid down, noting the length, and breadth of them, the entrances and go out town and wither to be avoided by taking other routes.

The team had a successful mission and Gage later sent them on a second mission to Lexington to gather intelligence, but the mission was cut short when the men were recognized and had to flee from town.

While General Gage's intelligence network was working well and he was suitably prepared for the possible military action, he made a major miscalculation regarding the intelligence gathering capabilities of the Colonists.

Early American Intelligence and the Sons of Liberty

Even before the Stamp Act was enacted in 1765, which imposed the purchase of a stamp from England for anything produced on paper, there was a loosely formed organization throughout the Colonies known as the "Sons of Liberty." The purpose of the organization was to continue the fervor for revolution, and while spying and espionage were conducted, there is no evidence that spying or espionage were part of their charter. The Massachusetts group was unique in that, unlike most of the others, it had an intelligence gathering mission with Paul Revere and Dr. Joseph Warren as active participants. Like other Sons of Liberty groups, the Boston group was tolerated by the British who knew where the group met but did not necessarily know who the members were. All members were sworn to secrecy by an oath administered on a bible. According to Paul Revere:

"We were so careful that our meetings should be kept secret, that every time we met, every person swore on the Bible that he would not discover any of our transactions but to Messers. Hancock, Adams, Dr. Warren, Dr. Church and one or two more."

It was later discovered that Dr. Church was, in fact, a British spy reporting all he learned to General Gage. The information Church provided to General Gage was more than hearsay. It was often the direct conversations of the Continental Congress. This knowledge gave General Gage a clear edge when planning his strategy.

While a great deal is not known about the Revere intelligence operation with Samuel Adams and John Hancock as members of the Provincial Congress, they knew of his operations and it is highly likely they relied on the Revere group to meet their intelligence requirements. It is known that in early 1774, Paul Revere carried secret information from the Committee of Correspondence in Boston to Samuel Cut of the Committee of Correspondence in Portsmouth, the location of Fort William and Mary. The message read:

> That orders have been sent to the Governors of their Provinces to deliver their several fortifications or castles to General Gage and that a number of troops had the preceding day embarked on board transports with design to proceed and take possession of said castle.

Revere relayed the following important intelligence, which reported that when the British order was received by the Rhode Island Assembly, the powder and shot at Fort George was removed by the Patriots and stored in Providence. He also brought news of the king's order in Council prohibiting the export of gun powder and military stores to America.

Upon receiving this intelligence the Committee at Portsmouth met and decided to take pre-emptive action. On December 14, 1774, about four hundred men assembled in Portsmouth and began a march to Fort George. With only five men on guard, the Patriots soon took the fort. The raid netted 103 boxes of powder that were soon loaded onto boats and sent to Durham. Tradition has it that this powder was used at Bunker Hill.

Fall of Fort William and Mary

The next night a party from Durham returned to Portsmouth, joined with a local group and took Fort William and Mary in Portsmouth the following morning. They carried off the light canons and small arms to Durham. This action is often called the first overt action of the Revolutionary War. To quote Reverend Alonzo Hunt on the capture of Fort William and Mary, he wrote:

> The daring character of this assault cannot be overestimated . . . It was an organized investment of a royal fortress, where the King's flag was flying, and where the King's garrison met them with muskets and artillery. It was four months before Lexington, and Lexington was resistance to attack, while this was a deliberate assault. When the King heard of this capture, it so embittered him that all hope of concessions was at an end. It made war inevitable.

This quote captures the importance of the fall of Fort William and Mary. It was not a defensive move but in fact the first offensive one of the Rebels against the British. The actions at Lexington and Concord that followed in four short months were the first defensive actions of the war. The victory at Fort William and Mary inspired the Colonists to believe that they could in fact beat the British.

Lexington and Concord

Through his roving agents General Gage knew that considerable stores of powder and other military supplies were cached in the towns of Lexington and Concord. So finally in spring 1775, he decided to deal with the situation. The increased activity of the British troops in preparation for the move was noted by Colonists who constantly observed the British troop activity. On April 15, 1775, Dr. Warren was informed by his spies that General Gage had detached some of his grenadiers and light infantry from regular duty and that there was unusual activity on British ships in the harbor. He needed to know why. It is highly suspected that the answer to the question was provided to Dr. Warren by none other than Margaret Gage—the American wife of General Gage—who reportedly told Dr. Warren, "The march is tonight. The target is Concord." Whatever the source, Dr. Warren now had all of the information he needed and went into action. He first contacted William Dawes and then Paul Revere to alert the two towns.

Before leaving on his ride, Paul Revere had devised a plan of action whereby other Patriots would be alerted to the impending action, employing lanterns in the tower of the old North Church. One lantern would signify that the British fleet was leaving the harbor and two lanterns would signify the troops are moving by land. Late on the night of April 18, 1775, Revere contacted the church sexton, Robert Newman, and Captain John Pulling to hang two lanterns in the steeple thus alerting the citizens in Charlestown and other local areas about the movement of the British troops.

That same night Dawes and Revere commenced their mission. Each departed Boston by a different route to lessen the chance of being stopped by the British. Their first destination was Lexington, and they successfully sounded the alarm. They then began the ride to Concord, joined by Dr. Samuel Prescott, an innocent traveler who enjoyed their company. Along the way the trio was stopped by a British patrol. In an attempt to escape, Dawes fell off his horse while Revere was taken into custody—the mission seemed doomed. However, Dr. Prescott, who obviously had been made aware of their mission, succeeded in jumping his horse over a fence and finished the mission. Concord was warned of the approaching British soldiers.

In addition to the riders spreading the alarm, the Colonists had perfected a unique alert system that they had used as early as the Indian Wars. Bells, drums, gunfire, and a trumpet were used to alert Massachusetts villages. The system was so efficient that people within twenty-five miles of Boston were aware of the army movements while they were still unloading boats at Cambridge.

For all these reasons the people of Lexington and Concord had enough warning to move the caches of powder and military supplies to new locations. Therefore the wonderful map that General Gage had created, based on his roving agents, had very limited value when his troops arrived in Concord on April 19, 1775.

Siege of Boston

Within days of the battles of Lexington and Concord, the Patriots initiated a siege of Boston by controlling the surrounding countryside and thereby causing a logistical and tactical problem for General Gage. As the overall commander of all British troops in America, he received intelligence reports from all the Colonies under British control. With the land routes around Boston now under Patriot control the only way he could receive intelligence reports from other Colonies was by ship.

Frustrated by the lack of intelligence, he instituted a plan to intercept mail between Boston and England, particularly letters addressed to Benjamin Franklin. Ship captains were instructed to go through the mail and if they found such letters deliver them to General Gage. In retrospect, this move was useless since General Gage did not know that Franklin had already returned to the Colonies! Unfortunately, that was not the least of his problems.

Gage had a serious logistics problem, he needed to feed his troops and horses, and due to the siege he had limited access to supplies. The Committee of Correspondence, aware of his dilemma, ordered that all livestock on Noodle Island, Hog Island, Snake Island, and part of Chelsea be driven inland out of British reach. On May 27, 1775, when General Gage learned of the order, he sent fifty Marines to Noodle Island to prevent the movement of the livestock. They failed their mission as the livestock had already been moved. In early June, Gage sent two-hundred troops to Noodle Island to retrieve much needed hay for the horses, but again the mission failed since the Patriots set fire to the island and destroyed everything of value. Had General Gage acted as soon as he learned of the Patriot proclamation, he may have had a different outcome.

As Gage worried about resupplying his troops, the Americans were busy reacting to intelligence information. It seemed that the British were about to occupy the Charlestown peninsula as well as Dorchester Heights which would have provided a protective perimeter for the harbor. While the information was invalid, the American reaction was noticed by the British who now understood the strategic value of Dorchester Heights and the area around it.

In early June, General Gage met with his three generals, Henry Clinton, William Howe, and John Burgoyne, to develop a four-prong attack on Dorchester Heights, Roxbury, Charlestown, and Cambridge. The date was set for June 18, 1775. Thanks to General Burgoyne, however, the Patriots knew all about the plan in advance. Burgoyne, apparently a talkative man, was overheard talking about the plan, and soon Dr. Warren was informed of the details. With little time to react, the Patriots soon occupied Dorchester Heights and ordered General Ward to fortify the peninsula on which Bunker Hill stood. Had Dr. Church not been ordered to Philadelphia by the Provincial Congress, he would have known of the Patriot's plans as a member of the Committee of Safety and passed the information on to General Gage.

Battle of Bunker Hill

The battle of Bunker Hill (also known as Breed's Hill) was fought on June 17, 1775. And while the British won the battle they now knew that their enemy was formidable. The losses on both sides were extensive. The British losses were 19 officers and 207 men killed and 70 officers and 758 men wounded or 40 percent of the men engaged. The American losses were estimated at 140 killed and 301 wounded. For the British it was a severe loss of troops. But for the Americans it was not only a loss of troops but also the loss of a very important figure for the Patriot intelligence efforts. Dr. Joseph Warren, a key intelligence operative in the New England area, had been killed. His death was a setback for intelligence gathering and he would be hard to replace.

While Dr. Warren's death was a blow to the Patriots, others did step forward and continue to obtain good intelligence. They ensured the intelligence was delivered into proper hands so they could react to the information.

Just three days after the battle of Bunker Hill, events unfolded in Philadelphia that would soon impact the Army of New England. On June 15, 1775, George Washington was named as the commander-in-chief of the Continental Army—an impressive title given that the Continental Army did not exist at that point! The military forces in the various states consisted of volunteer militia groups with the exception of one area. That area was New England where the Colonies of Massachusetts, Rhode Island, and Connecticut had united to form what became known as the Army of New England.

WASHINGTON ASSUMES COMMAND OF THE ARMY OF NEW ENGLAND

Washington was quick to move to the Boston area and make the Army of New England the core of the new Continental Army. He arrived in Cambridge on July 2, 1775, and, on the morning of July 3, 1775, he stood in front of the troops, drew his sword, and took command of the Army of New England, which also contained militia groups from Virginia, Maryland, and Pennsylvania that had been sent north to assist with the siege of Boston. These militia groups merged together and became known as the Main Army of the Continental Army.

Washington, while aware of the intelligence operations in the Boston area, wasted no time in establishing his interest in acquiring good intelligence. He had learned its advantages during the French and Indian War when he was quoted as saying, "There is nothing more necessary than good intelligence to frustrate a designing enemy & nothing that requires greater pains to obtain." He quickly went into action and just twelve days after assuming command, his account book contains the following entry:

July 15, 1775
$33.33 given to _____ to induce him to go into Boston to establish secret correspondence for the purpose of conveying intelligence of the enemy's movements & designs.

The absence of a name in the entry is by design as Washington ordered that no names of people employed in intelligence work were to be entered in the book.

Washington's Use of Deception

Washington's skillful use of deception soon came to the forefront of his new army. When he arrived in the Boston area he was told that the Patriots had three-hundred barrels of gun powder—more than enough for another battle. However, that number was derived prior to the battle of Bunker Hill. The number derived on August 6, 1775, was a grand total of six barrels, enough for only nine rounds per rifle. If this would have become common knowledge to the British, it would have given them a definite edge in a future battle. Washington immediately went into a plan of deception. He had his agents spread word throughout Boston that the Americans had 1,800 barrels—enough for an entire army. At the same time, he made sure that the American troops heard the same deceptive information. Since the troops didn't know this information was false, it raised their morale. The British never realized they had been duped—and this was only the beginning.

Not long after taking command, Washington was pressured by the Continental Congress to drive the British out of Boston. With this in mind, he had a conference with his generals on how to do just that—at Dorchester Heights.

Dorchester Heights

A frontal attack on the British was dismissed in favor of fortifying Dorchester Heights and forcing the British to leave Boston Harbor. On October 15, 1775, General William Howe arrived in Boston and replaced General Gage as the British commanding general in America. General Howe had served in America previously and had been in the battle of Bunker Hill. He was quick to assess the value of Dorchester Heights, a fact that Washington was soon made aware. He also received a report sent to him by John Hancock of an agent in London who stated that a large number of cannons and four-hundred artillery soldiers were being sent to Boston. When these reinforcements arrived Howe would go on the offensive.

Washington knew he had limited time to accomplish the task. He quickly developed a plan centering on Dorchester Heights. The plan called for about forty-four heavier guns to be brought to Dorchester Heights under cover of night from Fort Ticonderoga along with fourteen mortars and one howitzer located at Roxbury. The guns would be used to fire upon British troops in and around the city, as well as the ships in the harbor. The artillery would also prevent a frontal attack by the British on Dorchester Heights. How was all this going to be done with utmost secrecy? By a series of deceptions:

- In order to move the guns from Roxbury to Dorchester Heights under cover of night, a distance of approximately two miles, Colonel Henry Knox had the wheels of 300 ox carts wrapped with straw to muffle the sound as they moved along.

- A bombardment of Boston from Roxbury, Cobble Hill, and Lechmere was ordered to mask the activities on Dorchester Hill.

- On the night of the bombardment, 2,000 men under General John Thomas hauled the heavy guns up the Heights and prepared fortifications. Frozen ground prevented digging fortifications, so instead they were made below the Heights and then taken up and emplaced.

- They created large wooden frames that were then filled with hay, twisted into bales, or compacted with twigs and tree branches. These same screens were also used to camouflage movements across the roads.

- Barrels were filled with earth and rocks. The filled barrels were then placed in front of the parapets, giving an illusion of strength. The barrels could also be rolled down the hill against an attacking force.

The entire operation was accomplished during the night of March 4, 1776, and the plan was so effective that the British had no idea what was happening that night. While the secrecy was excellent, the Americans also had the advantage of a thick fog rolling in that completely obscured any activity on Dorchester Heights.

When all was in readiness, the work party left the Heights and was replaced by 3,000 fresh troops under the command of General Artemas Ward. Another 4,000 troops stood by at Cambridge for an attack by boat across the bay on Boston in case the British attacked Dorchester Heights.

All communications in and out of Boston were cut off and Generals Heath and Sullivan inspected the lines to ensure that all the necessary preparations were made. Regiments were ready to move in the event of a British attack. Finally, General Washington issued orders to his troops stressing the importance of the task at hand. A real morale booster.

The British were caught completely off-guard. In late February 1776, a British spy known only as "Junius" reported to the British that the Americans were going to bombard the town of Dorchester, but the warning was ignored.

On the morning of March 5, 1776, General Howe awoke to a beautiful clear day—until he looked at Dorchester Heights and saw the American fortifications there. He was shocked! When he saw what had happened in one night he said that, "The rebels have done more in one night than my whole army could do in months!"

General Howe's immediate reaction was to deploy 2,000 troops to Castle William from where he planned to attack Dorchester Heights that night. His fellow generals discouraged him, but he was adamant, only to be undone by a violent storm hitting the area that afternoon making an attack impossible. After consulting with his generals, Howe decided he had no choice but to evacuate Boston and move to Nova Scotia.

British Depart from Boston

On March 7, 1776, General Howe declared that he had no intention of destroying Boston as long as the Rebels did not attack his troops during the evacuation. The British sailed out of Boston on March 17, 1776, with over 8,000 soldiers and 1,000 Loyalists who were bound for Halifax.

General Washington had prevailed! Now that the British Army had departed from Boston (and essentially the entire region of New England), General Washington planned his next move. Realizing that the British would be returning to the Colonies and probably to New York City, he also would move his Continental Army there. And so on April 4, 1776, the Continental Army left not only Boston but New England and moved south to New York City.

But Washington did not abandon the New England area to only militia support with no Continental Army present. On the same day of his departure from Boston the Continental Congress authorized the Eastern Department covering all the New England colonies. Congress also named General Ward as its first commander.

SUMMARY

Intelligence activities played a major role in the early events of the Revolutionary War in New England. For the Patriots, it was in many cases an individual or small group effort, such as the Sons of Liberty, but all were effective in their own way. While the British had Loyalist spies operating in the area, they underestimated their enemy and it cost them dearly.

The New England area was the first area to really feel the brunt of the impact of the American Revolutionary War. When the military action began, local militia groups were the only means of countering the British, a situation that existed in all of the Colonies. General Washington arriving on the scene changed the command structure for the militia. All militia groups and the newly formed Continental Army had one commander, and it did make a difference.

When Washington arrived in Boston there was already a fragmented intelligence operation functioning there. The value of this early system soon proved itself to Washington and he quickly came to rely on their input. While these operatives did not move to other departments when Washington left New England they provided Washington with an awareness of the value of intelligence as well as how to acquire good information.

To ensure that the concept of a central geographic command remained after the Continental Army left, Washington established the Eastern Department that remained an active department until November 1779 when it was abolished. The center of the military action moved south, where the armies could fight year round without stopping for winter quarters.

~~~

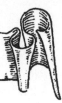

DR. BENJAMIN CHURCH JR.

DR. BENJAMIN CHURCH JR. WAS A RESPECTED CITIZEN OF Massachusetts. He was a Harvard graduate, a London trained physician, a participant in the Boston Tea Party, a member of Paul Revere's Sons of Liberty group, a member of the Committee of Correspondence for Massachusetts, a Massachusetts delegate to the Provincial Congress, the first chief surgeon for the Continental Army—and a spy for the British!

The "why" Church did what he did remains a mystery, but there is evidence as to the "when" and the "how" of his spying endeavors. Correspondence of the royal governor of Massachusetts as early as 1772 refers to information passed to the governor by Dr. Benjamin Church. As a prominent citizen of Massachusetts, Church's frequent associations with the governor would raise no eyebrows.

The "how" is simple. When he was in Massachusetts and wanted to pass information on to General Gage, he would go into British controlled Boston "to replenish his supply of medicine," when in fact he would actually meet with General Gage. When he would be in Philadelphia or out of Boston, he relied on written communications. The letters were always unsigned, normally in English, although one was in French and one was in cipher. When in Philadelphia, the letters would be in a second envelope and addressed to a person in Newport, who would then deliver them. When in Massachusetts, he used local couriers to take the letters into Boston while it was under siege. Loyal couriers were the essential element of Dr. Church's communications. He frequently used relays to further security.

But in spring 1775, Church became frustrated as three of his attempts to have a letter delivered to Boston were foiled by siege participants. In July 1775, Church tried again. He wrote a letter in cipher, and enclosed it in an envelope addressed to "Major Cane, Boston, On His Majesty's Service," and gave it to a woman who had been his mistress to deliver. What happened next is best described by General Washington in his report to the Continental Congress after the courts martial. It states:

> *I have now a painful though necessary duty to perform, respecting Doctor Church, the Director of Hospitals. About a week ago, Mr. Secretary Ward, of Providence, sent up one Wainwood, an inhabitant of Newport to me with a letter directed to Major Cane in Boston, in occult letters, which he said had been left with Wainwood*

some time ago by a woman who was kept by Doctor Church. She had before pressed Wainwood to take her to Captain Wallace, Mr. Dudley, the Collector, or George Rowe, which he declined. She gave him the letter with strict injunctions to deliver the letter to either one of these gentlemen. He, suspecting some improper correspondence, kept the letter and after some time opened it, but not being able to read it, laid it up, where it remained until he received an obscure letter from the woman, expressing an anxiety as to the original letter. He then communicated the whole matter to Mr. Ward, who sent him up with the papers to me. I immediately secured the woman, but for a long time she was proof against every threat and persuasion to discover the author. However she was at length brought to a confession and named Dr. Church. I then immediately secured Dr. Church and all his papers. Upon the first examination he readily acknowledged the letter and said it was designed for his brother Fleming, and, when deciphered, would be found to contain nothing criminal.

What Washington does not include in his statement to the Congress (probably so as not to reveal a code breaking capability), is what he did when he initially received the letter. He needed to see the underlying text. With this in mind, he privately gave one copy of the cipher text to Reverend Samuel West, and another one to Elbridge Gerry to recover the actual text. Within a day, both men returned with their translations, and when compared, the two texts agreed word for word. Washington now knew he had the original text. He knew that Dr. Benjamin Church was a traitor and moved to have him arrested.

While the text is not addressed to a person and is unsigned, there are several clues in the text as to the identity of the author:

(PAGE 1)

I hope this will reach you. Three attempts have I made without success in effecting the last. The man was discovered in attempting his escape but fortunately my letter was sewed in the waistband of his breeches. He was confined a few days during which time you may guess my feelings but a little art and a little cash settled the matter. Tis a month since my return from Philadelphia. I went by the way of Providence to visit mother. The committee for warlike stores made me a formal tender of 12 pieces of cannon, 18 and 24 pounders, they having to a previous resolution to make the offer to General Ward.

To make a merit of my services, I sent them down and when they received them they sent them to Stoughton to be out of the danger, even tho they had formed the resolution. As I before hinted of fortifying Bunkerhill, which together with the cowardice of the clumsy Col. Gerrish and Col. Scammon were the lucky occasion of their defeat. This affair happened before my return from Philadelphia. We lost 165 killed then and since dead of their wounds. 120 now lie wounded. The chief will recover. They boasted you have 1400 killed & wounded in that action. You say the rebels lost 1500, I suppose, with equal truth. The people of Connecticut are raving in the cause of liberty. A number from this colony from the town of Stanford robbed the King's stores at New York with some small assistance the New Yorkers lent them. These were growing turbulent. I counted 280 pieces of cannon from 24 to 3 pounders at Kingsbridge which the committee had secured for the use of the colonies. The Jersies are not a whit behind Connecticut in zeal. The Philadelphians exceed them both. I saw 2200 men in review there by General Lee, consisting of Quakers & others inhabitants in uniform with 1000 riffle men & 40 horse who together made a most warlike appearance. I mingled freely & frequently with the members of the Continental Congress. They were united, determined in opposition, and appeared assured of success. Now to come home – the opposition is becoming formidable. 18 thousand men brave & determined with Washington and Lee at their head are no contemptible enemy.

Adjutant General

(PAGE 2)

Gates is indefatigable in arranging the army. Provisions are very plenty. Cloaths are manufacturing in almost every town for the soldiers. 20 tons of powder lately arrived at Philadelphia, Connecticut & Providence upwards of 20 tons now in camp.

Saltpetre is made in every colony. Powder mills are erected constantly employed in Philadelphia & New York. Volunteers of the first fortunes are daily flocking to the camp. 1000 rifflemen (in 2 or 3 days recruits) are now levying to augment the army to 22 thousand men. 10 thousand militia are appointed in this government to appear on the first summons. The bills of all the colonies circulate freely and are readily exchanged for cash. Add to this that, unless some plan of accommodation takes place immediately, these harbours will swarm with privateers. An army will be raised in the middle provinces to take possession of Canada. For the sake of miserable conulsed empire, solicit peace, repeal the Acts, or Britain is undone.

This advice is the result of warm affection to my King & to the realm. Remember I never deceived you. Every article here sent you is sacredly true. The papers will announce to you that I am again a member for Boston. You will there see our motley council.

A general arrangement of offices will take place except the chief which will be suspended but for a little while to see what part Britain takes in consequence on the late continental petition. A view to independence grows more & more general. Should Britain declare war against the colonies, they are lost forever. Should Spain declare against England, the colonies will declare a neutrality which will doubtless produce an offensive & defensive league between them. For God's sake, prevent it by a speedy accommodation. Writing this has employed day. I have been to Salem to reconnoitre but could not escape the geese of the capitol. Tomorrow, I set out for Newport on purpose to send you this.

I write you fully. It being scarcely possible to escape discovery, I am out of place here by choice and therefore out of pay and determined to be so unless something is offered in my way. I wish you could contrive to write me largely in cypher by the way of Newport, addressed to Thomas
(PAGE 3)
Richards's merchant. Inclose it in a cover to me intimating that I am a perfect stranger to you but being recommended to you as a gentleman of honour, you took the liberty to inclose that letter in treating me to deliver it as directed, the person as you informed being at Cambridge. Sign some fictitious name. This you may send to some confidential friend in Newport to be delivered to me at Watertown. Make use of every precaution or I perish.

Dr. Church's court martial was held in October 1775, with General Washington as the president of the Board. He was found guilty, but the sentencing became a problem. The Articles of War did not contain references to "civilian espionage" and similarly a civilian espionage act did not exist for the Colonies.

To correct the situation, the death penalty clause for civilian espionage was added to the Articles of War on November 7, 1775; however, Washington would not allow it to be retroactive therefore sparing Dr. Church's life. He remained in jail (first in Connecticut and later in Massachusetts) until 1780, when he was exiled to the West Indies due to ill health. He sailed on the sloop Welcome Aboard but never arrived because of a severe storm en route. The ship sank and all passengers drowned. To Colonists, it seemed his death sentence had been carried out.

Dr. Church's wife and children fled to England where they received a pension from the Crown.

(NOTE: When the U.S. Constitution was adopted in 1787, Article III, Section 3 stated "The Congress shall have power to declare the Punishment for Treason." However, it was not until 1918 that Congress defined the punishment for treason as the death penalty.)

VI

The Middle Department/ Main Army

MAJOR EVENTS

1776

Forced abandonment of Ft. Lee, NJ, November 1776

Washington's army crosses Delaware River at McKonkey's Ferry, PA, December 1776

First Battle of Trenton, NJ, December 1776

1777

Second Battle of Trenton, NJ, January 1777

Battle of Princeton, NJ, January 1777

Battle of Bound Brook, NJ, April 1777

Battle of Short Hills, NJ, June 1777

Battle of Brandywine, PA, September 1777

Paoli Massacre, PA, September 1777

Battle of Germantown, PA, October 1777

Battle of Fort Mifflin, PA, November 1777

Fall of British river forts defending lower Delaware River, PA, October 1777

Philadelphia falls to British, October 1777

Battle of White Marsh, PA, December 1777

Winter quarters at Valley Forge, PA, December 1777

1778

British evacuate Philadelphia, PA, June 1778
Battle of Monmouth, NJ, June 1778

1779

Battle of Newtown, PA, August 1779

1780

Battle of Connecticut Farms, NJ, June 1780
Battle of Springfield, NJ, June 1780

The Middle Department was established on June 15, 1775, just one day after the establishment of a Continental Army and the same day that George Washington was named its commander-in-chief. The Middle Department was initially responsible for New Jersey, Pennsylvania, Delaware, and Maryland. Delaware and Maryland were subsequently transferred to the Southern Department. The Middle Department was frequently referred to as "The Main Army" since General Washington was the commander of the department throughout the war, as well as being the commander-in-chief of the Continental Army.

After the battles in New York City, Long Island, and White Plains, the Main Army entered New Jersey and remained in the area of the Middle Department throughout the war. The only exception was when Washington's army moved into the Southern Department to counter General Cornwallis. At that time, two important command decisions were made. First, the command of the geographic area of the Middle Department was passed on to the militia commander during Washington's absence, and second, Washington did not assume command of the Southern Department during the time he was there. His mission was very specific while General Greene's was much broader in scope. General Greene continued to command his forces, focusing primarily on South Carolina preventing British forces from assisting Cornwallis while General Washington was focused totally on the attack at Yorktown.

The Middle Department did perform its military role particularly in the areas of New Jersey and Pennsylvania in battles such as Germantown, Trenton, and Camden. The majority of the military activity in this department took place in New Jersey, in large part due to the proximity of New Jersey to New York City, which was held by the British. New Jersey ranked first for amount of military activity within a state by the Continental Army, but South Carolina had the most battles, fought predominately by militia troops.

British-occupied New York City and Long Island became high-interest areas. In fact, New Jersey became known as the "Crossroads of the Revolution," as both

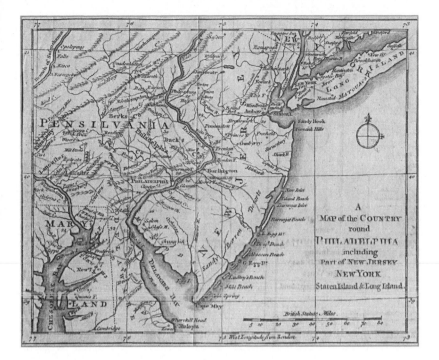

armies moved through the state on their way to battle. In addition, it also represented the dividing line between the north, where fighting stopped during the winter months, and the south, where the fighting could be continued on a year-round basis.

Although New Jersey, Pennsylvania, Delaware, and Maryland all served in the Middle Department, each state represented a diverse and non-homogeneous population. Each state had its own character and it was not always in the favor of the Rebels. In New Jersey, for example, the population was split between the Loyalists and the Rebels. The split was so divisive that, in 1777, armed conflict erupted in the state between the two elements. As a result of the conflict many Loyalists fled to New York City where they continued their support of the British.

Pennsylvania, on the other hand, was still predominately a Quaker (religious order based on pacifism) state at the time of the Revolution. Many Quakers lost their property due to their refusal to sign the Writs of Assistance, which gave the British authority to search their homes for smuggling activities. When the war broke out, there wasn't a single military organization in the entire state. Eventually, volunteer companies were formed that became known as the Military Associates, which actively supported Washington's campaign during 1776–77.

During the Revolutionary period, there were two distinct and separate areas of Pennsylvania. The first was a predominately Quaker area located in the eastern part of the state including Philadelphia, and the second was in the western part of the state, centered on what was then called Fort Pitt, which later served as the headquarters of the Western Department. The second area was predominately non-Quaker, which provided troops for the Continental Army.

Mission of Middle Department

So, why would George Washington move his troops from New York City to New Jersey and take charge of the Middle Department? The name of the department tells it all. By having the Main Army located in the territory of the Middle Department, Washington could move his troops either north or south in order to provide military support as required, which he did prior to the battle of Yorktown. At the same time, Washington wanted to be in the proximity of New York City since it was the British military headquarters. By creating the spy ring on Long Island in 1778, he could keep a close watch on British activities and their plans. Washington also knew that the British were interested in maintaining their hold only of the southern colonies—they were the money makers with the production of cotton and tobacco. By having the Continental Army firmly placed between the British headquarters in New York City and the southern colonies, it was very difficult for the British forces in New York to support their southern counterparts.

INTELLIGENCE OPERATIONS

Washington Recruits Agents

When Washington entered New Jersey with his army, he had two intelligence problems: the first was tactical and the second was strategic. The first and most pressing was to establish an intelligence capability within the state for military operations. He already had his system of military aides tasked with intelligence operations. He was aware of at least one rebel spy ring—that of the Joshua Mersereau family, who lived in northern New Jersey and had supported Washington during his time on Long Island. Beyond this group, Washington had to be careful when recruiting since New Jersey was a major Loyalist state. Fortunately, he was not in the state very long before he found willing agents to provide him with tactical intelligence. An example of this was demonstrated by an agent's report and map given to Washington before the battle of Princeton. The tactical intelligence flow to Washington continued throughout the war and often from unexpected sources.

On the strategic side, Washington was well aware of the need for continuing strategic intelligence regarding the activities of the British continental headquarters in New York City. His time and efforts, however, were taken up in the other colonies. He established a foothold in New Jersey, and it was not until the summer of 1778, after the battle of Monmouth and after the British fell back to New York City, that he was able to take action to correct the situation. He tasked his intelligence aide, Major Benjamin Tallmadge, to organize a network in the New York City area known as the Culper Ring. Located strategically on Long Island and controlled by Tallmadge, the sole task of the Culper Ring was to provide Washington with information regarding the British headquarters and its activities. Under Washington's tutoring, the members were trained in the use of invisible ink, coding and decoding of messages, and the use of aliases. The Culper Ring proved to be highly successful in keeping Washington informed of the intentions of the British Army. Its mission never changed—it was always directed solely against New York City and Long Island. It remained active until the end of the war.

In addition to the Culper Ring, Washington used individual spies in his efforts against the British command. In the fall of 1780, Washington desperately wanted to kidnap the traitor Benedict Arnold for a trial by the Continental authorities. To accomplish the task, he recruited Sergeant John Champe to "desert" to the enemy and work his way to New York City, where he was to kidnap and bring Arnold back to Washington. Unfortunately the plan failed, but not due to Champe's efforts. That same year Sergeant Daniel Bissell was recruited to "desert" to the enemy and collect intelligence. His desertion was accepted by the British and he remained behind enemy lines for two years, before reporting back to Washington.

The intelligence activities of the individual states of the Middle Department follow.

New Jersey

When Washington and his troops entered New Jersey in November 1776, the fox hunt began, with Washington as the fox and Cornwallis as the master of the hounds. Washington was stalling for time until the army was united with General Henry Lee, who was intentionally lagging in his arrival from New York. His tactic was to keep the army moving, and rely on locals to keep him informed about the movement of the British Army. After entering New Jersey via Newark, Washington moved on to New Brunswick leaving Newark as the British arrived. From there, he left for Princeton and finally Trenton—all with the British in pursuit. At this point, he crossed the Delaware River into Pennsylvania, where he was joined by 4,000 local militia troops. Washington cleverly ordered that all the boats along the Delaware River be secured on the west side of the river, thus creating a barrier for the British Army. When the British arrived at the Delaware River on December 18, General Howe received a cannonade from across the river and decided to stop there to go into winter quarters, a common practice for both armies. It was during this campaign that General Howe coined the nickname of "The Fox" for General Washington.

The British Army may have gone to winter quarters as the Continental army expected them to do, but Washington wanted to go on the offensive. He needed to prove to his army, as well as the populace, that they could win this war. Colonel Joseph Reed, one of his trusted aides, wrote a note to Washington saying "that something must be attempted to revive our expiring credit, give our cause some degree of respect, and prevent the depletion of the Continental money, which is coming in very fast — but even a total failure cannot be more total than to remain in our present situation." Washington replied "that the game was about up." After reviewing all the facts at hand, Washington decided that the Hessians at Trenton would be the target.

Battle of Trenton

The British decision to go into winter quarters was quickly recognized by General Washington, who immediately sent out agents to gain intelligence about the deployment of British forces. They reported back that the British forces' major commands were located at Trenton, Burlington, Princeton, Port Amboy, and New Brunswick. The Hessians, because of their brave actions at the battle of Fort Washington in November of 1776, had the honor of being placed in the forward position. They were placed at Burlington and Trenton with outposts at Mansfield Square and Black Horse Tavern. The theory being that if the Colonials did attack any of these posts, the Hessians with their military tenacity would provide time for the British Army to react in a positive manner.

Once the point of attack was determined, the date had to be decided. General Washington chose to attack on the 26th of December for a very wise reason: he had learned that the Hessians would celebrate Christmas by feasting and drinking in great quantities—a celebration that would make the next day a recovery day.

How Washington knew this fact could have been due to a member of his intelligence network, a German named Christopher Ludwick, known as "The General's Baker." Ludwick had served in the German army, and had once again infiltrated into the Hessian camp, as he had done on Staten Island. His mission was to ascertain if the Hessians would be celebrating Christmas in their usual drunken way as they had when he was in the Hessian army. Since there were many German-speaking people in the area, his presence went unnoticed. Discovering that the celebrations would happen, Washington now knew he had the advantage. Local legend has it that a spy by the name of John Honeyman informed Washington about the Christmas celebration. However, no official record of John Honeyman is known to exist. His story is apparently an anecdotal account created by an unknown author.

As Washington's army prepared for the attack, the Hessians were totally unaware of the activity across the river. Colonel Johann Gottlieb Rall (also spelled Rahl), the Hessian commander, ate Christmas dinner at the Green Tree Tavern and played cards there with the local rector. Later that evening, a Loyalist came to the tavern and passed a note warning Colonel Rall of the attack, but he merely folded it and placed it in his waistcoat. Later, after the attack had been mounted, Colonel Rall's body was found with the folded note in his waistcoat. In a period of just over two hours, the Continental Army captured 1,000 arms, several cannons and ammunitions stores, and captured 896 Hessians—all at a loss of four soldiers. Knowledge of the enemy's habits gave Washington a distinct advantage before battle. Washington had turned the tide—with intelligence largely responsible for his victory.

Second Battle of Trenton — The Fox Escapes

As Washington was well aware, the British would not allow his victory at Trenton to go unchallenged. He returned to Trenton after a short respite for his troops and prepared for the arrival of Cornwallis and his army. Knowing that he would be greatly outnumbered by the British, he planned carefully and accordingly. An attack on Princeton seemed like the most obvious solution. A successful attack there would provide much needed supplies as well as relief for the troops—both mentally and physically. On the night of December 31, 1776, Washington received the following letter from General Cadwalader, which strengthened his plan to proceed to Princeton:

Sir   Crosswix (N.J.) 31st Decr 1776
    A very intelligent young Gentleman is returned, just now, from Prince Town, he left this yesterday Morng & got in about 12 or 1 O'Clock. He would have returned last Night but General Lesley, who commands & Col: Abercombie would not suffer him to go off. He made his escape this Morng early, & informs,

that from the best Information he could get, there were about 5000 men—consisting of Hessians & British Troops—about the same Number of each. I have made a rough Draught of the Road from this place; the Situation of the Cannon & Works begun & those intended this Morng. He thinks there are not so many as they report. He conversed with some of the officers & lodged last Night with them(americans). They enquired what were our Numbers; He mentioned abt 16000, from the best accts. They did not believe we had more than 5 or 6000, that many were forced into the Service, & that they were deserting in great Numbers every day. No Sentries on the back or East side of Town. They parade every Morng an hour before day, and some Nights lie on their Arms, an Attack has been expected for several nights past- the men much fatigued, & till last Night, in want of Provisions when a very considerable number of Waggons arrived with Provisions from Brunswick. All their Baggage sent to Brunswick, where there are but few men. This confirms the Acct I sent you last Night. About 50 light Horse at Prince Town, one half quartered at Scudders Mill, the other on the West of the Town. He enquired if any Troops were on the Road. They say there are none on this Side of Brunswick, some Hessians arrived yesterday (tis said from Brunswick. I suppose they were those that landed at South Amboy, as I cannot hear any thing of them in this neighbourhood.

A Party of our light Horse brought in this Morng to Cranberry, about 30 Cattle, left by the Hessians, in general, poor. I recd your Letter last Night, by Express. Our Spy was near the Party of Chasseurs, when they were taken & says an Assistant Qr Master Gen. or Commissary was with them. The Enemy had heard it. Major Mifflin is just setting off with a Party of 200 from Cumberland. I am, Sir, with great Respect, Your Excellencys most obt Servt.

John Cadwalader

With this information in-hand and knowing he had a head start on Cornwallis, Washington advanced his troops toward Princeton. A victory there would provide him with much-needed supplies, as well as a morale booster both for his army and the populace as well. He patiently waited until January 2, 1777, when he learned that Cornwallis had arrived at last. He ordered General Edward Hand to engage Cornwallis' advancing troops in a delaying action, which lasted about six hours, thereby allowing Washington to begin the movement of troops to Princeton. Additionally, he set up what appeared to be a defensive line of infantry troops along the south side of the Assunpink Creek. When Cornwallis arrived late in the day, he decided to wait until the morning to attack, gloating that, "At

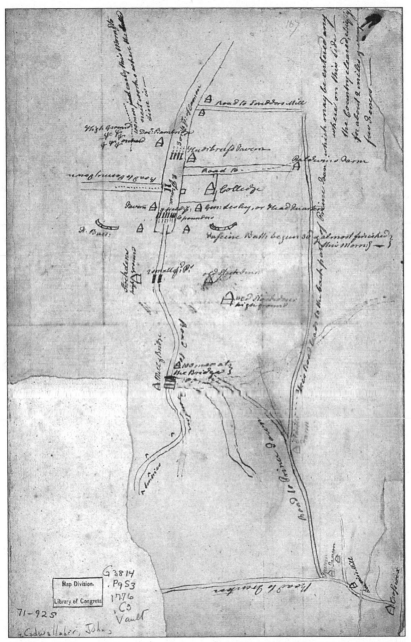

ENCLOSED WITH CADWALADER'S LETTER WAS THIS HAND-DRAWN MAP OF PRINCETON.

last we have run down the fox and will bag him in the morning."To make matters worse for the British, Washington used one of the oldest military tricks in the book: deception! He ordered some troops left behind to build fires in areas where the British would be sure to see them, and to shout orders audible to the British. Meanwhile, he commanded the remainder of his army to silently move out of the area toward Princeton. Cornwallis roused on January 3, 1777, to a rude awakening. Washington and his army were nowhere to be found, and cannon noises could be heard in the distance. Realizing that Washington moved to Princeton overnight, Cornwallis quickly relocated his army to New Brunswick, in order to protect his supplies stored there. Needless to say, the attack was successful for the Continental Army, garnering supplies and providing the Colonies with a newly found confidence in their army.

During this period, both armies moved their defensive positions many times. When scouts informed Washington that Cornwallis retreated to New Brunswick, he decided to move to Morristown to establish winter quarters for his victorious army. Both sides remained in winter quarters until April 1777, when Cornwallis attempted to draw Washington out by showing signs of taking his own army out of winter quarters. Washington, however, was aware of the ruse—most likely due to the spying activities of the Mersereau family in northern New Jersey. The family closely followed the movements of the British and reported them, usually in person, to General Washington. When Cornwallis realized Washington wouldn't react, he finally evacuated New Jersey and returned his army to Staten Island in June 1777. Shortly thereafter, Washington turned over the defense of New Jersey to the state militia and moved his army to the Highlands of New York, fully aware that good intelligence and deception techniques had played a major role in his New Jersey victories.

British Intelligence in New Jersey

The British maintained an intelligence awareness of the Continental Army's activities in New Jersey largely through Brigadier General Cortlandt Skinner, who served as the New Jersey attorney general when the British evacuated the colony. In that same June when the British Army left New Jersey, he remained behind to set up Loyalist networks in New Jersey, all of which would report to him. He situated his headquarters on Staten Island, and continued to report on New Jersey for the remainder of the war. His presence was not known to Washington, but as the war shifted south Skinner's value to the British diminished.

Pennsylvania

Even before Washington's move to the Highlands of New York, he had received reports of increased activity in New York City. His agents were reporting that General Howe was planning an assault on Philadelphia. The "when" question was finally answered when Washington was advised that on July 23, 1777, General Howe and his troops sailed from New York with the destination of Philadelphia. Washington waited. He knew that he would be alerted to the movement of the British fleet up the Chesapeake Bay area, as well as the destination of the ships. He then received reports from agents along the shores of the Chesapeake Bay that the ships had landed at Head of Elk River on August 25, 1777, along with an estimate of the troops involved. Most importantly, he now knew the route to be taken by the British.

Washington's Eyes and Ears in Philadelphia: John Clark

Just a few short weeks before he moved his troops into Pennsylvania, Washington knew he would need to build an intelligence network in and around Philadelphia, which was the largest city in the Colonies at the time. He selected one of his young intelligence officers, John Clark, for the mission, and sent him south in advance. Clark soon had an extensive network of spies operating in the area. While he himself rarely went into the city, he did remain in the periphery allowing his agents to come to him, as he felt a variety of persons going in and out of the city was much less suspicious than one person constantly going in and out.

Clark's network failed to forewarn Washington of the British advances against Paoli and Germantown resulting in considerable casualties. Clark was able to report the casualty numbers from these battles. These numbers were important to Washington, who was in a constant conflict of attrition. Losing a battle was still considered a win if the British had more casualties.

Washington considered Clark to be one of his own personal spies. They thought alike and worked as a team. Their relationship is well demonstrated by the following exchange that took place in November 1777. Clark recommended that "according to Sir William's desire," Washington should draw up a false statement concerning the number and condition of the American Army and "your intended movements," which would then be dutifully delivered to Howe for his misinformation.

Delighted by the scheme, Washington replied to Clark, "you have fallen upon an exceedingly good method of obtaining intelligence and that too much secrecy cannot be used, both on account of the safety [of Clark's spy] and the execution of continuance of your design, which may be of service to us." Washington then provided the false information he wished to have delivered to Howe:

"I'd have you mention that General Gates, now having nothing to do to the Northward [Burgoyne's invasion from Canada having been defeated], is sending down a very handsome Reinforcement of Continental Troops to this Army, whilst he with the remainder of them and all the New England and York Militia, is to make an immediate descent on New York [City], the reduction of which is constantly spoken of... and that Genl. (Philemon) Dickinson is at the same time to attack Staten Island, for which purpose he is Assembling great numbers of the Jersey Militia; that the received opinion in our Camp is, that we will immediately attack Philadelphia on the arrival of the Troops from the Northward, and that I have prevailed upon the Legislative Body to order out two thirds of the Militia of this State for that purpose; that you have heard great talk of the Virginia and Maryland Militia coming up, and in short that the whole Continent seems determined that we use every exertion to put an end to the War this winter; that we mention the forts as being perfectly secure, having sent ample Reinforcements to their support."

With winter coming, both the Americans and the British were about to settle down in winter quarters. General Howe planned to assault the American army, hoping to deal it a death blow, but Clark's agents discovered their plan through idle gossip. They successfully managed to provide a continual flow of intelligence to Washington regarding important details of the attack. The encounter, now known as the battle of White Marsh, resulted in a failed attempt by the British to rout the American army. Through Clark's efforts, Washington knew in advance of their plan and could therefore plan his defenses accordingly. The British defeat was a major disappointment for General Howe.

Washington and Clark were of a single mind when it came to intelligence and deception. Their close collaboration continued until January 1778, when Clark was forced to resign his commission due to poor health. However, the network that Clark had built in and around Philadelphia continued to support Washington until the Continental Army left the area in June 1778.

A Quaker Lady Joins the Revolution: Lydia Darragh

While Washington was heavily dependent on Clark and his spies, he did have another unique source of information from a Quaker woman, Lydia Darragh. She quietly ran a family network in support of the Continental Army for the entire time they were in the Philadelphia area. Lydia collected the information and her husband, William, would record it on small bits of paper in his own created shorthand. These papers were then positioned on large metal buttons called "mold buttons," that Lydia would cover with material to match the coat. Wearing the coat, Lydia's son, John, would then cross into the American camp area to deliver the buttons to Lydia's brother, William, an American army lieutenant. From there, the message would be deciphered and delivered to Washington. No one knows what specific intelligence Lydia passed this way with one exception.

General Howe began planning what he'd hoped to be a surprise annihilation of Washington and the Continental Army; he even increased the size of his army. The increase of troops meant some would need to be housed by locals, a requirement enacted by the British. General Howe required a room to be used as his council

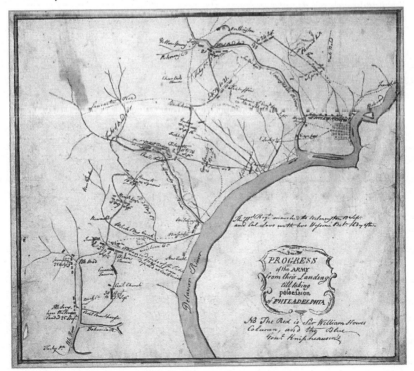

ORIGINAL MAP OF VALLEY FORGE REGION

chamber and he chose Lydia's home for this purpose. On the night of December 2, 1777, a British officer instructed Lydia to put the family to bed early since they wished to use the room that night without interruption. The group gathered and Lydia, through a partition, was able to listen to their conversation. She discovered that the British would march out of Philadelphia by night on December 4 to attack Washington's army. According to her report, with their superior force and the unprepared condition of the enemy, the British seemed confident in their victory.

Lydia knew she had to get this information to Washington, but wasn't sure how to execute that task. In order to maintain security, she did not tell her husband what she had heard. She decided it had to be hand delivered, and since she had a British pass that allowed her to cross the British lines, she would be the one to deliver the message. She left Philadelphia, walking toward the American army until she ran into an American officer, probably Major Allan McLane, one of Washington's intelligence officers. When McLane heard the information Lydia brought he said, "that every intelligence from the city agrees that the enemy is in motion and intends a great strike." This was important information and had to be delivered to Washington at once. Lydia returned home exhausted but pleased with herself.

The battle of White Marsh did take place, but not with the result that Howe wished for. Washington and his army remained intact and in place. The casualties on both sides were fairly equal, but the British inability to crush Washington's army led to the resignation of General Howe and his return to England. And that spring the British evacuated Philadelphia.

A Horseshoe at Valley Forge

In December 1777, after the skirmishes at White Marsh, Washington took his army into winter quarters at Valley Forge, given its advantage of defensibility about thirty miles east of Philadelphia. Washington cleverly placed his troops in a horseshoe shape, with the open end of the shoe facing west. This arrangement not only provided easy access for his intelligence agents to his headquarters (they kept coming as long as he was at Valley Forge), but it also made it possible for food and supplies to be delivered.

One good example is the Oneida Indians, who had substantial lands in the east. That year they had an abundant crop of corn. Realizing the need for food for the troops at Valley Forge, the Oneida Chief Skenandoah sent supplies of corn from central New York State to Valley Forge. An Oneida woman, known to the English as Polly Cooper, accompanied the supplies and remained at Valley Forge to teach the troops how to cook the corn. It is entirely possible that through her contacts with the various Indian tribes she was able to keep Washington informed as to the intentions of the Indians. When she left Valley Forge, she was presented with a shawl belonging to Martha Washington.

(It should be noted that Washington set up winter quarters in the Middle Department on two other occasions, both times at Morristown, New Jersey. The first was in January 1777, and the second would be in the fall of 1779. In the case of the January 1777 encampments the conditions were more severe than later at Valley Forge.)

As spring 1778 approached, Washington's network of spies in Philadelphia began to report rumors of General Clinton moving the main part of his army out of Philadelphia. Based on these reports, Washington prepared his army for the chase. On June 18, 1778, Washington moved his troops out of Valley Forge in pursuit of Clinton and his army. It wasn't until June 28 that the two armies collided in the battle of Monmouth. The battle was considered by most to be a draw, as the British continued their retreat to New York, but in Washington's mind it was a victory. His troops, trained by Baron von Steuben, a professional soldier from the Prussian army, performed in a highly disciplined manner in a combat situation. He now had what he considered a professional army.

The battle of Monmouth was the last major battle to be fought in any of the northern departments of the Colonies. The British hope of cutting off the southern colonies from the north had failed. After the British entrenchment in New York City, Washington moved his troops to White Plains, New York, in the Highlands Department from where he hoped to launch an attack on New York City.

Deception Plan for Invasion of New York

While no other major battles were fought in the Middle Department after the battle of Monmouth, the Middle Department did contribute to the overall deception scheme leading to the battle of Yorktown. In the summer of 1781, when Washington began to move his combined French and American forces south, the geography of New Jersey was a central part of the deception plan to convince the British his target was New York City. Washington had French troops in their very distinct uniforms clearly visible on the north shore of New Jersey, and in a stroke of genius, he had built a complete camp, ovens and all in New Jersey. This gave the British spies ample proof that his army was coming to New Jersey prior to an invasion of New York City. The deception plan had once again fooled the British. Due to the perceived threat from Washington, they were forced to keep troops in New York City that would have been more useful in the south.

SUMMARY

Despite the metaphorical rollercoaster the Middle Department went through, it did fulfill its mission of serving as a barrier between the northern colonies and those of the south. From a low at Valley Forge to an absolute high in 1781, Washington's use of intelligence proved to be critical in both areas. First, at both the battle of Trenton and the battle of Princeton, advanced intelligence by untrained agents provided Washington information that gave him the upper hand as he planned his tactical maneuver. Ludwick's report of the activities of the Hessians on Christmas and the sketched map of Princeton provided by a young man were immensely essential to maintain an edge over the British forces. The second use of intelligence, developed in the Middle Department and used throughout the entire war, was deception. Washington became a master of this art and his actions became a model for his generals (and even much later in World War II). Officers who served under Washington in the early days of the Middle Department and learned the techniques of intelligence later went on to command departments of their own where they employed many of the methods of intelligence they had learned in the Middle Department. General Nathanael Greene is a good example of such an officer.

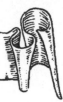

a person of interest
in the middle department

SERGEANT DANIEL BISSELL

DANIEL BISSELL, BORN ON DECEMBER 30, 1754, IN WINDSOR, Connecticut, was raised on a farm with the typical but rudimentary amount of education. In 1775, after the battle of Lexington and Concord, he enlisted as a fifer in the 8th Connecticut Regiment. Later that same year, he re-enlisted as a corporal in the 5th Connecticut Regiment for the duration of the conflict. He participated in the battles of White Plains (1776), Trenton (1776), and Monmouth (1778), where he was wounded in the cheek by a piece of shrapnel. By this time a sergeant, he was highly respected for his military performance, as well as his innate intelligence and trustworthy character. At one point, he had served as the paymaster for his unit. His leadership in battle gained him the respect of the men he commanded.

In 1781, General George Washington felt the need to send an agent into the New York area to gather information about British forces. He wanted to know the number of troops and, if possible, their future plans of attack. When Washington asked his staff for a candidate to undertake this mission, Colonel Herman Swift of the 2nd Connecticut Regiment and one of Washington's most trusted officers, recommended one of his sergeants, Daniel Bissell. Colonel Swift was aware of the photographic memory and total recall exhibited by Sergeant Bissell—a great asset for a spy. With Washington's approval, Colonel Swift approached Sergeant Bissell, explaining the purpose of the mission and most importantly what would be required of him. Sergeant Bissell would feint a desertion from his unit and go behind enemy lines for a period of about two weeks. It was explained to him that if he was captured, the Continental Army would confirm him as a deserter—a rather heavy price to pay. Despite this fact, Bissell readily agreed and prepared to depart.

His mission in his own words

The best way to describe his mission is from an affidavit in his own words, which he provided at the age of sixty. He said:

> *State of New York, Ontario County, ss: I, DANIEL BISSELL, of Richmond,*
> *of more than sixty years of age, do testify and say, that on the thirteenth day of*

August 1781, Col. Herman Swift, of the 2nd Connecticut Regiment, called on me early in the morning, and stated to me that he dined at Head Quarters the day before, and His Excellency found it necessary to send within the British lines, to ascertain their position and force, some person, and that I was determined on for the undertaking, and further stated that His Excellency conceived that the great danger was in passing the several examinations. After some further conversation the subject passed between us, I agreed to accept the perilous tour. Col. Swift then directed me to go to a certain place near Head Quarters, where Col. David Humphrey would meet me. Soon after I arrived at the place appointed, the Colonel came and put into my hand a paper, requesting me to go to some bye-place and read it over, through the course of the day, then destroy it, go to my Regiment, get some refreshment, put on and carry with me two suits of clothes, wear in my watch, silver buckles, &c., which I wore in the American army, so as it should have the appearance of deserting; (note: Still further to avoid suspicious and secure the accomplishment of the design in hand, Bissell was entered and published in the official returns, as a deserter from the American army. His real character and design were thus known only to Washington and a few of his principal officers. The astonishment and mortification of his numerous friends, when they heard him returned as a deserter, can be better imagined than described; though his character was afterwards satisfactorily vindicated) and at the time the army was on the parade for evening roll-call, quit the Regiment, go to a bridge between the army and Col. Schammel's Light Infantry, where I should meet Col. Swift, who would give me further instructions. Col. Swift directed me to call on Col. Schammel at his marquee at nine o'clock in the evening; and Col. Schammel went with, and conducted me by his Camp guards and sentinels, and informed me that he had ordered off all guards and patrols from the North River road (until after midnight) down as far as Croton Bridge, that being the extend of our lines. I was then to answer (if hailed) 'friend of Britain.' The paper Col. Humphrey gave me was as follows, to the best of my recollection:

"As Gen. Arnold (note: the traitor Arnold in the British service) is now in Virginia, with all the new raised corps, there will be no recruiting parties in New York; and as the fleet is now at the Hook, consequently there will be no press (gang) in the city; and with the money you carry in, you can get a protection from the Mayor or Police of the city, to go to Lloyd's Neck, thirty miles on Long Island, to cut wood for the Crown. After this, you will return to King's Bridge or Laurel Hill, and view the works there, obtain the number of each regiment, the number of men each

contains, by whom commanded, their several alarm posts, the number of cannon mounted in each work. You will view all the works on York Island in the same manner; get the whole number of regular forces, distinguishing the British from the foreigners; the number of new raised corps, and also the number of militia enrolled for the defense of the city. Get what information you can of their works and force at Powler's Hook, also that of Staten Island. Obtain the number of Shipping in the Harbour, and that at the Hook; and when you have completed your business here, you will pass over to Brooklyn, view the works there, ascertain their force on Long Island. When you have got the business completed, the seventh or ninth night, be at a place called Whitestone, not far from Lloyd's Neck, where a boat will attend to fetch you off. In case you cannot attend on one of those nights, you will then make you escape off at the east end of Long Island."

Becoming a deserter

There are several points to be made before continuing Bissell's story. First, to officially be labeled a deserter is no small matter, especially for a man very obviously dedicated to the cause of his country. He would forever be branded as a traitor by his family, his town, as well as the soldiers he had served with in the Continental Army. Second, the letter Bissell was instructed to give Colonel Schammel was an authentication of who he was. Bissell claimed that when he caught a glance of the opened letter, it was a blank sheet of paper—a prearranged signal. Third, it must be noted that General Washington did not inform Sergeant Bissell of any of the other intelligence activities he was orchestrating in the New York area. Washington wanted information from various sources that he could compare and validate—what today we call "independent sourcing." In this case, however, Bissell had no secure channel to report any of the intelligence he developed, since he was a one-man operation. Washington received no information from Bissell prior to his return—which was a year later.

And now to continue Bissell's story in his own words:

"Then followed all the probable questions that would be asked me, in the several examinations, together with their answers. But when I arrived at New York, to my great disappointment, I found that Gen. Arnold had returned and had established his recruiting parties in every place where deserters could come in; that the British fleet had got into New York and shut out the French fleet; and that the press-gangs were in every part of the city; that the Commander-in-chief, Sir Harry [sic] Clinton, had issued a late order that there should be no

more protections given to deserters. After avoiding the press-gang for three days, and being attacked with a violent fever, (note: Mr. Bissell has been heard to say that he had fully possessed himself of the details of the proposed attack on New London, when he was attacked with illness and thus prevented from making any use of his knowledge, as he dared not attempt to swim the river in his enfeebled condition.) I caused my name to be enrolled in Arnold's regiment. I was soon after sent to the Hospital at Flushing, in December following removed back to York Island (Harlem Heights), put into a barn which was their Regimental Hospital, where I remained until May. Here my suffering was truly great; without fire the greatest part of the time, only wood allowed for the purpose of cooking our pork and pease; without attendance, but one additional blanket to two men; without shifting my clothes for three months; covered with head and body lice; unable to walk. In this situation, I was taken out of the Hospital to do Quarter-Master Sergeant's duty, for said Regiment, by Capt. Robert Rowley, who acted also as a Quarter-Master to the same; and through his kind attention to my health, I owe my escape from them."

Bissell completes his missions

Sergeant Bissell escaped after thirteen months behind enemy lines by bribing a boatman to take him across the Hudson River to New Jersey. From there he returned to the Continental Army. His time as the quartermaster sergeant in the British Army provided him with detailed information regarding many facets of the British military, including morale issues, logistics, level of supplies, and strategic planning. There is no record of the information he brought back, but he states that it took him two full days to write it all down on paper. He seemed to be remembering these details from memory since he destroyed all his notes when it became too dangerous to keep them. Washington was amazed as he stood before him and relayed all the information he had gathered without a single note.

Again, it is important to make a few points relative to Bissell's account. First, being in New York as a deserter was dangerous as General Clinton had voided any protection for them. Second, Bissell joined Benedict Arnold's Corps, where he became sick, which was the only way he would get any medical attention.

After his return, Bissell was offered a chance to be transferred to the Invalid Corps and receive a pension, but he declined saying, "This I declined on the ground that my Country was poor and it would be of no advantage to me." At this point he was placed in the 2nd Connecticut Regiment and remained there until the war was over.

Honorary Badge of Military Merit

The value of Daniel Bissell's intelligence, along with his brave actions, which provided support to the Colonial efforts was recognized by General Washington on May 9, 1783, when Bissell became one of the three men to receive the Honorary Badge of Military Merit. His citation reads:

"I, GEORGE WASHINGTON, Commander-in-Chief of the American Army, &c., &c., &c., "To all to whom these Presents shall come, sendeth Greeting:

"Whereas it hath ever been established maxim in the American Service, that the Road to Glory was open to all, that Honorary Rewards and Distinctions, were the greatest Stimuli to virtuous actions, and whereas Sergeant DANIEL BISSELL of the Second Connecticut Regiment, has performed some important service, within the immediate knowledge of the Commander-in-Chief, in which his fidelity, perseverance and good sense, were not only conspicuously manifested, but his general line of conduct throughout a long course of service, having been not only unspotted but highly deserving of commendation.

"Now, therefore, Know Ye, that the aforesaid Sergeant BISSELL, hath fully and truly deserved, and hath been properly invested with, the Honorary Badge of Military Merit, and is entitled to pass and repass all Guards and Military Posts, as freely and as amply [as] any Commissioned Officer whatever; and is further recommended to that Notice which a Brave and Faithful Soldier deserves from his Countrymen.

"Given under my hand and seal, in the Highlands of New York, this Ninth day of May, A.D. 1783

"Signed, "GEORGE WASHINGTON, (L.S.)

"Registered, "JONATHAN TRUMBULL, Secretary."

Legend has Daniel Bissell tied to the present-day Purple Heart medal. During the early days of the war, Bissell was at a dance and was dancing with a young lady named Rhoda Hurlbut (later to become his wife). As a clumsy dragoon passed Miss Hurlbut he accidently caught his spur on the bottom of her purple dress, ripping off a strip. Daniel Bissell picked up the strip, folded it like a heart, and pinned it on the inside of his jacket, where he wore it for the remainder of the war. When George Washington heard this he is reported to have said "Ah, a Purple Heart."

Post-War Life

After the war, Daniel Bissell did not choose to return to Windsor, Connecticut, where he was still listed as a deserter. He settled initially in Randolph, Vermont, and later moved to Richmond, New York. He returned to active duty in the army as a lieutenant with the 16th Regt. U.S. Infantry to fight the Indians in what has become known as "The Adams War" (1798–1800). He died in Richmond, New York, on August 21, 1824, and was buried in the local cemetery. His tombstone reads: "Daniel Bissell, Died August 21, 1824, Aged 70 Years. He had the confidence of Washington and served under him."

However, Daniel Bissell was considered a deserter by his hometown of Windsor for over 180 years. Finally, in 1919, a rock was placed on the Bissell Farm designating it as the birthplace of Daniel Bissell, Patriot Spy. The plaque on that rock states: "Birthplace of Daniel Bissell, Patriot Spy of the American Revolution, 1754 – 1824."

Sergeant Daniel Bissell has been recognized by the U.S. Army Intelligence branch for his work in the Revolutionary War. His name is now listed in the Military Intelligence Hall of Fame, established by the Military Intelligence Corps of the United States Army in 1988 at Fort Huachuca, Arizona.

According to the Connecticut Archives, a poem was written by a compatriot of Bissell. It reads:

> *Daniel Bissell of Windsor, The Revolutionary Spy*
> *A man: a strong, courageous, upright man,*
> *Who did his duty as it came to him,*
> *In those troublous days that tried the hearts of men,*
> *Despising suffering, and even death, for his country's cause.*
> *A spy: the crown of martyrdom put from him by a kind Providence,*
> *Which the crown of large success his labors gave, instead;*
> *And to complete his work sufficient strength,*
> *And to his home and friends returned him safe.*
> *And we; who think perhaps we live in times far less severe,*
> *But problems have to solve no less obscure,*
> *What cheer from this compatriot, who has gone before?*
> *"Our country first, be strong, to God the rest."*
> *A Tribute of a Compatriot Kinsman*

His willingness to undertake such a mission and be branded as a deserter speaks clearly about Bissell's character. With his known photographic memory and total recall, we can only guess at the intelligence value of his extended mission. However, it must have been quite extensive for General Washington to decide to honor him with the Honorary Badge of Military Merit—one of only three given out during the Revolutionary War.

The intelligence he relayed to Washington, while not of immediate tactical use, offered a wealth of knowledge regarding many aspects of the British Army. Bissell's reports provided Washington with extensive information regarding supply levels, morale, number of troops, and logistical support. Thus affording Washington valuable background knowledge for the long-range strategic planning for final victory.

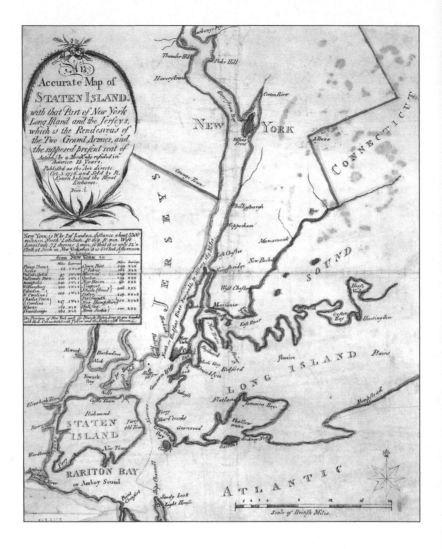

An
Accurate Map of
STATEN ISLAND,
with that Part of New York
Long Island and the Jerseys,
which is the Rendesvous of
the Two Grand Armies, and
the supposed present seat of
Action, By a Sketch who resided in
America 15 Years.
Published as the Act directs.
Oct. 3. 1776. and Sold by R.
Lynn behind the Royal
Exchange.
Price -

New York is W by S of London distance about 3300 miles in North Latitude 41 deg. 6 min. West Longitude 74 degrees 3 min. so that it is 5 of the Clock at Noon in New York when it is 5 of Clock Afternoon

from NEW YORK to

	Miles	bearing		Miles	bearing
Perops Town	32	S W b S	Crown Point	220	N N E
Jersey	27	S W W	St. Johns	300	N N E
Perth Amboy	27	S W b W	Montreal	340	N N E
Baltimore Town	210	S W b S	Quebec	559	N N E
Annapolis	240	S W b S	New Haven	40	E N E
Williamsburg	300	S W b S	Newport		E N E
Edenton	505	S W b S	Rhode Island	200	E N E
N. Carolina		S W b S	Boston	240	N E b E
Charles Town	647	S W b S	Portsmouth		N E b E
S. Carolina		S W b S	New Hampshire	320	N E b E
Albany	164	N b E	Halifax		E N E
Ticonderoga	202	N N E	Nova Scotia	500	E N E

The Province of New York and its Islands hown here is pea bounded with Red. Connecticut with Yellow and the Jerseys with Green.

NEW YORK

CONNECTICUT

JERSEY

LONG ISLAND

STATEN ISLAND

RARITON BAY
or Amboy Sound

ATLANTIC

SOUND

Scale of British Miles.

VII

The New York Department

MAJOR EVENTS

1776

Washington arrives in New York City

General Howe arrives on Staten Island

Battle of Long Island

Battle of Kip's Bay

British take New York City

Battle of Harlem Heights

Nathan Hale hanged as spy in New York City

Battle of White Plains

Battle of Fort Washington

THE HISTORY OF THE NEW YORK DEPARTMENT IS ONE OF CHAOS due to early developments in the war. The New York Department was established on June 25, 1775, encompassing all of the Province of New York. The department was formed in anticipation of the British Army movement from Nova Scotia to New York City. However, that did not happen until July 3, 1776, when the British landed on Staten Island. This gave the Patriots time to refine the department structure. When the Middle Department was formed on February 27, 1776, the New York Department was merged into it. The merger, however, only lasted less than two months, and on April 14, 1776, the Northern Department was formed. This department included all of the Province of New York north of the Hudson Highlands. The remainder of the New York Department, consisting of New York City and Long Island, ceased to exist with the occupation by the British on September 15, 1776. Washington moved to White Plains in early October 1776.

The focus of the war had shifted with the evacuation of Boston on March 7, 1776, and the move to Nova Scotia by the British. This deployment was seen by Washington as temporary, since the British would undoubtedly return, and this time, with a focus on New York City, a known Loyalist town. This belief led Washington to move his army to New York City in an attempt to thwart the British plans.

When Washington came to New York City in April 1776, it was the second largest town in the New World with a population of 25,000; but more importantly, it was a major port city for the profitable import/export business predominately with Britain and the rest of Europe. It was a Loyalist town with many merchants amassing a fortune by dealing with the British government. Washington did not find it a particularly friendly town when he arrived. In fact, within three days of his arrival, on April 17, 1776, he sent a letter to the New York Committee of Safety stating his concern about the number of residents who had not come over to the side of independence as they continued to work for the British. He did not find any effective intelligence networks in operation to assist him. In fact, for the eight months Washington and his army were in the New York area, he had little success in recruiting agents to gather intelligence for him. And in the case of Nathan Hale, a volunteer, it turned into a disaster. While Washington and his army had only a short stay in New York City, it proved to be a learning experience for Washington as it reinforced his strong desire to have an effective intelligence operation.

Washington arrived in New York City with a 19,000-man Continental Army. From intelligence reports, he knew approximately when the British would be leaving Nova Scotia and sailing to New York and he knew he would be outmanned by the British forces. With this in mind, he split his troops between Manhattan and Long Island in anticipation of the British arrival. In July 1776, when General Howe arrived at New York City, he brought 32,000 troops who immediately occupied Staten Island, a 101-square-mile island southwest of Manhattan and Long Island running closely along the New Jersey shore. The north section of the island was an ideal launching area for attacks on both Brooklyn and Long Island. This island became the prime target area for Washington's intelligence gathering efforts against the British.

WASHINGTON'S INTELLIGENCE EFFORTS

When Washington deployed to New York City in 1776, he wasted no time in attempting to establish an intelligence network among the civilian population, but only successfully recruited two men to spy for him. The first was Haym Solomon, a merchant who was well-connected with the British activities of the port. The second was Hercules Mulligan, a tailor known as "the fashionable clothier of Queen Street," whose clientele was largely comprised of Loyalists. Their reports to Washington provided him with some of the activities of the Loyalists in the city. The reports were generally not of a military nature as Mulligan's contacts were, in the most part, from the civilian population.

Once the British had landed on Staten Island, Washington's intelligence target became real. He needed to know exactly how many British troops were there and the plan of attack. Initially, his only source of information came from the Mersereau family who were successful in penetrating the British encampments on Staten Island, and on August 21, 1776, reported the following to Brigadier General William Livingston:

- General Howe had about 35,000 British troops on Staten Island

- 20,000 of these troops were preparing to land on Long Island

- The British wagon train was prepared to move, and all but two of Howe's field guns were already aboard ship for transport.

By the time Washington received the information, its timeliness had expired despite its accuracy. On August 22, when the British landed on Long Island, due to his lack of intelligence Washington was not sure if it was the major offensive or just a raid. This need for current information almost cost Washington his army. He arrived on the scene that same day and was quick to perceive the crisis at hand. In order to save his army from the British trap of encirclement, he ordered an evacuation of the troops to Brooklyn by boat across the East River during the night. Heavy fog provided excellent cover and the evacuation was accomplished without the British gaining any knowledge of it happening. The wheels of the wagons were wrapped with straw to muffle the sound, and the troops were told not to talk (a similar technique to that used for Dorchester Heights in Boston). The lack of good intelligence impacted the efforts of both sides. Each side was in a learning curve of how to anticipate the movements of the other army.

At this point Washington, who had retreated to Brooklyn Heights, was in dire need of current intelligence regarding the movements and intentions of General Howe's troops, located south of him in New York City. His only way to obtain such information was to send volunteers behind enemy lines. Having no cadre on hand to perform this mission, he turned to his generals to find a volunteer.

First, Washington contacted Generals William Heath and George Clinton and asked them to recruit volunteers to become spies, but no volunteers came forward. Washington then turned to Lieutenant Colonel Thomas Knowlton, the commander of a unit called Knowlton's Rangers, reputed to be the first intelligence unit of the U.S. Army. Washington's instructions to Knowlton were simple and direct, find a volunteer to go behind enemy lines and collect intelligence of value to the Continental Army. The initial response to his search is best characterized by Lieutenant James Sprague, who stated "I am willing to fight them, but as for going among them, & being taken & hung up like a wild dog, I will not do it."

Nathan Hale

Eventually a young captain by the name of Nathan Hale, a Connecticut schoolmaster, stepped forward and volunteered to undertake the mission. He was young and typically not a person to go unnoticed in a crowd—he was above the average height of his fellow citizens, with flaxen reddish hair, freckles, and a distinguishing powder burn scar on his face—hardly one to work in the shadows. The only instruction given to him by Colonel Knowlton was to go behind enemy lines, collect intelligence (not further identified), and then return. He had no direct contact with General Washington, who was unaware of the volunteer, most likely by design. Hale wasn't given codes, ciphers, or "sympathetic" (invisible ink) to use in order to secure his notes.

With no further instructions and carrying his Yale diploma, Hale left Harlem Heights by boat on September 12, accompanied by Sergeant Stephen Helmstead. Initially landing on Long Island, he worked his way into New York City. Whatever he learned remains a mystery, as does his arrest on September 21, 1776. The very next day, Nathan Hale was hanged, and purportedly uttered his famous quote, "I only regret that I have but only one life to give my country." His hasty execution may have been due to General Howe's belief that the massive fires in New York City were caused by the Rebels, which is probably not true.

The irony of the situation is that almost simultaneously with the execution of Nathan Hale on September 22, an American by the name of John Davis did succeed in infiltrating the British lines and returned with answers to many of Washington's intelligence questions, such as the disbursement of troops, placement of cannons, and readiness for battle.

Hale is thought of as the first American hanged for spying—which may or may not be true. In 1543, the British Parliament passed The Treason Act, which stated that acts of treason that were committed outside the realm of England would be tried within England. The act was reaffirmed in 1772, and the British tried to use the Act in the *Gaspee* incident in Rhode Island, but could not gather enough evidence. But it is entirely possible that Nathan Hale is not the first American hanged for spying as it could be someone who was tried and executed under the Treason Act in Britain—no records exist either way.

Washington learned several important lessons from the Hale episode. First, he learned that he needed to have a personal role in the selection of the volunteers who were going on intelligence missions. They needed to be "vetted" to ensure that the candidate had the capacities to complete the task at hand. Second, he realized that very specific instructions must be given to the agent as to what information he wanted. And third, provisions must be made to provide a way of securing the information either by cipher or invisible ink. An expensive lesson, but Washington was able to quickly turn the lessons learned from Nathan Hale's death to his advantage.

Counterintelligence

Another problem facing Washington during those early days was that of counter-intelligence. He frequently received reports that contained information of potential and possible counteraction. One report spoke of British intentions to kidnap and transport him to England, where he would be put on trial for treason. A second report reached him claiming that the British were planning to secure Kings Bridge, the only land route from Manhattan, in order to trap and destroy the Continental Army. Most of this information came via New Yorker Henry Dawkins, who overheard the information while in jail for counterfeiting. Whether any truth existed in these reports was up to Washington to decide. Militarily, he knew of the importance of the Kings Bridge and had taken steps to protect it in case his troops had to leave Manhattan. As for the kidnapping threat, he knew of this possibility, and did on occasion move his headquarters as a precaution. These early dealings with rumor and spurious information provided him with an excellent baseline of experiences that proved very helpful during the course of the war.

In summer 1776, 56-year-old Christopher Ludwick enlisted in the Continental Army. He was known in Philadelphia as the "Gingerbread Man" for his baking skills. As discussed in the Middle Department chapter, Ludwick (who spoke German) was useful in his role against the Hessian troops of the British Army, but he would also play a larger role in a Committee of the Continental Congress known as "The Committee of Three." The Committee of Three, established in August 1776 and originally composed of James Wilson, Thomas Jefferson, and Richard Stock, was established to develop psychological warfare. It was "to develop a plan for encouraging the Hessians and other foreigners employed by the King of Great Britain, and sent to America for the purpose of subjugating the States, to quit in this service."

Within a week, George Washington informed the Committee the plan had been put into several channels. On August 18, 1776, Ludwick was summoned to Washington's headquarters and was soon sent off on his first assignment. He was to enter Staten Island as a deserter to gather intelligence and talk to the Hessian troops, attempting to reabsorb them into the American military. Washington assigned Ludwick to oversee affairs involving the Hessian prisoners. He served as an interpreter, clandestinely gathering intelligence. When the Continental Army left New York City in early October 1776, Ludwick moved with the army and continued his activities.

When Washington decided to leave the New York area, he knew he would need to have effective intelligence gathering in the city. He began a program now known as a "stay-behind" program. This program established teams that in the event the enemy captures the territory, they will stay behind and become the basis of an intelligence network behind enemy lines. Later, in 1779, when Washington was in the Pennsylvania area, he became acutely aware of the need for increased intelligence from New York City. Spy networks were successfully established in both New York City and Long Island, unrelated to the stay-behind agents. The primary source of intelligence from the area came from the Culper Ring under Benjamin Tallmadge. The Culper Ring was targeted strictly against New York City and Long Island and they provided Washington with his main source of intelligence regarding the British headquarters in the city.

SUMMARY

Military efforts in New York City served as a time for Washington to hone his spymaster techniques. He learned the importance of careful selection when it came to spy candidates. But more importantly, he discovered that not all of his spies would be successful in their missions, no matter how much vetting was involved.

As he was refining his techniques, Washington was astute in ensuring that his central core of officers was well-briefed on their responsibilities in the world of espionage. He may have lost the battle of New York City, but the experiences there served him very well for the duration of the war. He had learned not only about the value of good intelligence but also how to organize an intelligence effort.

In a more general sense, he came to realize that in most future battles between the two armies, the British would outnumber the Continental Army—he would have to adjust his tactics accordingly. Accurate intelligence regarding the size of the enemy force would be critical to his success.

CHRISTOPHER LUDWICK, WASHINGTON'S BAKER

ONE OF GENERAL WASHINGTON'S SPIES AND A USER OF PSYCHOlogical warfare had a very unique and un-American background. Christopher Ludwick, born in Germany, had a highly varied career before coming to America at the age of thirty-four. He had served in the Austrian army in the war against the Turks, and survived the 17-week siege of Prague, after which he joined the Prussian Army. After peace had been declared, he became a sailor and traveled the high seas for seven years. In 1753, he sailed for America with twenty-five British pounds sterling of clothing, which he sold for a 300 percent profit. When he returned to London that same year, he became a baker. But he did not stay in London for long. His business endeavors carried him to Philadelphia, where he established a profitable bakery business. He became a well-known citizen, particularly in the German community. Active in this community, he was one of the founders of the German Society of Philadelphia and, in 1774, was elected to the Committee of Secret Correspondence for Philadelphia.

In the summer of 1776, at the age of 56, he enlisted in the Continental Army as a private and his skills as a baker were soon noted. In 1777, he was appointed to be the Baker General for the Continental Army, a position in which he served well.

However, there was another area for which Christopher Ludwick was ideally suited. He was a gregarious individual, who would prove to be of value as a weapon against the Hessian troops of the British Army. About the same time he entered the Continental Army in August 1776, the Continental Congress created a committee to be engaged in psychological warfare against the Hessian soldiers. The Committee of Three proposed a plan to Washington, who soon informed John Hancock, President of the Congress, that he had accepted the plan and put it into several channels. Christopher Ludwick was one of those channels. On August 18, 1776, General Washington summoned Ludwick to his headquarters. He was well aware of Ludwick's German language capabilities and also of his outgoing personality—a perfect fit for the Hessian project. Ludwick agreed with the plan and soon posed as a deserter behind enemy lines on Staten Island for his first mission. He returned with the required intelligence. His intelligence career continued as he frequently went behind enemy lines to talk with the Hessian troops, trying to convince them to come over to the American side.

After Washington's forces left New York City, Christopher Ludwick was soon put in charge of the German prisoners. He served as the interpreter, thereby gaining intelligence information and he also developed a psychological warfare program for the prisoners. His plan was: "Let's take them to Philadelphia, he urged, and there show them our fine German churches. Let them see how our tradesmen eat good beef, drink out of silver cups every day, and ride out in chairs every afternoon; and then let us send them back to their countrymen, and they will all soon run away, and come and settle in our city and be as good whigs as any of us."

The plan was later expanded to place Hessian prisoners in towns in the York and Lancaster areas, both of which had considerable German populations. His plan proved successful. On March 8, 1777, Ludwick officially submitted a petition to Congress in which he stated:

> That many of the Hessians and Waldekish Prisoners of War, especially the single men, are so well pleased with this country and the way of its Inhabitants that at all events they would rather prefer to settle here than to return to the dreary abodes of Bondage from whence they came. That the working of such like men for wages at their respective trades or in agriculture might in some measure relieve the public of the burden of maintaining them but what is still more be of service to the inhabitants who are greatly in want of journeymen and labourers, and that your grant of the enlargement of their persons with the permission to breathe in the open fragrancy of American air would be to them a renewed instance of American public benevolence and lay them under further Obligation to a generous and merciful Enemy.
>
> Your Memorialist begs leave to propose and on behalf of these unhappy strangers within your gates to pray for a special act of Grace or a resolve of your Honorable Assembly. That a provident discreet and humane German person be appointed to muster at Philadelphia and Lancaster those Prisoners who would do as aforesaid go to work, provide masters and Employers for them, be their counsel and solemn Witness in Contracts which they may make with their employers, register their names and places of abode and the substance of mutual contract, take a promise of Obligation from such Employer that he will see his

labourer forthcoming when required or if he should leave him give notice to the Guardian of the German Prisoners of War. So that they or either of them in Case of an exchange of prisoners should be agreed upon by the Parties at War, or of any Prisoners disturbing the public peace might be returned to the place where prisoners of War properly belong.

The plan worked so well that on November 16, 1777, John Hancock wrote to Washington the following:

"Request that you will negotiate an exchange of the Hessian prisoners at Elizabethtown under the care of Mr. Ludwick, as soon as possible. They have been treated in such a manner during their stay in this city, that it is apprehended their going back among their countrymen will be attended with some good consequences."

The Hessian troops were exchanged and, as Ludwick had predicted, deserters of Hessians to the Colonists increased. The pension records of Frederick Sivert, a Hessian soldier, are a good example of Ludwick's work. They read:

Frederick Sivert, an early settler in Sand Hill District, born Hesse Casel, Germany, came to America early part of Revolutionary War. Was a Hessian solder in service of Great Britain, was captured by Americans under General, 26th December, 1776, at Trenton, NJ. While a prisoner of war, he learned from German citizens the real condition of the country and cause of the war, enlisted in the Continental Army and fought to the close of the war for the independence of the colonies. Married Martha Curtis, settled on Big Wheeling Creek.

Ludwick's work in the intelligence field did not end in 1776. Prior to the battle of Trenton, December 26, 1776, Ludwick had infiltrated the Hessian camp and when he returned he provided the information that the Hessians would be celebrating Christmas and not be on the alert. Washington attacked the camp and scored a major victory. Also in 1781, with the arrival of the French troops to assist the Colonists, a deception plan was developed to convince the British that they would be attacking New York City. The French troops halted in New Jersey and began to develop a permanent camp. It was all a deception. They went so far as to develop a huge bakery at Chatham, with the help of Ludwick who also built ovens there that were never used.

Ludwick returns to civilian life

Christopher Ludwick remained with the Continental Army until the end of the war after which time he returned to Philadelphia. His fortune was gone, but he started anew and became a wealthy man once again. When he died on June 14, 1801, his will provided for the establishment of an institution "for the schooling and education gratis, of poor children of all denominations, in the city and liberties of Philadelphia, without exception to the country, extraction, or religious principles of their parents or friends." The funds initially went to the Philadelphia Society for the Establishment and Support of Charity Schools. Since 1872, the Society has been known as the Ludwick Institute. His tombstone reads:

On every occasion his zeal for the relief of the oppressed
Was manifested, and by his last will,
He bequeathed the greater part of his estate for the
Education of the children of the poor of all denominations, gratis.
He lived and died
Respected for his integrity and public spirit,
By all who knew him.
Reader, such as Ludwick.
Art thou poor, Venerate his character.
Art thou rich, Imitate his example.

VIII

The Canadian Department

MAJOR BATTLES

1775

Campaign of Montreal / Fort St. John's / Fort Chambly
Battle of Quebec

1776

Battle of Saint-Pierre
Battle of Trois-Rivieres

MINOR BATTLES

1775

Battle of Ile aux Noix

1776

Battle of the Cedars
Battle of Sorel

IN 1763, WHEN THE TREATY OF PARIS ENDED THE FRENCH AND Indian War, the territory known as New France became the Province of Quebec under British rule. In 1774, the British Parliament passed the Quebec Act, which defined the province as all territory south to the Ohio River and west to the Mississippi River, all of which was important to the American fur traders. The Quebec Act also restored the Roman Catholic religion as the main religion for the territory, and allowed French civil law to remain in effect. These actions were seen by the Colonists to be one of the so-called "Intolerable Acts" passed by the British Parliament.

Even before the revolution happened, Canada was on the minds of the Colonists. In fact in 1774, the Massachusetts Committee of Correspondence sent a representative, John Brown, to Canada on a very specific mission. He was to invite American merchants in Montreal and Quebec to send delegates to Philadelphia, who would help plan the revolution. The goal was to have the Canadians join forces with the American Colonies.

As the revolution became a reality, Canada was eyed suspiciously by the leaders in the Colonies as the best route for a British invasion force to enter the Colonies; however, the Continental Congress was unsure of how the situation should be handled. Initially, on June 1, 1775, the Congress forbade the invasion of Canada by Colonial forces as Congress declared that the Colonies were in a state of defense not offense. It wasn't until George Washington had become the commander of all Colonial forces that Congress changed their minds. On June 27, 1775, Congress authorized General Philip Schuyler to "invade and hold Canada," which led to the establishment of the Canadian Department.

The Canadian Department was established on February 17, 1776, and abolished on July 2, 1776. During its short lifetime, six commanders were named to head the department. Two of whom died during their tenure—General Richard Montgomery from battle wounds and General John Thomas from smallpox.

The Canadian Department was set up initially for military and political reasons—all incorrect. From the military aspect, the department's formation was a reaction to rumors that Governor Guy Carleton was planning to move an army down through Lake Champlain and Lake George and into the Hudson Valley. Hardly possible, since at that time, Carleton had at most eight hundred British troops in Canada. From the political point of view, the Continental Congress felt that since the French part of Canada (known as New France) had only been part of the British Empire since 1763, they might possibly join the Colonists in their fight for independence. Hence, a plan was created to capture Quebec—it did not happen. After the disastrous retreat in the summer of 1776, the Canadian Department was officially dissolved on July 2, 1776, and incorporated into the Northern Department. The Canadian involvement did not cease in 1776, but merely shifted to the Western Department (where later in the war, American forces crossed into Ohio, Indiana, and Illinois—all within the Province of Quebec).

While the Canadian Department has a short history, it contains a true historical irony. Two individuals, one British and one American, were involved in the combat of 1775. John André was a young British lieutenant from the 23rd Foot Unit who was captured at Fort John's in November 1775, and held as a prisoner-of-war, first in Lancaster and later in Carlisle, Pennsylvania, until he was exchanged in December 1776. American Benedict Arnold was wounded at the battle of Quebec in December 1775. Later these two men would be linked forever in the history of the American Revolution with the defection of Benedict Arnold and the capture and execution of John André—his accomplice.

The Invasion of Canada

Initially the invasion was a single force to be led by General Schuyler; however, Schuyler became ill and General Richard Montgomery took command. Montgomery and his force left Fort Ticonderoga and aimed to capture Montreal and Quebec. But Benedict Arnold convinced Washington that a second prong advancing through Maine focused directly at Quebec would split the British force, thereby increasing the Americans' chance for success. Not surprisingly, nothing went according to plan. Schuyler's force arrived in Canada in August, and Arnold did not arrive until November. While Montreal was captured with relative ease, the campaign for the city of Quebec fared poorly, and wound up with a six-month siege, from December 1775 to May 1776, when General John Burgoyne finally arrived with sufficient reinforcements to relieve the siege.

Canada remained a point of interest, and finally in January 1778, the Continental Congress authorized a second invasion of Canada. Intelligence sources had informed them that the British could not replace their losses at Saratoga until May of that year, and also that the new alliance with the French might sway the inhabitants of Quebec. While Washington eventually warmed to the proposal, and when Marquis de Lafayette, a Frenchman, was offered the command for the invasion, Washington advised him to take it. In his eyes, a Frenchman leading the invasion may bring the province to the American cause.

When Lafayette reached Albany, he found a total lack of resources, both in men and supplies. Since it was winter, Lafayette knew he had to transport the men using wagons and sleighs. His efforts to acquire transportation and the volunteers to drive them came to naught, and the invasion was inevitably cancelled. He learned through intelligence sources that Governor Carleton was reinforcing his defenses along the invasion route. Finally, in March 1778, all plans for another attempted invasion of Canada were aborted, and military actions in Canada shifted to the west and centered on Fort Detroit in the western Province of Quebec.

Politically, Canada remained an agenda item but by 1780, Congress had abandoned all thoughts of invading Canada with the hope of their joining in the revolution. Nevertheless, in 1782, when the American peace proposal was presented to the British delegation in Paris, it contained a demand that Canada be ceded to the United States. Britain refused, as did the French, and therefore the clause was dropped prior to the final treaty agreement, which was signed on November 30, 1782.

INTELLIGENCE DEVELOPMENTS
American: A Ragtag Operation

The Canadian Department existed during the early days of the new republic before intelligence operations were effective. One example of the inept use of intelligence occurred in the fall of 1775, when General Benedict Arnold was ordered to take his troops to Canada. To plan his route, he based his march on a map drawn in 1759 by the explorer John Montresor. This map was the only one available and it may well have been planted by the British to confuse the enemy. The map did not indicate distances and locations were missing. Using this map, Arnold estimated that it would take three weeks to join up with General Richard Montgomery in the Quebec area. His troops left Cambridge on September 13 and didn't arrive at Quebec City until November 15, two full months later as a result of the faulty map and poor intelligence. They were joined by Montgomery on December 1, 1775, at Pointe aux Trembles, which happened to be located twenty miles from Quebec City.

That wasn't the only example of poor intelligence involving Benedict Arnold though. Prior to his departure, Arnold did minimal advance intelligence work. Not only were his troops ill-prepared for the severe winter weather, but he also took troops whose enlistments ran out in December 1775. Both of these missteps led to dire consequences, such as medical problems caused by cold weather and troops returning home when their enlistments ran out.

In June 1776, once again faulty intelligence played a major role in the defeat of the Continental Army at Trois-Rivieres, a defeat which resulted in the end of the Canadian campaign. Prior to launching the attack, the American generals had no idea how many British troops they would be facing (they were actually outnumbered by the British four to one) or how strong the fortifications were. Rather than scouting ahead to reconnoiter the terrain for the best approaches, the Americans hired guides to lead the army. The guides were, in fact, British Loyalists who led the army into the swamps to languish for quite some time. In another planned action by troops of General John Sullivan, an attack on Fort St. John's had been split in two for a two-pronged attack. Loyalist guides, who led the columns, managed under cover of darkness to maneuver the two columns into positions facing each other, which resulted in the two columns firing on one another.

To make matters worse, in May 1776, the Americans belatedly learned that fifteen British warships with reinforcements and cannons were anchored on the St. Lawrence River. It was considered by many historians to be the most serious intelligence failure of the entire eight-year war.

There were occasional successes though. In the fall of 1775, Colonel Seth Warner's regiment was stationed at Longueuil during the siege of Fort St. John's. The regiment had been alerted that the British were sending eight-hundred troops to relieve the ones at Fort St. John's. The troops would be sent by boat and would land at Longueuil, where Warner would be in place with his troops. When the British landed, they suffered major casualties.

While the military action was ongoing, covert intelligence operations were also underway. On February 15, 1776, based on input from the Committee of Secret Correspondence, Congress authorized a covert operation in an attempt to encourage the residents of Canada to become a "sister colony." A French printer was sent to Canada by Benjamin Franklin to "establish a free press for the frequent publication of such pieces as may be of service to the cause of the United States." Three members of Congress, Benjamin Franklin, Samuel Chase, and Charles Carroll, were named to head the operation, and later Father John Carroll was added to the group to assist with the Catholics in Canada. The Committee was empowered to:

- Raise six companies of militia in Canada

- Offer sanctuary in the thirteen colonies "for all those who have adhered to us"

- Allow some authority over American forces in Canada

The operation had very limited impact due to the inability of the American commissioners to actually provide more than promises for Canadian defection. In addition, the excesses and brutal treatment against the Canadian population by the American forces and the general failure of the American military operation worked against the commissioners. The Canadians saw the risk too great and a failed operation would not prove to be beneficial to them. They were content under British control.

British: Three Professionals at Work

Unlike the American side, the British had two very strong professionals in senior positions in Canada who knew how to acquire and use intelligence. The first was Sir Guy Carleton, who was the governor general of the Province of Quebec and stationed in Quebec and the second was Colonel Henry Hamilton, who served as the lieutenant governor and superintendent of Indian Affairs at Fort Detroit. These two men were very adept at working with the Indians, particularly Hamilton, who had served in Parliament and had acquired a strong diplomatic skill and utilized it to collect information for the use of officials in both Detroit and Quebec. They had organized Indian intelligence gathering organizations. In addition, Hamilton and Carleton maintained close communications and kept one another advised of any intelligence developments.

In striking contrast to the American intelligence efforts in Canada, these two British professionals, while not trained as intelligence operatives, knew what information was required and how to obtain that intelligence and performed the duty extremely well.

While not in Canada during the time period of the Canadian Department, the third Brit that should be noted is General Frederick Haldimand, who replaced General Carleton in 1778. Haldimand was fluent in French and was successful in keeping the French in line with the British. He also had an extensive intelligence network both in Canada and the Mohawk area of New York. The following letter sent by Haldimand to General Henry Clinton is an example of the extent of his network:

21 June 1781

Doctor SMITH of Albany, my best intellingencer, is just come in his having escaped from the Hands of the Rebels on the Way to Jail.

He attributes his being seized to his having given you late intelligence and suspects some of your Domestics of betraying him to Washington, who wrote the Commissioners of Conspiracies that a Plot was on "Foot, and SMITH was immediately ordered to be seized and loaded with irons.

Should his suspicion be well founded, I hope he will arrive time enough to prevent greater Evil.

No Victuallers yet arrived or heard of. I shall be obliged to purchase at vast expense.

Frederick H(aldimand)

(Sir Henry Clinton)

Indians: Led by a Mohawk

Indians played a role in the Canadian Department, predominately due to one man, Joseph Brant, a Mohawk chief. While still in his youth, Brant had come to the attention of John Johnson, the superintendent of Indians Affairs. Johnson selected him to be sent to the Moors Charity School for Indians located in Lebanon, Connecticut. There he studied the classics and learned English. Upon his return, he became a leader in the Mohawk tribe, as well as in the Six Nation Confederacy. In early 1776, he traveled to England with Johnson where he met with King George, became a Mason, and was treated royally by English society. He returned to Canada in August 1776, a true supporter of the British Empire. He used his influence as a Mohawk chief among the Indians in both Canada and northern New York to keep the Indians loyal to the British. Brant's leadership of the local Indians not only inspired them to fight for the British, but also helped use them to gather intelligence.

INDIVIDUALS IN INTELLIGENCE

American

UNIDENTIFIED FRENCH PRINTER–Virtually nothing is known about a French printer sent to Canada by Franklin and his Committee.

JAMES BOWDOIN, A DRAFTSMAN AND AGENT—Bowdoin was a draftsman sent by General William Heath into Halifax to acquire detailed information about the defenses in place. He successfully completed the mission, providing detailed plans of the Halifax harbor to include specific military works and depths of the surrounding waters. He later went on to become the first president of the American Academy of Arts and Sciences.

DOMINIQUE L'ECLISE, SCHUYLER'S BEST—Little is known about this Canadian, who served as an agent for General Philip Schuyler, beyond the fact that he was detected, his property was confiscated, and he was imprisoned. However, his work must have been of value since when General Washington was advised of L'Eclise's status, he went to the Continental Congress on his behalf. On October 2, 1776, Congress granted Washington authority to pay L'Eclise's debts amounting to $600 and $60 plus one ration a day "during the pleasure of Congress" as compensation for his contribution to the cause of the American Revolution.

CLEMENT GOSSELIN, A FRENCH CANADIAN SOLDIER—Gosselin fought with the American troops in Canada at the battle of Saint-Pierre, where he was eventually captured. Upon his release in 1776, he went into hiding since he served with the Americans. His intelligence activities, if any, are unknown during that time period. On November 28, 1778, he sent a report on the status of the British forces in Canada to General Washington (now in Washington's papers). He remained in the army for the rest of the war.

British

JOHN ANDRÉ (A SPY?)—The later activities of John André are well known, but his time in Canada is much less clear. He spoke French and the French in Canada were a concern of the British. The possibility exists that he was used as an agent against the French. It is known that while in a prisoner-of-war status in Carlisle, Pennsylvania, he was caught surreptitiously handing a letter to a person that was written in French. No local could read it so the contents were not known. Additionally, when André was paroled and escorted to British lines, he was careful to observe the route, and reported all his findings to his superiors once released.

SIR GUY CARLETON—Carleton served twice as the governor of Quebec, as well as the governor of Canada from 1785 to 1795. In 1782, he replaced General Henry Clinton as the commander-in-chief of the British forces in America. He was wounded in the battle on Lake Champlain in 1776, and was given a peerage in 1786. Sir Guy Carleton had mastered both the art of spymaster and intelligence user prior to the American invasion of Canada. He used both British Loyalists and Indians in his intelligence operations.

COLONEL HENRY HAMILTON—In 1775, Colonel Hamilton was appointed lieutenant governor and superintendent of Indian Affairs at Fort Detroit. This was one of five lieutenant governor positions in the

Province of Quebec. Hamilton became adept at handling the Indians and at keeping Governor Carleton informed on the Indian activities in his area of Canada. Captured by George Rogers Clark at Vincennes in November 1779, he was held as a prisoner until 1781, when he was paroled and returned to England. He came to Canada once again in 1782 to become the deputy governor at Quebec. He later was transferred to Antigua, where he died in 1796. His intelligence work was highly valued by Governor Carleton as he was his eyes and ears in the western areas of Canada.

SUMMARY

The Canadian Department was short-lived as a military department. Unlike most of the other areas in this early stage of the war, thanks to the work of Henry Hamilton and Sir Guy Carleton, the British did have a working intelligence system operating in their area. While heavily dependent on the local Indians, it did provide information for the use of the British against their American foes.

Later in the war, the western area of Canada, particularly around Fort Detroit, became the responsibility of the Western Department. However, Washington's interest in Canada did not end when the Canadian Department ceased to exist. In May 1780, he instructed General Heath to send agents into Canada to collect information about Halifax in support of a French requirement for information on the British defense works there. Washington directed that the persons sent should be those "upon whose firmness and fidelity we may safely rely." He further suggested that it should be a draftsman.

The Canadian Department may have been de-established, but Canada remained an intelligence target. Even later in the war when the emphasis shifted to the south, there continued to be an interest in Canada. Around 1781, a young Colonial officer named Captain David Gray posed as a deserter and was recruited to be the courier for Colonel Beverly Robinson, a Tory intelligence officer. He later served as the courier for Major Oliver DeLancey Jr., who had replaced John André as head of the Secret Service in New York. For two years, Gray served as the primary courier between DeLancey and the British in Canada. For this entire period, all communication was read by the Rebels prior to its delivery to British authorities in Canada. He returned to the Continental Army with his name expunged from the deserter list by order of General Washington.

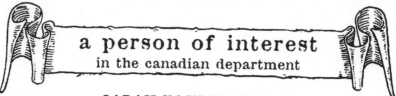

SARAH KAST McGINNIS

SARAH KAST MCGINNIS WAS BORN IN 1713. SHE LIVED IN THE Mohawk Valley in the colony of New York, where she was an unabashed Loyalist (Tory). After her husband's death in the French and Indian War, she was left with eight children to rear on the family farm. To add to her income, she joined her son-in-law in his trading business, becoming well-known to the local Mohawk Indians.

When the Revolutionary War broke out, McGinnis, an outspoken Loyalist, felt the full wrath of the Rebels when her home was burned down with her son in it. Her property was taken from her and auctioned off to a Rebel family. Sarah, at the age of 64, her daughter, and granddaughter were sent to prison at Fort Dayton (now Herkimer, New York). They later escaped to Fort Stanwix, where General Barry St. Leger found them and sent them on to Canada, arriving there in August 1777.

After the battle of Oriskany in August 1777, the British were having trouble controlling the Mohawk Indians, who had joined them in the battle. While still loyal to the British they wanted to fight the white man using their Mohawk ways (guerilla tactics) and not those of the British. The British needed to keep the Mohawks loyal to their side in the conflict. British Colonel Daniel Claus, a family friend and superintendent of Indians, knowing of Sarah's knowledge of the Mohawk language and customs, asked Sarah McGinnis to perform a special mission for the British. He asked her to return to New York and live among the Mohawks. This would serve as a counteraction to the Americans, who were trying to coax the Mohawks to become their ally. It would be her mission to keep the Mohawks aligned with the British.

McGinnis accepted the mission and soon was en route to the major Mohawk village. When she arrived, she was greeted by many old friends. The Indians showed her a Wampum belt, a sign of friendship, they had received from the American General Philip Schuyler. McGinnis told them the belt was an evil message and they should bury it. She remained with the Mohawks near Genesee, New York, until the spring of 1778, keeping the Mohawks loyal to the British and also keeping the British informed.

In the fall of 1779, she was once more asked to live with the Mohawks, but this time was accompanied by her son George, a lieutenant in the Indian

Department. Similarly received, she was greeted with joy and a meeting was called to hear what she had to say. As a result of her advice, many of the Mohawks moved north to Canada to avoid the ongoing slaughter by the Rebels.

After the war McGinnis moved permanently to Canada as a Loyalist. She petitioned the British government for a land grant and money to cover her losses during her time in New York with the Indians. She received a small amount of money, but no land grant. She died on September 9, 1791, in the Province of Ontario. In 1998, a certificate was finally issued, making Sarah Kast McGinnis an official United Empire Loyalist, an after-the-fact honor given to those American settlers who remained loyal to George III during the American Revolution and who resettled in Canada or other British provinces.

Sarah McGinnis's voluntary efforts of living with the Mohawks were beneficial to the British, as she was highly respected among the Indian tribes. Her word carried significant impact and helped ensure that the Mohawks continued to side with the British.

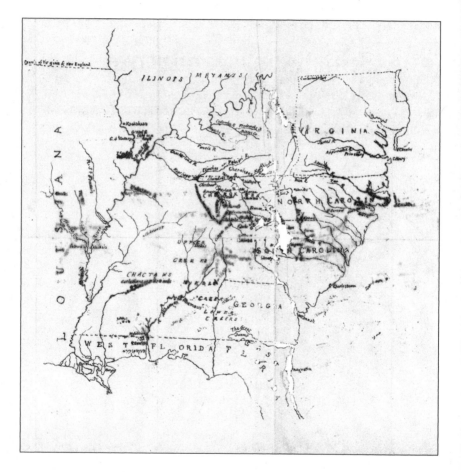

CHAPTER
IX

The Southern Department—
Where the War Was Won

MAJOR BATTLES

1776
Burning of Norfolk, VA
Battle of Fort Moultrie, SC

1778
Battle of Savannah, GA

1779
Second Battle of Savannah, GA

1780
Siege of Charleston, SC
Bird's invasion of Kentucky, KY
Battle of Camden, SC
Battle of Kings Mountain, TN
Battle of Cowpens, SC
Battle of Guilford Court House, VA

1781
Battle of Eutaw Springs, SC
Battle of Yorktown, VA

1782
Battle of Blue Licks, KY

MINOR BATTLES

1776
Battle of Moore's Creek Bridge, NC

1778
Battle of Alligator Bridge, GA

1779
Battle of Kettle Creek, GA
Battle of Beaufort, SC
Battle of Brier Creek, SC
Battle of Stono Ferry, SC
Battle of Savannah, GA

1781
Siege of Ninety-Six, SC

1782
Battle of Combahee River, SC

THE SOUTHERN DEPARTMENT WAS ESTABLISHED ON MARCH 1, 1776, and was composed of the colonies of Virginia, North Carolina, South Carolina, Georgia, and Maryland and Delaware were added later. It should be noted that the western borders of the colonies of Virginia, North Carolina, and South Carolina extended to the Mississippi River, well beyond the Appalachian mountain range.

The Southern Department was formed in reaction to the burning of the city of Norfolk, Virginia, on January 1, 1776. On that day, Lord Dunmore (John Murray) the royal governor of the state of Virginia, along with many of the Loyalists living in Norfolk, fled the city due to harassment by the Rebels. After boarding ships in the harbor, Lord Dunmore ordered the bombardment of the city, causing massive destruction. The war had finally come south. The Southern Department was unique in that while most of the other military departments went into winter quarters due to local weather conditions, the weather in the Southern Department made it possible to have year-round military operations. Except for the burning of Norfolk in January 1776, the battle of Moore's Creek Bridge in February 1776, and the battle of Savannah in December 1778, the Southern Department remained relatively quiet until 1779. At that time, the British decided to force a disbursement of the Continental Army by carrying the war to new areas such as the South. From that time until the end of the war, the Southern Department was the most active of any of the departments. It is interesting to note that all of the major battles of the war after the battle of Monmouth Court House in New Jersey, fought on June 28, 1778, were fought in the Southern Department including the decisive defeat of the British at Yorktown.

At the time of the onset of the Revolutionary War, the South was a complex mix of Loyalists, Rebels, Indians, and a large population of slaves, who were the main concern of the southern plantation owners. Who would the slaves support in the event of war? On November 7, 1775, Lord Dunmore, the British governor of Virginia issued a proclamation stating that if slaves left their masters and joined his "Ethiopian Regiment," they would be granted freedom when the war ended. Over three hundred slaves followed his call.

The Southern Department was the most independent of all of the departments, and it has the distinction of being the only department to have its command structure severely damaged twice. The first was at the surrender of Charleston, when the headquarters of General Benjamin Lincoln was destroyed, and again on August 16, 1780, at the battle of Camden, where General Horatio Gates was in command.

After General Nathanael Greene took command on October 17, 1780, things changed for the better. He made contact with General Francis Marion, also in the Southern Department, and ordered him to organize an espionage network behind the enemy lines. Greene also instructed Marion to continue making his raids to ensure that Cornwallis felt unsecure.

An important aspect of the war in the south was the geography. There were two distinct areas of interest. First, there were the more populated areas, predominately along the coastal areas of the Colonies such as Norfolk, Charleston, and Savannah. From the military aspect, these areas were well-suited for traditional military tactics. The second area, however, was not. It was the wilderness areas of the colonies of Virginia, North Carolina, and South Carolina, as well as the areas now known as West Virginia, Kentucky, and Tennessee. All these lands were inhabited by Native Americans and required a very different set of military tactics such as Indian and guerilla. Generals such as Greene were more adept at adopting both types of tactics as opposed to the British, who still clung to structured battle.

Another concern for the Continental Army in the Southern Department was the area south of Georgia. The British were in Florida, the Spanish in Louisiana, and the French influence was still strong in the Louisiana area. All of these various countries were capable of stirring up mischief against or in support of the Southern Department. And some did.

Indians — A Constant Threat

The majority of the Indians located in the Southern Department were of the Cherokee, Creek, or Chickasaw tribes. Like the Indian tribes of the Western Department, they were acutely aware of the settlers violating the Proclamation of 1763, made after the close of the French and Indian War. This proclamation forbade settlers from going beyond the Appalachian Mountains. Subsequently, when the Revolution broke out, the British used this fact as a reason for the Indians to align themselves with their cause. In the South, the Cherokee, Creek, and Catawba tribes initially were convinced to remain neutral in the conflict. However, in May 1776, a delegation of Shawnee, Delaware, and Mohawks met with the Cherokees and Creeks and convinced them to actively go on the warpath in support of the British. The tribes represented a constant problem for the Southern Department which continued the remainder of the war— particularly in the areas of the department that bordered on the Western Department, called the Ohio and Illinois territories.

While the strong propaganda efforts of the British to keep the Indians in the Western Department on their side had proven to be successful, there was not a similar case of triumph in the Southern Department. There the Indians were more swayed by what they heard from local Loyalists. The following quote of Thomas Jefferson very clearly states the southern view of the Indian:

> *I hope the Cherokees will now be driven beyond the Mississippi and that this in future will be declared to the Indians the invariable consequences of their beginning a war. Our contest with Britain is too serious and too great to permit any possibility of avocation from the Indians. (April 5, 1780)*

INTELLIGENCE DEVELOPMENTS
The Individual was Supreme

With the exception of its last commander, General Nathanael Greene, none of the commanders of the Southern Department had been exposed to the intelligence operations of General Washington. They had no real concept of how to obtain useful intelligence, or how to use it if they had it. Two of the early commanders, Generals Charles Lee and Horatio Gates, were too busy actively seeking appointment as the commander-in-chief of the Continental Army rather than tending to their command. Generals William Howe and Benjamin Lincoln both lost major battles due to their lack of efforts to obtain valuable intelligence, and they were subsequently replaced.

The last commander of the Southern Department, General Nathanael Greene, was a very different commander than those who came before him. He had a real grasp of what kind of intelligence he needed to gather, based on his involvement in the activities on Long Island where major espionage efforts were ongoing. General Greene worked closely with George Washington, where he learned the value and techniques of intelligence gathering and use. He even had a man on his staff at the Southern Department who had been trained in code breaking and had actually broken British cipher messages associated with Cornwallis' army. All of this experience served him very well in the Southern Department.

Intelligence activities in the Southern Department when compared to those of the more northern departments varied greatly. While there were established spy networks in the north, they did not exist in the Southern Department. Espionage was more of an individual effort and in some cases, such as with the Seviers, it was a family effort against the Indians. Ranger and Indian scout companies were formed in the various militias in an effort to keep in contact with the Indians and ascertain their intentions. Though all of these efforts were just as useful as those of the north, because they were much more individual they were more difficult to direct and manage.

One other major variation of the intelligence operations of the Southern Department was the greater role of women. Not only was the number greater, but the role they played was different from the more northern areas. These women were frequently pioneer women, meaning they were not afraid of traveling through unknown territory and they were also quite adept at horsemanship. They often acted alone and quite willingly took risks usually associated with their male counterparts. These strong Southern women were a major asset in the Southern Department.

The British intelligence efforts were equally fractured. They depended heavily on the Loyalists, who remained in the area for their intelligence. As the war dragged on more and more Loyalists continued to leave the area, leaving a narrow channel for intelligence.

However, intelligence operations were actively involved in some of the critical battles of the Southern Department, both the more traditional military battles, as well as the guerilla actions. Starting with the most northern colonies of Maryland and Delaware, the individual efforts in each colony of the Southern Department follow. The persons included represent only those for whom proof of their work exists—so they are only a portion of the intelligence activities of the time.

MARYLAND AND DELAWARE: GUARDIANS OF THE CHESAPEAKE BAY

Although the Maryland and Delaware units were not transferred to the Southern Department until April 1780, the activities of these two colonies throughout the war are included with the Southern Department.

Delaware and Maryland saw no battle action take place within their boundaries, but their geography played a major role during the Revolution because of one factor—the Chesapeake Bay and the Atlantic Coastal area. Delaware natives could and did keep an eye on ships arriving via the Delaware River and proceeding to Philadelphia. More importantly, the Maryland colonists kept watch on the Chesapeake Bay for British naval activity especially during two separate times. The first came in July 1777, when British General Howe, accompanied by 15,000 troops, entered the bay. The second was prior to the naval battle between the French and the English in 1781.

In July 1777, General Howe left New York with a ship convoy of 15,000 troops, with the intention of entering the Chesapeake Bay and debarking at the headwaters of the bay, a location known as Head of Elk (present-day Elkton, Maryland). As he entered the Chesapeake on August 22, Colonists spotted the armada and immediately passed word to General Washington about the impending attack. Then two days later Colonel Henry Hollingsworth, the deputy quartermaster general, alerted the Continental Congress to the impending disembarking of the British troops. This intelligence was given to General Washington on August 26. Washington proceeded with Generals Greene and Lafayette to Head of Elk to perform their own reconnaissance, which was to establish the size of the British force. The reconnaissance was unsuccessful due to inclement weather, however the task did establish that the troops were there and would soon be on the move.

Colonel Hollingsworth was ordered to remove all the food supplies from the path of the British. At the same time, Washington established fortifications along the roads to prevent the British from advancing to Philadelphia. The intelligence provided by his agents afforded them with enough time to move the stores and assume a defensive stance, but the British would still enter Philadelphia on September 29, 1777.

The Head of Elk event is an excellent example of how quickly intelligence could be moved in a fairly restricted area. In 1781, Washington, reacting to intelligence reporting, moved his combined French/American force by ship to Virginia. The following entries are from a journal written by James Thatcher:

3 Sept crossed the Schuylkill River and on the 6th arrived at Head of Elk River in Maryland. Having marched over 200 miles.

8 Sept An express has now arrived with the following intelligence that Comte De Grasse has now actually arrived at the mouth of the Chesapeake bay, with a fleet of 36 sh[ips] and three thousand land forces, which are landed and have joined our troops under Marquis de La Fayeette, in Virginia. (in fact the 36 ships and 3,000 troops now under Marquis de la Fayette arrived at the mouth of the Chesapeake Bay on 30 August).

11 Sept sailed at four o'clock pm. for head of Chesapeake Bay.

13 Sept Sailed from Annapolis but soon called back to the harbor of Annapolis. This is in consequence of intelligence of a naval action between the French and the British near the mouth of the Chesapeake Bay. (The Battle took place between 5 and 9 Sept). Also received intelligence that General Arnold had returned to Virginia from his Connecticut raid.

15 Sept The gratifying intelligence is announced that the naval engagement between the French and the British has resulted in the defeat of the British with considerable loss and the French now are in sole command of the Chesapeake Bay . . . We can now proceed on our expedition.

16 Sept We obeyed the signal for sailing.

25 Sept Reached the harbor between Jamestown and Williamsburg, where the greatest part of our transports arrived in the course of the day, and the troops disembarked and encamped.

From the above entries two points can be made. First, it took approximately eight days for current intelligence reports to reach Washington in the Maryland area from the Tidewater area of Virginia. And secondly, it shows the reliance Washington had on his intelligence input as well as his patience in not acting until he had adequate intelligence input on which to base his decision.

Individual Spies

TENCH TILGHMAN, A CONFIDANTE OF GENERAL WASHINGTON— Colonel Tench Tilghman from the Eastern Shore of Maryland had become a confidential aide-de-camp to General Washington. In that position he would have not only seen the intelligence coming into the headquarters but also would have been directing some of the agents collecting the data.

Colonel Tilghman was with General Washington at the surrender of Cornwallis at Yorktown. As an indication of the esteem Washington had for Tilghman, he selected Tilghman to have the honor of delivering the letter to Congress in Philadelphia announcing the surrender. That letter read:

To The President of Congress, Head Quarters near York

October 19, 1781
Sir, I have the Honor to inform Congress, that a Reduction of the British Army under the command of Lord Cornwallis, is most happily effected . . . .
Col. Tilghman, one of my Aids de Camp will have the Honor to deliver these Dispatches to your Excellency; He will be able to inform you of every minute circumstance which is not particularly mentioned in my Letter, his Merits, which are too well known to need my observations at this time, have gained my particular attention, and could wish that they may be cohonored (honored) with the Notice of your Excellency and Congress.

Your Excellency and Congress will be pleased to accept my Congratulations on this happy event.

VIRGINIA:
CRITICAL INTELLIGENCE WINS THE DAY

At the time of the Revolution, the state of Virginia also encompassed what today are the states of West Virginia and Kentucky (all will be treated as one herein).

The major battles in Virginia were the burning of Norfolk (1776), Bird's invasion of Kentucky (1780), the battle of Guilford Court House (1781), the battle of Yorktown (1781), and the battle of Blue Licks (1782). There were no major battles in West Virginia, but over thirty minor skirmishes occurred in the area.

Prior to the battle of Yorktown, General Lafayette was ordered by George Washington to perform a shadow operation against Cornwallis, but not to engage him in combat. To do this, Lafayette needed useful intelligence, and with the help of such men as Colonel James Innes, this was accomplished.

Efforts to kidnap General Benedict Arnold while in Virginia did occur. The first was in March 1781, when an attempt to capture Arnold as he took his daily ride along the Virginia coast of the Chesapeake Bay was foiled by British ships anchoring in the area at the time of the proposed operation. The second was again in 1781, when Thomas Jefferson ordered General John Muhlenberg to capture Arnold, but this too was foiled due to tight British security.

Virginia had two distinct areas of conflict during the Revolution. The first was centered on the Atlantic coastal area, specifically the Norfolk area. This area is where the armies of the two combatants met and ultimately forced the surrender of Cornwallis. Here the intelligence requirements were military in nature, both tactical and strategic, focusing on the enemy army to ascertain its whereabouts and its intention. Individuals, many of whom were known to the commanders and not established networks, supplied much of the information obtained by both sides.

The second area was the frontier area, where combatants were predominately Indian tribes facing local militias. There the intelligence requirements were much more local and of immediate need. Where were the Indians and when and where will they strike? Each of the militia groups acted independently with both "Indian spy companies" and individuals who served as Indian spies.

Attempt to Kidnap Thomas Jefferson

The British military had two primary kidnapping targets—one was George Washington and the other was Thomas Jefferson, the drafter of the Declaration of Independence. In both cases, their intent was to ship their quarry to England for a show trial of treason and a hanging in London.

Jefferson, then governor of Virginia, became the main target in 1781, when Benedict Arnold, now a British general in charge of his American Legion, landed at the mouth of the James River in January. He immediately attacked Richmond in an attempt to not only capture Jefferson but other members of the Virginia General Assembly such as Patrick Henry. The attempt failed as Jefferson and the delegates fled Richmond ahead of the attack.

Several months later, when Cornwallis relocated his army from the Carolinas to Virginia, where Jefferson and the Virginia Assembly were now located in Charlottesville, Cornwallis decided to once again attempt to capture Jefferson. He ordered Colonel Banastre Tarleton to take his regiment to the Charlottesville area, where he was to capture Jefferson. Colonel Tarleton quickly organized his troops and began the quick march to Charlottesville. When the regiment entered Louisa County on June 3, 1781, about forty miles from Charlottesville, they passed by the Cuckoo Tavern, where perchance a Virginia militia captain was asleep on the tavern lawn. The captain, Jack Jouett, awoke and listened to the troop chatter as they passed, which is how he learned their mission. He quickly mounted his thoroughbred horse and arrived at Monticello ahead of the British column. The governor listened over breakfast, and then ordered Jouett to proceed to Charlottesville and warn the others. Jefferson barely escaped, but he stayed on his property and watched the British search for him. The plot had failed once again, thanks to an alert horseman.

Individual Spies–Eastern Area

JAMES ARMISTEAD—James Armistead was a slave who with his master's permission volunteered to serve General Lafayette prior to the battle of Yorktown. He was asked to go behind the British line to gather intelligence, which he accepted. He soon was noticed by the British and Cornwallis asked him to return to the American side to spy for him. Thus he became a double agent—a real one for Lafayette and a bogus one for Cornwallis. The intelligence he brought back to Lafayette was a major asset to him in planning for the attack on Yorktown.

COLONEL JAMES INNES, MERCHANT IN DISGUISE—Colonel James Innes, a prominent lawyer in Virginia, served as a colonel under

General Lafayette. As Cornwallis waited in Williamsburg, Innes, at the request of Lafayette, established what he called a "line of intelligence," both north and south of the York River. As this was his home area, he was able to convince members of the local population to work with him in gathering intelligence. His recruits were local tradesmen, many known to the British for their work, which was a perfect cover. They would enter the British camps with goods to sell—those goods being supplied as necessary by Colonel Innes. According to Colonel Innes, the line north of the York River was particularly productive. As an incentive, Lafayette offered ten guineas to anyone who could prove he had been in a British camp and even more if they brought back useful information.

On February 11, 1782, Colonel Innes wrote a letter to Governor Harrison of Virginia relating to him his line of intelligence, and asking for state support of the intelligence effort. That letter reads:

Sir: During the late campaign in that state. While the British Army was in possession of Williamsburg I was spoken to by the major general marquis Lafayette on account of my acquaintances with the inhabitants of that city and its vicinity to use any efforts to establish a line of intelligence with the British Army—both on the north and south sides of York river. To enable me to effectuate this object with the more certainty, the Marquis directed me to promise a premium of ten guineas to those persons, whom I might employ, provided they could give an undeniable proof of their having been in the British encampment and greater rewards—should they bring material information—I was happy enough to make such arrangements as answered the general's wishes. The persons whom I had engaged as Intelligencers on the both sides of York River were, I have been told, compensated by the occupiers for their tools and new goods. First, those on the Gloster Side, from whom many material services were derived. Having so accepted the Marquis' demand of me a performance of my promises, to which, as the Marquis has now left the Continent, I shall be compelled in light of his Excellency may dispose that ought to be relieved by the interference of the State.

Governor Harrison did respond to the request of Colonel Innes and payment was made to the members of the intelligence line.

PRIVATE CHARLES MORGAN, SUCCESSFUL DESERTER—Very little is known about Private Charles Morgan of the New Jersey Regiment except for a short period of time when he served under General Lafayette in 1781. At that time, Lafayette was in pursuit of General Cornwallis in southern Virginia. Once Lafayette had Cornwallis pinned down on the peninsula at the mouth of the York River, he realized he was in need of detailed information concerning the British and their plans. He needed a volunteer to feint a desertion and enter the British camp. He soon found Morgan.

Private Morgan had been noticed previously by Lafayette for his bravery and also his friendly manner, a good combination for a man undertaking such a task. When asked by Lafayette to undertake the task Private Morgan was quick to accept the challenge with one condition: if he was caught and hanged, General Lafayette would place an article in the New Jersey papers, stating that Morgan was not a deserter but a Continental Army agent on a mission. Lafayette agreed. After several more visits with Lafayette to "rehearse" the answers he would give when queried by the British, Private Morgan "deserted" and went over to the British side.

Upon arrival, he was asked why he deserted and his reported response was: "I have been with the American Army from the beginning of the war and I went into the contest with all my heart and soul. While I served with George Washington I was perfectly satisfied and I would have gone until the end, but when they put me under the charge of a Frenchman I felt that it was time to call a halt. I was unwilling to fight under a foreigner. I did not like it, I chafed under it, and finally made up my mind to desert and here I am." His story was accepted and he was assigned to a British unit, but not before he was taken to see General Cornwallis.

General Cornwallis asked Private Morgan a number of questions: How many men did Lafayette have under his command? Morgan answered with a number that was considerably lower than the real number. Second, how long would it take for Lafayette to move his troops across the river? Morgan answered three hours. Surprised, Cornwallis said he must have meant three days, but again, Morgan answered three hours. He told Cornwallis that Lafayette had special boats capable of ferrying the troops across the river. At this point General Cornwallis turned to his staff with concern realizing that if that were true his scheme would not work. It would have to be revised and he put his staff to work doing just that. During the next few days, Cornwallis had several more interviews with Morgan who continued to supply the general with disinformation—mostly self-generated.

Private Morgan joined a British unit and with his hail-fellow, well-met personality soon became good friends with four of the British soldiers in the unit. He soon convinced six soldiers to desert with him and to join the American army and that is just what they did. Private Morgan arrived back in the Continental Army camp with the six British soldiers in tow as well as a Hessian guard they passed along the way. Lafayette ordered the men to be fed and clothed and enlisted in one of the units.

The intelligence that Private Morgan was able to relay to General Lafayette made it clear to the general that he did not have to change his plan of operation but to proceed as planned—a major advantage not only for Lafayette but for George Washington as well, since they were in constant communication.

It is not possible to place a true value on the impact of the disinformation provided to General Cornwallis by Private Morgan or on the information that Morgan relayed to General Lafayette. But one cannot help but think that the very effective agent work done by Private Morgan may have had a definite impact on the battle of Yorktown. General Lafayette wanted to promote Morgan to corporal but he refused the promotion as he felt his talents lay more in just being a regular soldier. The only reward received by Private Morgan was, at his request, the return of his cherished musket which had been given to another soldier when Morgan "deserted."

TUNIS MUCKELVAINE, INTERMITTENT INDIAN SPY—The chronology contained in the pension records of Tunis Muckelvaine provides an excellent example of just how individual the spying efforts were in the Southern Department, particularly in support of the local militia. His records state:

AUGUST 1776–Volunteered as an Indian spy for three months under Captain Robert Davis in what is now Pendleton County.

He was ordered to spy westward from the North Fork and Seneca to the top of the Allegheny Mountains. He was discharged in November 1776.

MARCH 1777 – Volunteered to serve six months as an Indian spy under Colonel Hutton. Ordered to spy from Evils Fort westward to the Allegheny Mountains. He was discharged in September 1777.

MARCH 1778 – Volunteered for six months as an Indian spy under Captain McCoy. He was ordered to spy westward in Pendleton County across North Fork and up the Seneca Creek. He was to report his findings every two weeks. He was discharged in September 1778.

MAY 1779 – Once again volunteered to serve six months as an Indian spy under Captain Trimble in what is now Pendleton County. Later was ordered to Randolph County to spy toward Buckhannon and to report back every two weeks. He ended this enlistment in December 1779.

APRIL 1780 – Volunteered as an Indian spy in Randolph County. He was ordered to spy from Wilsons Fort to Buckhannon, then back to Westfalls Fort in Tygarts Valley, fifteen miles above Wilsons and down the valley by Cassaday's Fort, and then to Beverly. He was ordered to report his findings every two weeks. He was discharged in October 1780.

MARCH 1781 – Volunteered again to serve as an Indian spy in Randolph County under Captain Bogard. He was ordered to spy in Randolph, Lewis and Nicholas counties reporting his findings to Buckhannon barracks and Cassaday's Fort. He was discharged once again in September 1781.

MARCH 1782 – Volunteered for three months as an Indian spy in the same areas as where he had served in March 1781. He was discharged in May 1782.

MARCH 1783 – Volunteered for a three month tour as an Indian spy under Captain Wilson and Colonel Westford. He was utilized in the same areas as those of 1782. He was discharged in June 1783.

His pension record goes on to state: "He served during the revolution from 1776 to 1783. He saw no general officers that he now remembers nor did he see any regular troops. He saw militia and Indian spies a kind of mixed service." It was a very individualistic effort from a man who dedicated a major portion of his life to protect the settlers, who were moving into a wilderness section of the new country.

Individual Spies–Western Area (present-day Kentucky)

DANIEL BOONE, MORE THAN JUST A PIONEER—In 1775, Daniel Boone and twenty-eight other employees of the Transylvania Company set out to establish trails and settlements in what is now Kentucky. They succeeded and, in 1775, the first settlement in Kentucky was founded and named Boonesboro. That settlement became the main center for Boone's activities. He was an active Indian scout supporting the local militia and in fact during the Revolutionary War he became a major in the local militia.

In 1778, Boone was captured by the Indians and he lived with them for six months. His escape and saving of Boonesboro can best be described in his own words from his account titled, *The Adventures of Col Daniel Boone*, published first in 1784:

> When I returned to Chellcothe, alarmed to see four hundred and fifty Indians, of the choicest warriors, painted and armed in a fearful manner, ready to march against Boonesboro, I determined to escape at the first opportunity.
>
> On the 15th (of June) before sunrise, I departed in the most secret manner, and arrived at Boonesboro on the twentieth, after a journey of one hundred and sixty miles during which I had but one meal.
>
> The Indians had spies viewing our movements (at Boonesboro), and were greatly alarmed with our increase in numbers and fortifications.

The Grand Councils of the nations were held frequently, with more deliberations than usual. Finally on the 15ᵗʰ of August the siege was lifted.

The Boonesboro episode is a prime example of the work of Daniel Boone for his adopted state of Kentucky. His intelligence activities, while not of use to the Continental Army, certainly did assist the militia. Daniel Boone lived long enough to see Kentucky become the fifteenth state of the United States on June 1, 1792. He died September 26, 1820, in his beloved state of Kentucky.

JAMES DUNCAN, INDEPENDENT INDIAN SPY—The pension records of Private James Duncan provide a clear picture of how unorganized the intelligence activities were in Kentucky, and also how freely the word "spy" was used:

> *He states that he was ordered to the Blue Lick but being tired & just off a long journey moving he did not go but was immediately ordered out to guard the forts in which service he was employed two months. He had no officer but was employed as a spy in guarding & protecting the forts mostly Englishe Station. He later joined Genl Clark's expedition against the Indians as a substitute for William Mayfield. He later returned home and was again employed in a tour of service of 2 months service as a spy and guard on the Red River in Tennessee ... He volunteered for an expedition under Capt. John Rains against the Indians. He with 8 or 9 others volunteered as spies. He later was ordered out again for 2 months as a spy near Palmyra on the Cumberland River. He was there for 40 days.... He never was mustered in or out of the Service.*

Was he truly a spy? No one knows for certain. It is probable that the authority who hired Duncan to guard the forts did so knowing of his intimate knowledge of the area and that he would keep his eyes open for unusual activity or signs of an unofficial spy.

JOSEPH KENNEDY—Joseph Kennedy served as an Indian spy under Daniel Boone in the Boonesboro area. He also served as an Indian spy for Major George Rogers Clark, involved in the defense of Kentucky from the Indians.

SIMON KENTON, CLARK'S INDIAN SPY—Simon Kenton was born in Virginia, but at the age of sixteen went west into the Kentucky territory. He became an Indian scout and was recognized for this talent. His official use as a spy began in 1777, when a commission arrived from Virginia giving the command of the colony to Major George Rogers Clark, with authority to appoint his officers. On March 5, the first militia of Kentucky was assembled and organized at Boonesboro and Harrodsburg. In 1821, Kenton recalled that event when he wrote to his friend General Robert Pogue stating, "Daniel Boone, James Harrod and John Todd captains, Joseph Lindsay as the appointed commissary - Silas Harlan, Samuel More, Ben Lynn, Thomas Brook and myself appointed as spyes. The whole country was then under the command of Major Cl__, ...'o was charged by the Governor of Virginia with the defense of the Western frontier." The number and pay of Clark's officers was fixed; he was allowed nothing for spies. But he appointed them regardless, because he needed them so much and for their payment he pledged the faith of Virginia.

Kenton continued his military career after the Revolutionary War. He first served with Anthony Wayne in the Northwest Indian War of 1790-94. He later became a brigadier general in the militia, and served in the War of 1812 including in the battle of the Thames in 1813.

In 1939, a gun collector purchased a Revolutionary War gun, and on close inspection found a birch bark message hidden in the gun. The message was faded but the initial part could be read as follows: For report on enemy pos... K 2nd Aug. Unfortunately the remainder of the message could not be recovered. However, the initials on the nameplate of the gun were "S.K." believed to be Simon Kenton, giving further credence to the originator of the message and what he was doing for the militia. Simon Kenton may be an unknown name today, but in his day he was a recognized Patriot who served his country both as a spy as well as a military soldier and scout.

JEREMIAH POWER, A SPY FOR FOURTEEN YEARS—Not all spies gave up their profession with the end of the Revolutionary War, which can be shown from the pension records of Jeremiah Power. His record states:

> *JEROMIAH POWER, Declaration: Jeremiah Power, a soldier of the Revolution, this day, came into Court and made this statement:*
>
> *On September 17, 1832, I am 78 years old, and I am a resident of Pendleton County, Kentucky.*
>
> *I came to the district of Kentucky in the fall of 1779, I was a ranger and spy against the Indians at Strode's Station on the waters of the Main Licking under Colonel John Edwards and continued in that capacity until 1793, during which time I was under several different commands: Capt John Morrison, Capt. David Hughes, Capt. James McMifflin and Capt. John McKentire.*
>
> *I was in the campaign on Vincennes on the Wabash River, under General George Rogers Clark in the fall of 1786, and at that time served as a spy. Col. Lewis Todd was my Colonel.*
>
> *In the winter of 1786, I returned to Kentucky. In the spring of 1787 was detailed as a spy and continued to act as such until Kentucky separated from Virginia and afterwards until October 1793.*
>
> *My name is not on the pension rolls.*
>
> *Witnesses: Robert Taylor and John H. Barker*

Jeremiah Power must have been a respected and well-known spy to be pressed into duty as many times as he was. Not many of the Revolutionary War spies followed his path, but he happened to be in an area that still had Indian tribes.

THE WETZELS, A FAMILY EFFORT—Living in what today we know as West Virginia, the Wetzel family provided three family members for the intelligence efforts in their area. John Wetzel, a militia member who served under General Andrew Lewis, had a company of Indian scouts who provided intelligence on the activities of the Indians in their area. His scouts were well known for their work and were active throughout the entire period of the war. Since John Wetzel organized his spies as a company that reported back to him, he was able to have a more complete picture of all the Indian activity in his entire area of interest.

On a less-disciplined level, Lewis Wetzel became a famous Indian scout during the war period in the western area of West Virginia. While a well-trained scout, he was also known to be ferocious and answered to no one. Undisciplined but effective, his feats of spying were so well known that on January 10, 1846, the county of Wetzel, West Virginia, was founded and named in honor of the Indian Scout Lewis Wetzel.

The third Wetzel, Martin, served in the Revolutionary Army including at the battle of Point Pleasant, but little is known of his spying activities.

Most of the intelligence gathered by the Wetzel family members was only of marginal interest to the military aspects of the war, which were focused on the eastern areas of the country; however, it did have a major impact on the settlers and their activities in the more western areas of the new country. There were many Indian scout (or spy) companies in the local militias, predominately in the western provinces. The survival of the local settlers depended on volunteers keeping an eye on the Indians in the area. The Indian scout or spy companies kept the Southern Department commander informed of Indian activities that may require use of his troops in the more western areas of his department.

NORTH CAROLINA:
THE BUFFER STATE BETWEEN NORTH AND SOUTH

North Carolina, like its neighbor Virginia, had a dual front. Tennessee was still part of North Carolina then and the "hot spot" of Indian activity. While there weren't any major battles fought in North Carolina, over forty minor skirmishes took place in the area. And though there are few surviving documents of spy activity, it is not to say espionage was not utilized.

Individual Spies – North Carolina

WILLIAM ALEXANDER—William Alexander served as the commander of a company of "volunteer spies" against the Cherokee Indians in 1776. The volunteers were fellow settlers, who wanted to protect their homes from constant Indian attacks.

ELIZABETH PLEDGE POINDEXTER, THE "PETTICOAT COURIER"—
Elizabeth Poindexter lived near the Yadkin River and was alert to the
activities around her. When skirmishes occurred in her area, she would
send messages through the Loyalist lines to the Rebels by sewing the
message in the lining of her daughter's petticoat. She is credited with
supplying intelligence to the Rebel forces that led to their victory over
the Loyalists at the battle of Shallow Ford on October 14, 1780.

Individual Spies – Tennessee

MARTIN GAMBILL—Martin Gambill was known as the Paul Revere
of the south, and with good reason. The story of Captain Gambill be-
gins in 1780, when Cornwallis planned a sweep north to attack Washington; however, the sweep had to be delayed since the Rebels had not
been subdued, making his rear section vulnerable to attack. Cornwallis
decided to send Major Patrick Ferguson into the mountain area to sub-
due the Rebels. Ferguson initially offered the Rebels an ultimatum, but
was duly ignored. At the same time, he alerted them to the impending
movement of his troops into the mountains. The result being the battle
at King's Mountain where local militias held the British to a draw.

Advance warning was needed in order to ensure that the militia
would congregate at the appropriate location. General Irwin McDow-
ell's troops, then in Watauga County, volunteered to serve by observing and tracking Ferguson's movements. They would burn large piles of
brush on the mountain tops as the British troops moved through. This
system was useful only in mountainous terrain where fire signals on
mountain crests could be observed from a substantial distance.

At this juncture, Colonel Isaac Shelby of Tennessee called a meeting of militia commanders at the home of John Sevier. Captain Martin
Gambill was one of the attendees. At that conference, it was decided to
intercept Ferguson's force before he could reach the mountains, and they
also decided that Sycamore Shoals in Tennessee would be the meeting
place for all militia units on September 25, approximately one week
later. The members of the meeting knew that a courier was necessary
to carry this information to all the militia groups scattered throughout
the area, and particularly to Colonel William Campbell, who at that
point was in Seven Mile Ford, Virginia, over one-hundred miles away.

Captain Gambill, who volunteered for the mission, was to deliver the message to Colonel Campbell, and also to dispatch couriers along his route to alert the various militia groups. He departed from the Sevier home on the afternoon of September 18. The exact route he took is not known, but on the morning of the 19th, he arrived at the home of Captain Enoch Osborne. As he emerged from Potato Creek, his horse dropped dead just short of the house. Captain Osborne provided him with a new horse (the second of three used for the journey) and departing from the Osborne farm, he traveled through the Comers Gap. At Thomas Bridge once again his horse fell dead from exhaustion. As before, he secured another horse and just after dark on the 19th, he arrived at the camp of Colonel Campbell.

As a result of the message Gambill carried, Colonel Campbell and his 400 troops arrived at Sycamore Shoals on the evening of September 24. Two days later, the united force of Crawford's troops of over 1,000 men began their march to join Colonel Cleveland's troops. They then began a southward march of about 380 miles that ended at King's Mountain (just over the border in South Carolina) where on October 7, 1780, the battle of King's Mountain occurred. This was a very important victory for the Rebel forces as the battle was won entirely by militia troops over British regulars. It also made Cornwallis realize that the western part of Virginia was going to continue to be a problem, in large part due to the heroic ride of Captain Martin Gambill, and the endurance of the troops who marched those 380 miles.

It can be argued that the ride of Martin Gambill had more of a direct impact on the American Revolution than Paul Revere. Why? Because General Cornwallis entered North Carolina with one thought in mind—subjugation. He expresses this thought in a letter to General Clinton saying: I am of the opinion that (besides the advantage of possessing so valuable a province) it would prove an effective border for South Carolina and Georgia and could be kept, with the assistance of our friends there, by a few troops as would be wanted on the border of this province if North Carolina should remain in the hands of the enemy.

Captain Gambill's ride to alert the militia troops halted this plan entirely. The battle of King's Mountain was fought completely by local militia (on both sides) totaling over 2,000, many having been warned by Gambill. The defeat of the British commander, Ferguson, at King's

Mountain ended Cornwallis' plan for North Carolina, and he subsequently retreated to South Carolina. It was the first major victory for the Colonials in the South, and it revitalized the revolutionary spirit, not only in the South but in the North as well. Militia troops throughout the Colonies now were looked upon with more respect and frequently compared favorably with the regular Continental Army.

SAMUEL RIGGS—In April 1834, Samuel Riggs filed an application for a Revolutionary War pension. In his sworn testimony for his pension application, he relates an interesting event that sheds light on how the term "spy" was used during the war. In this case it has two meanings—the first use of "spies" equates to "scouts" or military men working overtly, while the second use equates to "spies" working covertly. His statement refers to the Sevier Campaign of December 1780, against the Cherokee Indians. It reads as follows:

> *Our spies having gone on and met the advanced spies of the Indians, made us acquainted with their situation, they had fallen back about two hundred yards from where they had encamped. Col. Sevier was leading one division and Major Tipton the other. Suddenly a gun was fired bout fifty yards off from the midst of a field of tall grass before us at Col Sevier – Major Tipton, a volunteer being next to Col Sevier jumped from his horse and fired at the Indian, who had discharged his gun at Col Sevier, and broke the Indian's leg. The Indians immediately jumped up and fired – our men jumped from their horses at the fire of the first gun and commenced firing – and immediately drove off the Indians.*

The mental picture of Indians appearing suddenly up in the tall grass resembles today's computer games. But the account does show how the word "spy" had a very general meaning that ranged from an actual spy to that of a scout. The difference was important since it could save your life. A scout normally wore his uniform and worked in close proximity of the troops. If he were to be captured as a scout, he normally would be held as a prisoner of war and not executed. A spy, however, did not go on a mission in his uniform but in civilian clothes and worked covertly.

If he was captured, the chances were that he would be tried and almost immediately hanged, as in the case of Nathan Hale.

THE SEVIER FAMILY—John, Valentine, Joseph, and James Sevier, all members of a prominent family, were active in the Tennessee area (then western Virginia) during the Revolutionary War.

John Sevier was the most prominent of the Sevier brothers, involved in fighting the Indians prior to and during the Revolution. This early experience proved useful when in 1776 and 1777, he was with Colonel William Christian during his campaign against the Cherokee Indians. At the request of Colonel Christian, John served as a spy throughout the campaign. After the campaign ended, his official intelligence work continued. His talents were first employed when he was appointed as lieutenant colonel for Washington County where Indians, horse thieves, and Tories required constant surveillance—it was a turbulent area. Later in 1780, he was left in charge of defense of the settlements in the county which required more intelligence work. His actions throughout the war give a clear indication that John Sevier not only acted as a spy, but also had an extensive "unofficial" network that provided him with valuable information. When the state government of Tennessee was formed in 1796, John Sevier was chosen as the first governor. Later in 1801, he served in Congress in the House of Representatives.

Valentine Sevier served as a spy to provide tactical intelligence at the battle of Point Pleasant in October 1774, during the Dunmore War. He continued to fight in the Indian Wars.

Robert Sevier and **Joseph Sevier** served in the militia. Joseph Sevier had command of a spy company in Tennessee employed against the Cherokee Indians.

NANCY WARD, A COLONIAL SYMPATHIZER—Nancy Ward, known as the "Beloved Woman," was a powerful female leader of the Cherokee. She ruled the Council of Women and had a seat on the Council of Chiefs. On at least two occasions during the Revolutionary War, she sent messages to John Sevier that the Indians were planning to attack the Watauga and Eaton Station settlements (1776). Based on her intelligence input the Indians attacked, but were repelled.

SOUTH CAROLINA: MAIN THEATER OF OPERATIONS

South Carolina was a colony with strong ties to the British. Many Loyalists were living in the colony at the time of the Revolution, and it became the center of military activity in the Southern Department. While most of the military action in the colony occurred along the coastal area where the major cities were located, some military action did occur deeper into the colony. The major battles in South Carolina were the battle of Fort Moultrie, the siege of Charleston, the battle of Camden, the battle of King's Mountain, the battle of Cowpens, and the battle of Eutaw Springs. All told there were over 103 military actions in South Carolina during the course of the war.

Two military spy rings operated during the war years in South Carolina. Both rings were unusual in that they were established by military authorities and not spontaneously by civilians. The first was established in 1780 by order of General Horatio Gates. After the fall of Charleston, he ordered Colonel Francis Marion (who became known as the "Swamp Fox" to the British as he used the swamp routes to escape from them) to set up a spy operation in Charleston. Later when General Nathanael Greene was in charge and Charleston had become a major shipping port for the British, a new spy ring was established under the control of John Laurens. Laurens had been an aide-de-camp to Washington, where he learned the value of intelligence. General Greene was aware of his reputation and his skills were put to good use in the Charleston area. However, in 1782, Laurens was killed on a raid, trying to prevent the British from garnering supplies.

Another excellent source of intelligence for the Rebels in South Carolina was female agents. For whatever reason, the number of female spies active in South Carolina is far above the other colonies in the Southern Department. The women were of pioneer stock, good horse people, and not afraid of the environment they lived in.

Females Spies in South Carolina

KATE MOORE BARRY, HEROINE OF COWPENS—Kate Moore Barry lived in Spartansburg County and was a true pioneer woman. Her mother was a Cherokee Indian and her father a settler. When the war broke out, she and her husband joined the local militia. Kate Barry volunteered to become a scout in her area, reporting anything she could. Being part Indian, she knew all the Indian trails, making her movements go relatively unnoticed. She often worked with her slave Cato. Early on, her abilities came to the attention of General Daniel Morgan as a good source of intelligence, and in 1781, she volunteered to scout for him. Her biggest accomplishment was warning General Morgan early in January 1781 that the British were approaching, and they were closer than previously known. General Morgan retreated based on this information. On January 16, he was advised by Barry that the British scouts were only five miles behind him. She also informed him that the British outnumbered his force. To counter this, Barry recruited all the local Patriots to join Morgan's troops for the impending battle. Based on this information, he decided on the meadow at Cowpens to make his stand. The British were defeated in a major loss, due in part to the scouting efforts of Kate Barry—hence the name "Heroine of Cowpens."

As a result of her advance warning, General Morgan was able to pick the spot most advantageous for their soon-to-be victorious battle. Unfortunately for Cornwallis, the loss at Cowpens and King's Mountain forced him to abort his plan and retreat north to Virginia, where he ultimately lost at Yorktown.

Kate Barry was very conscious of the value of timely intelligence. Legend has it that she once had information that was critical to deliver, but she was alone with her two-year-old daughter. She reportedly tied the child to a bed post, rode off to deliver the message, and came home to untie her daughter.

EMILY GEIGER, A WELL-TRAINED COURIER—Emily Geiger was a member of a wealthy family living in Newberry County during the Revolutionary War. She was a strong Patriot and a well-trained courier, and wanted to do her part to support the cause. That opportunity came to her in June 1781.

General Nathanael Greene had learned through his intelligence system that the British Army in South Carolina had been divided between Charleston and the interior of South Carolina—it was the perfect opportunity to strike quickly. His troops were located at the fork of the Enoree and Broad rivers, and General Thomas Sumter's troops were camped at Watersee. It was critical that General Sumter be alerted to General Greene's plan—a message had to be couriered to Sumter as soon as possible—but by whom was still a question to all including General Greene.

Emily Geiger learned of the quandary and convinced General Greene that she could deliver the message. As a woman, she was less likely to be suspected of being a courier for the Rebels, plus she was horse-savvy and knew the terrain. It was enough to persuade General Greene. Having been trained by George Washington, General Greene used his intelligence acumen. He had Geiger memorize the contents of the message in case she had to destroy it in route. Worst-case scenario, she could still deliver the information orally to General Sumter. Once General Greene was satisfied that Geiger knew the contents of the message, she departed on her mission.

Near Fort Granby, Geiger was stopped by some British sentinels of Lord Rawdon. She was immediately suspected of devious actions since she was a young woman riding in difficult terrain at night. She was taken into custody and questioned by Lord Rawdon, who ordered her to be searched. Since she was a woman, they had to find another woman to conduct the search. While they were tracking down another woman, Geiger tore the message into small pieces and ate them. Consequently, when she was searched nothing was found and she was released. Geiger continued her journey and arrived at General Sumter's camp where she delivered the message verbally. General Sumter soon joined the main army at Orangeburg. The success of the battle of Eutaw Springs can be attributed to the actions of Emily Geiger.

HARRIET PRUDENCE PATTERSON HALL, A PETTICOAT COURIER— In the company of two other women, Harriet Hall rode into Charleston during the siege to gather medical supplies. They passed freely by the British, collected their supplies, and returned once again past the British guards. However, while in Charleston, Hall had delivered an important message to the American commander, which she had hidden in her petticoat.

LAODICEA LANGSTON, THE CONSTANT INFORMER "DARING DICEY"—Laodicea Langston, known as "Daring Dicey," lived in the Laurens area of South Carolina, which was populated heavily by Loyalists. As a Rebel, Daring Dicey found it very easy to glean intelligence from the Loyalists, after which she would ride across the Enoree River and inform the Rebels. She served in this role throughout the war period.

There was a group known as "Bloody Cunningham and his Scouts"—so called because of their particularly cruel actions. Dicey learned that this group was planning a raid on a group of Whigs living in an area known as The Elder Settlement, which was about twenty miles from her home. Dicey decided to warn them of the impending attack. She rode the twenty miles, warned the group, and was back in her home in time for her father's breakfast. When the Cunningham gang arrived at the settlement, it was deserted.

GRACE AND RACHAEL MARTIN, TWO CRAFTY WOMEN— Grace and Rachael Martin were sisters-in-law living in the outback of South Carolina. Around 1780, two British soldiers came to their home. They were couriers on their way to deliver messages and wanted to be fed and rest, which the women graciously allowed. When the couriers left, they were soon waylaid by two young men who took their messages and turned them over to the Rebel troops. What they did not know was that, in fact, the two young men were actually the two sisters-in-law dressed as men. The messages were delivered to General Nathanael Greene, who was most appreciative. The ladies' adventure didn't end there though. When they arrived back home, the two British couriers once again stopped at their home for a meal, having no idea that the two women serving them had actually been the culprits who waylaid them

British Spies in South Carolina

AN UNLUCKY "DESERTER"—In April 1782, when General Francis Marion departed Charleston headed into the area of the Cooper and Santee rivers, he had an uninvited guest with him—a Scotsman passing himself off as a deserter. He traveled with Marion's force for a while and then drifted off in the direction of the Loyalist Scottish settlements along the Pee Dee River. In short order, unrest began in the area and General Marion was informed that British Major Gainly was involved in encouraging the Loyalists to cause trouble. The pretended deserter was among the Highlanders to join the Gainly effort. General Marion reacted to the uprising, succeeded in putting it down, and in the process caught the Scotsman as he attempted to return to Charleston.

GEORGIA: THE LOYALIST STATE

There were two major battles in the state of Georgia, both of which occurred in Savannah. The first was in 1778 and the second was in 1779. There were over twenty-five military actions in all in the state.

The Patriots in Georgia were fermenting for revolution. In 1775, the royal governor of Georgia, James Wright, was concerned about his state's loyalty to the crown and decided to take action to quell the sentiment for revolt. He sent a letter to General Gage in New York requesting a British ship to appear off the coast of Georgia, hoping to impress the Georgia population and help keep them loyal to the crown. That letter, however, did not go directly to General Gage but was instead intercepted by members of the Georgia Committee of Secret Correspondence. The seal was broken and the enclosed letter was replaced by a new letter. In the original letter, Governor Wright reported that there was "no probability of quietude in Georgia," and he had requested of Admiral Samuel Graves "Immediate assistance—at the very least a sloop or warship of some sort." He also expressed a fear that the Patriots would seize the gun powder stored in his state. Those responsible for stealing the letter were also responsible for altering those points in the forged letter. The new letter stated that "No danger is to be apprehended," going on to say that the apparent rebellion was by no means real and that there was "nothing formidable in the proceedings or designs of our neighbors of South Carolina." And as to naval support, the new letter stated that "I now have not any occasion for any vessel of war." The new letter assured General Gage that Georgia was loyal and no additional support was needed. The fraudulent letter was received and no vessel was sent to Georgia. It wasn't until later that Governor Wright discovered what had happened to his original letter.

As in the other Southern Department colonies, most of the intelligence activities in Georgia were planned and carried out by individuals. One such individual was Nancy Moran Hart.

NANCY MORAN HART, MISTRESS OF DISGUISE—Nancy Moran Hart was a true frontier woman in Georgia. She was over six feet tall, which allowed her to disguise as a man. She frequently pretended to be a half-wit or peddler selling eggs as she wandered through the British camps. On one occasion in February 1779, she was able to provide General Elijah Clarke with information that led to his victory in the battle of Kettle Creek. The Georgia Patriots' victory at Kettle Creek ended the movement in Georgia to remain loyal to the United Kingdom. The

British had eyes on Spanish Florida, and if they made a move in that direction, Georgia would have been a major entry route.

British Operatives in Georgia

While little is known about British intelligence operatives in the Southern Department they obviously existed since the populations of many areas were strongly Loyalist. However, there is one outstanding example in the personage of Alexander McGillivray.

ALEXANDER MCGILLIVRAY, CREEK INDIAN LEADER AND SPYMASTER (1750–1793)—Alexander McGillivray was the son of a Scottish father and a Creek Indian mother. His father was a very successful Indian trader and his mother was a highly respected woman in the Creek hierarchy. Alexander's early life was among the Creeks, but at the age of twelve his father decided that he needed a formal education and he was sent to Charleston to study the Classics. Later, at about sixteen he went to Savannah and worked in a counting house for a short period. Not finding this to his liking, he returned to the Creeks at Hickory Ground where he met Colonel John Tait, a British officer. Tait knew that since Alexander's father was a Loyalist and his estate in Georgia and all his properties had been confiscated by the state, Alexander could be won over to the British side. And he was.

McGillivray soon became a chief among the Creeks and a person of great power. His strength was not on the military side and he led only a few of the Indian raids. On the other side he was superior at diplomacy and leadership in general. Theodore Roosevelt remarked that it was McGillivray's "consummate craft" and "cool and masterly diplomacy" that enabled the Creeks "for a generation to hold their own better than any other native race against the restless Americans." He soon rose to be not only the leader of the Creeks but also the Chickamauga's and later the Seminoles. In one of his rare military ventures he led the Creeks in assisting the British in the battle of St. Augustine in 1780.

But how does Alexander McGillivray have an impact on intelligence operations during the Revolutionary War? As the Creek leader, he no doubt had an intelligence network within the tribe. Inspired by Colonel Tait, he could use that network to acquire information of use to the British forces in the area. There can be no doubt that both the British and the Spanish recognized the value of this man as an ally. His influence was extensive, he was smart and world-wise, and had a wide network for information gathering. While there is little direct evidence of the value of his network, the following letter written on October 9, 1783, to the acting captain general in Havana is some indication of his value:

My Dear Sir:

About the middle of last month there arrived here Alexander Maguilberi (sic), half son of a Scotchman and an Indian woman, of the wind clan, sister of the Indian Chief named Red Shoes. Who, though formerly under our monarch, put to the sword the Spanish settlers on the Excambra River, and in other habitations in the vicinity . . . The said Maguilberi, I am informed, has more influence among the Creek Nations than any other person, and because he was educated at Charleston, the English named him Commissary for the Upper Creek Nations. But when the English retired from the Florida Coast, he called at St. Augustine, his accounts adjusted and his salary paid and the English bade him farewell, as he preferred to remain in his own land with the Indians, his wife and family. He has informed me that the English General MacArthur who was in St. Augustine, urged him to hold the Indians in readiness, to recommence the war, and that case they were called anew to such activity it would be for the good of the Indians. At the same time Maguilberi assured me that he preferred peace, and to that end, accompanied by some Indian chiefs, had come to solicit the establishment of a trade with the . . . . He, as well as various other Indians friendly to us will refuse to gather at a Congress offered them by the Americans in Augusta and Savannah.

Arthuro O'Neill

There can be no doubt that both the British and the Spanish recognized the value of this man as an ally. His influence was extensive, he was smart and world-wise, and had a wide network for information gathering.

After the war, Alexander McGillivray was well-known by the newly formed government of the United States. In 1790, George Washington invited him to attend a conference in New York City that resulted in the Treaty of New York City in an attempt to pacify the southern border. He went on to become the president of Pensacola as well as a member of the Masons. He died on February 17, 1793. No one is certain as to how important this man was to the British intelligence efforts in Georgia and Florida. It is probable that the information developed by the Creek Nations would have been given to McGillivray who in turn would pass it on to the British Colonel Tait. With his prominence and good standing among the British it would have been easy to pass along such intelligence.

French Operations in Georgia

In the summer of 1779, the Rebel governor of South Carolina, John Rutledge, and General Benjamin Lincoln were desperately looking for help to save Georgia from British control. To assist them in their cause, they enlisted a French admiral, Charles Hector d'Estaing, who had just won a major victory against the British off the coast of Grenada. Admiral d'Estaing agreed and set about enlisting a corps of free men of color for the project. The goal was to lay siege to Savannah, Georgia, an important town of about eight-hundred people with a small port.

D'Estaing arrived in the Colonies on September 9, 1779, with a corps of about 5,000 men, 500 to 800 of which he had recruited on the isle of Hispaniola. Arriving at Savannah, he attempted to get the British to surrender with no luck. Finally, when the American troops joined his force on September 23, the plan of attack was drawn up.

On the evening of October 8, 1779, the allied generals held a meeting to fix the details of the impending attack. What they did not know was that a member of the Grenadier Company of Militia, posing as a guard at the entrance to the tent, heard all the details of the plan. The guard, Sergeant Major James Curry, then defected to the British side and informed them of all the details of the planned attack including the planned location of the assault.

When the assault began, the British were already emplaced on Spring Hill. The assault was a disaster for the French and American troops with over 1,000 casualties, making it one of the bloodiest battles of the entire war—and all because of an American deserter. Sergeant Curry was eventually captured at the battle of Hobkirk's Hill in South Carolina and was summarily hanged the same day for his treason.

Simultaneous to the battle of Spring Hill, General Henry Clinton was loading troops to invade Charleston on transports at New York. If d'Estaing had won the battle, the British would never have attacked Charleston. The operation would have been cancelled and quite possibly the war would have been shortened.

SPANISH OPERATIVES IN THE SOUTHERN DEPARTMENT: THE COLONIST'S FRIENDS

Oliver Pollock, an American businessman in the New Orleans area, became a major asset in the American Revolution, particularly in the Southern Department. Recognized early on for his potential value he became a member of the Secret Committee of the Continental Congress. During the war period, he successfully acquired much needed supplies and succeeded in getting them to the Colonies. He became a close friend of the governor of New Spain, Bernardo de Gálvez, and that friendship proved extremely valuable to the Colonies. Gálvez permitted the American privateers to bring their captured British ships into the port of New Orleans, and he closed the Mississippi to all British ships but continued to permit the American ships to transit the river. In 1778, with the help of Gálvez, Pollock managed to obtain a loan of $70,000 from the Royal Treasury of Spain. That money was used to purchase equipment for the successful expedition of General George Rogers Clark at Kaskaskia and Vincennes.

In addition to Pollock, the Spanish, as of January 1778, had an "observer" by the name of Juan de Morales in the city of Charleston, South Carolina, reporting back to Galvez on the status of the war.

Additionally, cattle raised in Texas were provided to the Colonial armies through the same Mississippi pipeline as the military supplies. The route was across Texas to New Orleans, up the Mississippi to the Ohio River at Fort Pitt, and then east by land. All this was coordinated by the Spanish agent.

Through the efforts of Pollock and his influence with the Spanish in the area just south of Georgia, the impact of the British in Florida was minimized. His influence with the Spanish assisted the Rebels by providing a buffer zone between the British in Florida and the Americans in Georgia.

SUMMARY

Intelligence activities in the Southern Department were not the highly sophisticated systems of the more northern colonies. In the Southern Department it was predominately an individual effort that produced the results. It is interesting to note that unlike the more northern colonies, there was a preponderance of women working in the world of intelligence in the south. This may be due to the fact that the southern states were not as developed as their northern counterparts and women in the south were of the frontier breed—better horsemen, stronger and more willing to strike out on their own into unknown territory. The intelligence activities in the Southern Department had an impact on the outcome of the war, King's Mountain and Yorktown being two examples. The battle at King's Mountain proved that the local militia groups could be the equal to the more professional British troops. And for Yorktown, the deception tactics of Washington as he moved south to Yorktown and the successful use of Rebel spies infiltrating Cornwallis's camp proved invaluable to the successful defeat of the British.

When the military actions shifted to the Southern Department, it became the main theater of conflict for the outcome of the war. Strong commanders, such as General Nathanael Greene with his grasp of the value of intelligence, provided the leadership Washington required. Without such leadership the war could have continued for a longer time and possibly have had a different outcome. A stalemate was not an option.

This is to certify that the Bearer by the Name of James Has done Essential Services to Me While I had the honour to Command in this State. His Intelligence from the Enemy's Camp were Industriously Collected and More faithfully deliver'd. He perfectly Acquitted Himself with Some Important Commissions I gave Him and Appears to me Entitled to Every reward his Situation Can Admit of. done under My hand, Richmond Novembr 21st 1784

Lafayette

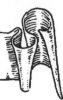

a person of interest
in the southern department

JAMES ARMISTEAD (LAFAYETTE)—SLAVE AND SPY

JAMES WAS BORN INTO SLAVERY ON THE PLANTATION OF WILLIAM Armistead, a major contributor to the Revolution, in Virginia around 1760. He served as a house servant and was well known to his master, whom he served on friendly terms. As the Revolution spread into Virginia, the patriotic feelings of William Armistead became infectious to his slaves to the point that in 1781 James asked to be allowed to join the Continental Army. His master would not allow this since when the war was over James would be a free man, no longer a slave. Consequently, James, now known as James Armistead, did not enlist in the Continental Army, instead his master had him assigned to the Marquis de Lafayette, his personal friend. Lafayette, realizing that Armistead was very intelligent, recruited him as a spy.

James Armistead entered the camp of General Cornwallis as an escaped slave and soon was pressed into service as a waiter in the officer's mess. In the mess, he overheard the officers talking about a variety of military subjects. At the same time, General Cornwallis was in desperate need of information regarding the Continental Army, and realizing that he had an asset at hand he soon recruited Armistead to return to the Lafayette camp to gather intelligence for him. James Armistead had now become a double agent, but only in name. The information he carried back to Cornwallis was all bogus. For example, in one case Lafayette employed the deception techniques taught to him by General Washington. A false document reporting the arrival of a large regiment of Patriot soldiers was created. It was written on a dirty piece of paper and carried to Cornwallis by Armistead, who claimed he found it along the road. Cornwallis believed him until the battle of Yorktown, when he knew he had been deceived.

According to Rex Ellis, vice president of Colonial Williamsburg's Historic Area, Armistead's role was critical to the American victory at Yorktown. He states, "If he had not given the information that he gave at the strategic time he did, they would not have had the intelligence to create the blockade that ended the war."

After the end of the war, James Armistead returned into slavery on the Armistead plantation. He could not be freed under the Emancipation Act of 1783 which states "whereas it appears just and reasonable that all persons enlisted as aforesaid, who have faithfully served agreeable to the terms of their enlistment, and have thereby of course contributed towards the establishment of American liberty and independence, should enjoy the blessings of freedom as a reward for their toils and labours." Since he technically had not enlisted he was therefore not a soldier. He remained a slave until freed by the Virginia Legislature on January 9, 1786, partly on the testimonial written by the Marquis de Lafayette and given to James Armistead on November 21, 1784, during Lafayette's visit to America. That testimonial states the following:

> *This is to certify that the bearer by the name of James, has done essential service to Me while I had the honor to command in this state. His intelligences from the enemy's camp were industriously collected and faithfully delivered. He perfectly acquainted himself with some important commissions I gave him and appears to me entitled to every reward his situation can admit to. Done under my hand, Richmond, November 21st, 1784*
>
> *Lafayette*

At that same time Lafayette gave James Armistead permission to change his last name from Armistead to Lafayette and for the remainder of his life he was known as James Armistead Lafayette. He died a free man on August 9, 1830.

In 1824, six years before his death, his portrait was painted in Richmond, Virginia, by the painter John Blennerhassett Martin. That painting today hangs in the Valentine Museum in Richmond, Virginia.

X

The Eastern Department

MAJOR EVENTS

1775
Battle of Freetown

1777
Danbury Raid
Battle of Bennington

1778
Battle of Rhode Island

1779
French Troops land at Rhode Island
Department abolished

THE SAME DAY THAT GENERAL WASHINGTON BEGAN TO MOVE HIS troops south to New York, April 4, 1776, the Continental Congress established the Eastern Department of the Continental Army. The new department consisted of the New England colonies of Connecticut, Massachusetts, New Hampshire, and Rhode Island. In addition, the Army of New England became the backbone of the new department. The Congressional action served to formalize what up to that point had been a loose confederation of the New England colonies.

The new department saw limited military action, mainly conducting raiding parties, with the exception of the more structured actions in Rhode Island in 1778. General Artemas Ward, who had previously commanded the Army of New England, was now commander of the new department. The Eastern Department was abolished in November 1779, when the Continental Army went into winter quarters in Morristown, New Jersey, and the British Army pulled out of Rhode Island. The campaign had moved south and there was no longer a British military presence in New England. In addition, the troops would be of greater value in the southern campaign, where Washington's troops were outnumbered.

INTELLIGENCE OPERATIONS

With the departure of the Continental Army from Boston, the emphasis of intelligence activities refocused to Connecticut and Rhode Island. For Connecticut, Loyalist operatives quickly shifted from reporting to the British headquarters in Boston to a new headquarters in New York City. Their reports led to two specific military actions in the colony of Connecticut.

The first occurred in April 1777 when, based on information provided by a Loyalist operative, British troops conducted a raid on Danbury, Connecticut, where they destroyed a major Rebel supply depot. Before the raid, a young woman named Sybil Ludington, learning of the raid, rode forty miles from New York City to Danbury to alert her father about the planned raid.

The second military action occurred in September 1778, when the American traitor Benedict Arnold led a British force in a raid on the Connecticut town of New London. The raid was an attempt to delay the combined American and French force from moving south against New York City. The raid also attempted to destroy the town, which served as a base for privateer activity.

The French Arrive in Rhode Island

In 1778, a Treaty of Friendship was negotiated between the French and American governments. As a result, the French government sent 2,800 French troops under Comte Charles d'Estaing to assist the Continental Army.

When Washington learned of the French mission to assist the American cause, he immediately went into action. He ordered General William Heath to send agents to Canada and Boston to collect information on Halifax defense works. He knew that this action would undoubtedly become known to British agents, and the information would be passed on to General Henry Clinton. In another deceptive move, he had a 1778 proclamation translated into French urging the Canadians to rise up and support the coming American/French invasion of Canada.

The French fleet sailed from France in April 1778, and arrived in American waters three months later in June 1778. Unable to land in New York City due to the presence of a British fleet and a high sand bar, the French fleet sailed for Newport, Rhode Island, which was currently held by the British. In order to drive the British out of Newport, the French, in cooperation with the Americans, decided to mount a joint mission to take Newport, Rhode Island, from British control. A plan was developed between the American General John Sullivan and Comte d'Estaing for a joint ground and naval attack on Newport.

However, General Clinton had received valuable intelligence that provided him with the exact size of the French force as well as their planned destination. With this information in hand, Clinton reacted. He ordered Admiral Richard Howe to gather a fleet to sail to Newport and counter the French fleet.

The two fleets met off the coast of Newport on August 10, 1778, and began to maneuver for position, but a violent storm arose and both fleets broke off the engagement. The British returned to New York and the French retired to Boston. After repairing the ships in Boston, the French returned to France. But this was not the end of the French involvement in Rhode Island. On July 12, 1780, the French once again arrived in America and successfully landed troops in Rhode Island who would later join with General Washington's army.

With the departure of the British from Rhode Island in 1779, there was no longer a significant British presence in the New England colonies. It became obvious that the war had shifted to the south and would not again return to the New England area. With this in mind, in November 1779, the Continental Congress abolished the Eastern Department.

SUMMARY

By creating the Eastern Department, the military in the New England area became the primary component of the Continental Army's military structure. The department now had a TO&E like the other departments, as well as a financial commitment from the Continental Congress. The military was no longer a loose confederation of colonial militia groups that was dependent on their colony for financial support.

General Washington now had an established command in the New England region—one that he could depend on to function in accordance with his overall strategy. The Eastern Department's handling of the arrival of the French fleet in 1778 stands as one of the many ways intelligence influenced his actions.

The abolishment of the Eastern Department in November 1779 was primarily predicated by the fact that the war had shifted to the more southern colonies. The troops from the Eastern Department would be of more value in the Southern Department where conflicts were still occurring, than in a department that was basically a peacekeeping operation.

~~~

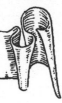

GENERAL JOHN GLOVER

J OHN GLOVER'S MILITARY CAREER BEGAN IN 1759, WHEN HE enlisted in a Massachusetts militia unit in Marblehead. In 1775, as a colonel, he led his troops to Boston to participate in the siege of Boston. General Washington noticed Glover and his ability to translate an order into action. For example, Washington asked Glover to acquire ships to intercept British supply ships thereby acquiring needed materials for his troops. Glover, using his own sloop, stopped the HMS *Hannah* and obtained 2,000 muskets, 100,000 flints, 30,000 artillery shells, and 30 tons of musket ammunition, all of which were in short supply in Washington's army. Washington appreciated his ingenuity.

When Washington moved to New York, Glover and his unit also made the move. Glover's association with Washington continued and they became close friends. When Washington realized he needed to evacuate his troops from Long Island, he turned to Glover, who devised a successful evacuation plan. The plan was a combination of land movements and the removal of troops by ships.

In 1778, Washington again turned to Glover. The French fleet carrying French troops to assist the Rebels was not able to use the port facilities of New York City and was forced to go to Newport, Rhode Island. Washington needed to be kept abreast of events in Newport. It is probable that Washington, knowing of the talents of now General Glover, sent him to Rhode Island to keep him informed of events there.

The following correspondence between General Glover and General Washington represents an excellent example of how well communications and intelligence flowed. The correspondence shows that while Glover reported enemy intelligence, he also included information about the Continental forces in the Eastern Department. Dated from September 12, 1778, until October 14, 1778, the correspondence focuses on the activities of the British in the Eastern Department, and the French ships of Comte d'Estaing off the shores of Rhode Island. At that time, General Washington was located in Westchester County, west of New York City, allowing for timely receipt of the intelligence contained in the letters. With a personal knowledge of Glover's talents, Washington could trust the validity of his reports.

Headquarters at Providence, September 12, 1778

General Glover desires the men to know that since the evacuation of the Island of Rhode Island on 30-31 last, the British have resumed their depredations along the coast of Massachusetts. On the 6th of this month General [Charles] Grey, of Paoli infamy, carried out an attack on New Bedford where his troops destroyed over seventy ships, burned the town, subjected women and children as well as the aged to insult and injury and murdered several of the town's citizens. The same terrible scenes were then visited upon the town of Fairhaven. Following this, on the 10th, General Grey landed his troops on Martha's Vineyard where they are reported to have carried off several thousand of sheep and 300 cattle as well as stealing some 950 pounds from the inhabitants of the island leaving them destitute to face the forthcoming winter. General Sullivan is determined to stop such inhuman violations and this brigade will soon be in receipt of orders to counter these activities.

Brigadier General John Glover
Glover's Massachusetts Brigade
General Sullivan's Division
Continental Army

Providence, September 23, 1778
Headquarters 15th Massachusetts Regiment

In response to the recent resumption of British attacks along the coast of Massachusetts, General Sullivan has ordered that supply depots be established to facilitate the quick response on the part of this army to similar depredations or to the possibility of a large scale invasion by an even greater force of enemy. The main supply depot will be established in the town of East Medway, Massachusetts and will serve as the principal distribution point for the other depots. Arms, powder and supplies are already being accumulated at that location including new cartridge boxes to replace those that proved so inadequate in the heavy rain encountered on the Island of Rhode Island.

In support of this object, this Regiment along with Colonel Sheppard's has been ordered to march at the soonest for East Medway to construct fortifications to protect the supply depot. The regiments are to break camp and undertake the march at ten o'clock tomorrow morning this 24th instant. All company returns

*are to be completed and submitted to the Regimental Sergeant Major by eight
o'clock tomorrow morning. Regimental officers are already in receipt of orders
including the order of the march. Platoon sergeants and corporals are responsible
for the men being mustered and ready to march at the command of their officers.*

*The distance from Providence to East Medway is approximately forty
miles and the Colonel expects this Regiment to complete the march and have
camp set up in no less than three days. All excess baggage will be left behind to
be forwarded later in company with the artillery train. This includes officers'
personal baggage. Priority will be given to tools required in constructing the
fortifications: shovels, mattocks, hatches, saws, axes, etc.*

*By order of
Timothy Bigelow
Colonel Commanding
15ᵗʰ Massachusetts Regiment
Brigadier General John Glover's Brigade*

---

*Providence, October 1, 1778
To His Excellency, General Washington
Pursuant to your request for frequent reports of the events
Pertaining to my command, I pen the following:*

Dear General,

*Your message informing me that General Clinton intended to send
reinforcements to General Pigot at Newport was both timely and accurate. At
7 o'clock this morning some thirty British ships were observed rounding point
Judith and by early afternoon had come to anchor between Conanicut Island and
the Island of Rhode Island. Several of the ships were obviously transports and
others of a more shallow draft that would allow them to come in closer to the shore
should the enemy wish to penetrate the numerous rivers that abound in this area.*

*Troops were seen being ferried ashore to the number of three thousand,
bringing General Pigot's forces to well over six thousand. It is not known if other
troops remained aboard the transports. It is presumed that the enemy intends to
continue the raids instigated by General Grey, and perhaps launch others more
deeply inland given his additional strength. You reported that General Grey
with his command has returned to New York. It might be that he will again*

be dispatched to this area to supplement the enemy's strength. Your promise to demonstrate again the New York lines if this appears likely to take place will, as you suggest, given General Clinton second thoughts with respect to making such a move.

The establishment of supply depots continues apace with the fortifications defending the central depot at East Medway well underway. Colonel Bigelow reports that all the redoubts and other works including the fascines should be completed within two weeks. Supplies are rapidly being accumulated and some already dispersed to the other depots.

Your Excellency. I hesitate, but feel that I must broach a sensitive subject. I have asked General Lafayette to again request that the Comte d'Estaing permit some of the troops that are aboard his ships to join this command so as to further enhance our flexibility to respond to any threatened enemy incursions. I have as of yet heard nothing of this request and given the past lack of support by our allies, I fear he may again claim that he can do nothing given the state of disrepair of his ships. If you could urge the Comte to augment the command with even a token force of French troops it would do much to raise the spirit of the men and bring the alliance into better repute among the officers of this command. I hope to hear from General Lafayette shortly and will apprise you immediately concerning his report.

I am with Great regard Your Excellency,
Your most obedient servant
Major General John Sullivan

Providence, October 10, 1778
To His Excellency, General Washington

Dear General,

It appears obvious that General Pigot plans some incursions into the interior portions of this command perhaps to interdict the transport of supplies from depot to depot or between Boston and Worcester to the central depot at East Medway. He has the ability given the strength of his command and the increased shipping he has received to dispatch forces to several points at once. The local militias have been of great service in reporting enemy activity and I believe that they will provide us with quick notification of future movements. However, the severalty of possible moves available to General Pigot places a great strain on this command to attempt to counter the numerous options.

We have had great news from General Lafayette, Admiral le Comte d' Estaing has agreed to forward a portion of the French troops under his command to our assistance.

They will march from Boston to East Medway and from thence to join our command here in Providence. They are expected to be in the vicinity of East Medway by the 14th inst. and here by the 21st inst. News of this will add greatly to the spirit of our troops.

It is unknown whether General Pigot would personally command any large scale raid, since it is reported that he has been in ill health of late. Command might devolve upon the detestable General Richard Prescott who, although having been twice our prisoner and been treated with great cordiality, has acted with what can only be termed bestiality toward our men who have been unfortunate enough to have become his prisoners.

Supplies continue to flow into the depots. The laboratories in Boston and Worcester and even in Springfield have been conscientious in replacing the powder ruined by rain or expended during the action upon the Island of Rhode Island. We now have a sufficiency for both artillery and muskets for any forthcoming action. Major General Heath in Boston has been most cooperative in responding to my request for articles for this command particularly in forwarding of 10,000 flints and replacing the defective cartridge boxes mentioned in a previous communication.

Be assured I will forward news of any future moves on the part of the enemy with the greatest dispatch.

I am with Great regard Your Excellency,
You most obedient servant
Major General John Sullivan

East Medway, October 14, 1778
General Glover at Providence has forwarded the following intelligence:

"Early in the morning of the 12th inst., a British flotilla consisting of some ten to twelve troop transports, a large number of barges and armed launches and escorted by three ships of the line, penetrated Mount Hope Bay *to land troops opposite Tiverton and Freetown in the vicinity of Swansea. They took advantage of the high tide to quickly move through the marshes to reach the Bay Road.*

The greater portion of the enemy has moved in the direction of Providence, and it is supposed might attempt to take the defenses of this city from the rear. The militia commander in Tiverton estimates the strength of the landing force to be in the several of thousands."

"A second force has apparently advanced rapidly through Rehoboth to Attleboro where they established a position blocking the Boston-Providence pike. Whether they intend to advance further from that point to threaten the depot at East Medway is unknown. They may simply be positioning this force to intercept any reinforcements intended for Providence."

Since receiving the above intelligence from General Glover, the enemy has been observed in the vicinity of Wrentham/Foxborough, and patrols may have penetrated as far as Norfolk, a mere seven miles from this post. The strength of the force while at Attleboro was estimated at above one thousand with at least two cannon.

In response to what appears to be a direct threat to this post, the following orders are to be communicated to the officers of this command:

Fifteenth Massachusetts Regiment
All soldiers of this regt. are to be taken off regular duties.

The regt. will immediately commence regular patrolling in the direction of Medway and Norfolk. All roads and possible routes of march of the enemy are to be patrolled aggressively.

The entire regt. will function as Light Infantry, and all those men who are not capable of carrying out rigorous activities to be organized as a fatigue component to assume all camp guard duties.

Those troops functioning as Light Infantry are to be issued sixty rounds of ammunition and rations sufficient for at least a two day absence from camp.

Fourth Massachusetts Regiment
Colonel Sheppard's Regt. will continue to fortify this in preparation for a possible enemy attack.

He will assume command of all troops not designated a force active patrol including the fatigue component of the 15th Regt. mentioned above.

In preparation for the defense of this post, Colonel Sheppard will also be responsible for coordinating the activities of his command with the French troops expected to arrive later today.

By order of Colonel Timothy Bigelow
Commandant, East Medway Depot

The information contained in the above letters provided General Washington with a very complete report of the British activities in the Eastern Department. The details ensured Washington that there was no need for more troops to be in the area—it was under control. The reporting also kept Washington informed about the French activities in the area.

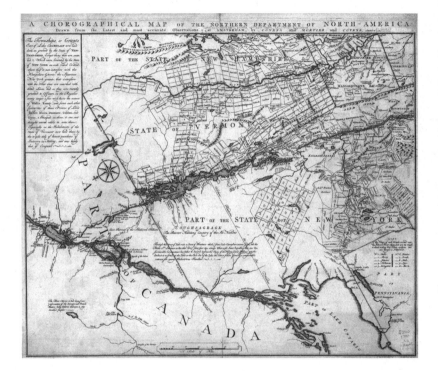

A CHOROGRAPHICAL MAP OF THE NORTHERN DEPARTMENT OF NORTH-AMERICA. Drawn from the Latest and most accurate Observations at AMSTERDAM by COVENS and MORTIER and COVENS Junior

XI

The Northern Department

MAJOR EVENTS

1775
Capture of Fort Ticonderoga
Battle of Fort Anne

1777
Battle of Oriskany
Siege of Fort Stanwix
Second Battle of Fort Ticonderoga
Battle of Freeman's Farm
Battle of Saratoga

1779
Sullivan's Expedition

THE NEW YORK DEPARTMENT WAS FORMED ON JUNE 25, 1775, shortly after the first battle of Fort Ticonderoga. Later on April 14, 1776, the Northern Department was formed, which consisted of the New York Department, New Jersey, Maryland, Delaware, and Pennsylvania—New York City and Long Island were not included as they were under British control.

Later, in 1777, the colonies of New Jersey, Delaware, Maryland, and Pennsylvania became a separate department known as the Middle Department.

The Northern Department consisted of diverse geographic areas, from cities to thick wildernesses. That diversity also held true for the population that ranged from the more sophisticated New York population to the rugged pioneer stock of upstate New York, though both consisted of Loyalists and Colonists. Additionally, New York's Indian population was vast and came to be known as the Iroquois Confederacy or Six Nations. Of the six tribes in the Confederacy, the Seneca, Cayuga, Mohawk, and Onondaga tribes sided with the British, while the Oneida and Tuscarora tribes sided with the Americans, causing a rift among the Six Nation Confederacy. Both the American and the British sides benefitted from their Indian allies.

INTELLIGENCE OPERATIONS

Before the establishment of the Northern Department, the intelligence activities in the area were controlled predominately by the Massachusetts Committee of Safety. This arrangement may well have had an ironic twist to it as Benjamin Church, a member of the Committee, was also a British agent. Any intelligence provided to the committee was probably passed on to the British by Dr. Church. A good example of this is the reporting in April 1775 by then smuggler Benedict Arnold that Fort Ticonderoga was in a dilapidated condition and could be easily taken.

Once the Northern Department was formed in June 1775, the intelligence gathering and interpretation became the responsibility of the department. The intelligence gathered prior to the battle of Saratoga added significantly to the outcome of that military event.

FORT TICONDEROGA 1775

Fort Ticonderoga, originally a French fort, had been ceded to the British in 1769 as a result of the French and Indian War. The fort was located on a narrow passageway between Lake George and Lake Champlain that provided access to the Hudson River Valley. Once in British hands, the fort wasn't considered viable and soon fell into disrepair. However, in the spring of 1775, even before the creation of the Continental Army or the Northern Department, the fort became a matter of high interest to the Colonials since it had eighty pieces of heavy artillery that would be very useful in the siege of Boston.

It is important to remember that the Fort Ticonderoga military action took place before George Washington was named as commander-in-chief of the newly formed Continental Army as well as the Northern Department. The various counter-productive actions that took place prior to the assault between Benedict Arnold and Ethan Allen as to the leadership of their combined force demonstrates the value of the formation of the Northern Department.

Planning the Attack

The actions of the three independent groups involved in planning for the assault on Fort Ticonderoga—Connecticut, Massachusetts, and The Green Mountain Boys—were initially conducted in isolation of the others, but later combined as follows:

CONNECTICUT: Prior to Arnold's report to the Massachusetts Committee of Safety, Colonel Samuel H. Parsons of the Connecticut militia had confided in Arnold that the forces besieging Boston needed cannons. Arnold gave him an account of the cannons located at Fort Ticonderoga, as well as the poor conditions of the fort for a military outpost. After hearing this information, Parsons convened an ad hoc group of Hartford, Connecticut, citizens to discuss the situation at Fort Ticonderoga. The group decided to initiate a plan to capture the fort on their own and without informing any other colony. Captain Noah Phelps and Benjamin Romans were dispatched to recruit and organize a troop for the effort. Edward Mott, a captain in Colonel Parsons' regiment, joined the group with five men. In all, over fifty-six men volunteered for the mission.

MASSACHUSETTS: In the spring of 1775, the first intelligence report regarding Fort Ticonderoga was received by Dr. Joseph Warren, head of the Massachusetts Committee of Safety. The report came from Benedict Arnold who had acquired the information while in the Montreal area working as a ship captain, merchant, and part-time smuggler. The report stated that "the Fort was in ruinous condition but it did boast of eighty pieces of heavy cannons, twenty brass, and, from four to eight pounders, as well as small arms, stores and a sloop. He further stated that Ticonderoga could not hold out an hour against a vigorous assault." Earlier in the year, a Connecticut member, John Brown, had made a covert trip to Montreal and his report also referred to the vulnerability of Fort Ticonderoga. His report indicated that the fort should be seized as soon as hostilities broke out. In early May 1775, the time appeared right to move against Fort Ticonderoga.

With the siege of Boston on-going, Arnold's report caused quite a stir among the Colonials and they reacted. They began to plan for an attack on Fort Ticonderoga. In the absence of a Continental Army, the Massachusetts Committee of Safety issued orders appointing Benedict Arnold as a colonel and commander, granting him a body of four-hundred men that he was to recruit himself from local militia groups or regular civilians. His mission was to march to Fort Ticonderoga and capture it for the Rebels. The objective was to acquire the cannons and move them to Boston. The first sanctioned offensive of the Revolutionary War was about to be underway based solely on intelligence reporting.

Ironically, Dr. Benjamin Church, a leader of the Massachusetts Committee of Safety, and also a spy for the British, wrote Benedict Arnold's orders. One can assume that Church informed the British General Gates of this action, but Gates was unable to react as his forces were under siege in Boston.

THE GREEN MOUNTAIN BOYS—The Green Mountain Boys was a quasi-legal militia formed in 1770 by a gathering of settlers in New Hampshire, with "Colonel" Ethan Allen as its commander. The group was formed for protection of New York over a land grant claim. Two of the group's members, Levi and Herman Allen, brothers of Ethan, were among the volunteers recruited by Captain Mott in Connecticut. Since Fort Ticonderoga was of interest to the Green Mountain Boys, the brothers informed Ethan about the Connecticut initiative, which led to a meeting in Bennington, Vermont. About 140 Green Mountain Boys and 70 men from the Connecticut militia attended, where they developed a plan to secure the roads to Fort Edward, Skenesborough, Ticonderoga, and Crown Point, and then execute a surprise attack on Fort Ticonderoga. Ideally, the plan was to be implemented in three days. Captain Noah Phelps was sent on an intelligence collection mission to scout Fort Ticonderoga.

In the meantime, Captain Phelps managed to go to Fort Ticonderoga, where he entered the fort disguised as a barber. When he returned, Phelps reported that the fort was poorly defended and unaware of any threat. But in February 1775, the commander of the fort, Captain William Delaplace, reported twice to General Gates about possible intelligence gathering missions at the fort, but Gates ignored the reports—Ticonderoga was not of military interest to him.

When Benedict Arnold learned that the Connecticut militia and the Green Mountain Boys were planning an attack on Fort Ticonderoga, he was indignant, but still unprepared. Since learning the troops were to gather at Castle, Arnold mounted his horse and rode off to meet with leaders of the group. He confronted Ethan Allen, their commander, with his written commission from the Massachusetts Committee and demanded that therefore he be the one to lead the force. Allen objected at first, but eventually agreed to issue joint orders during the mission. The surprise attack was successful, and the fort was captured, with the remaining cannons and military supplies removed to the Boston area.

This episode shows the importance of the department organization set up by George Washington and the Continental Congress. If the Northern Department had existed before the battle of Fort Ticonderoga, the confusion before the attack wouldn't have been as substantial. Not to mention, General Schuyler would have been in command. It would have been his responsibility to organize such an attack and elect the commander for the action.

GENERAL BURGOYNE'S OFFENSIVE

After the first battle of Ticonderoga in July 1775, the Northern Department's activity was limited until the early months of 1777. On February 15, 1777, the New York Committee of Correspondence reported to George Washington details of a plan developed by General John Burgoyne, which was to move his army down the Hudson River Valley. There he would connect with General Henry Clinton's army, in so doing cutting the Colonies in half. Burgoyne's plan was in American hands thirteen days before it was even presented to King George III for approval. This information now focused the Northern Department with two new missions: to prevent General Burgoyne's army's passage down the Hudson River Valley, and also to control the Indian tribes in the department. General Philip Schuyler, commander of the department, knew what his intelligence staff needed to acquire:

- The size of Burgoyne's army

- Where it was located in Canada

- When would Burgoyne's army head south through New York State

- What route would the British Army take

Burgoyne's plan soon became evident. It would be a three-prong campaign composed of three separate columns. Burgoyne led his column of 8,000 men down the Hudson River Valley toward Albany. Colonel Barry St. Leger led his column with 1,000 men from the east of Canada along the Mohawk River—mainly serving as a decoy. General Clinton was to lead his column up the Hudson River with the intention of meeting Burgoyne. Now Schuyler knew his force of 3,000 was outnumbered by a 2 to 1 ratio, making the placement of his troops critical to provide tactical advantage. However, Schuyler had an important intelligence advantage—it was difficult to disguise the British Army's route when 8,000 troops were being moved with a very large baggage train, which frequently lagged and delayed potential tactical moves.

Burgoyne, on the other hand, probably had a good estimate of the number of Rebel troops he faced, as well as the location of critical American forts along the proposed route; however, he was unsure of the status of the manning at each fort. He also was unsure early on if General Howe and his army would leave Philadelphia and proceed up the Hudson River to support his move south.

Both sides utilized Indians as scouts and information gatherers to accomplish their intelligence requirements, and both typically had excellent results. In some cases though the information the Indians provided was slanted to benefit the Indians rather than the British or American combatants.

Burgoyne's Army Begins the Advance

And thus the chase of the Fox and the Hound continued. Intelligence activities played a distinct role in the outcome of the campaign. Even before Burgoyne's army moved out of Canada on June 16, 1777, the friendly Oneida Indians, in the spring of 1777, warned the Colonists of the impending advance of the British into the Mohawk Valley. A similar report was received from Silas Towne of Oswego, New York, who was sent to Canada by General Schuyler soon after Burgoyne's arrival. His mission in Canada was to ascertain what Burgoyne was planning. After arriving, Towne was arrested and placed in a prisoner-of-war camp but his escape to New York allowed him to pass on the intelligence to General Schuyler. Towne's report further validated what the Oneida Indians had reported earlier.

When Burgoyne's troops moved down Lake Champlain in June 1777, an Indian vanguard laid down such an effective screen that the Colonists did not realize how close they were to Fort Ticonderoga. Even when Burgoyne's army arrived at Fort Crown Point and camped about four miles from the fort, the Colonists still had no idea they were there.

In June 1777, young Sergeant Moses Harris, from the Duchess County Regiment, was sent on a mission, presumably as a courier and dressed in civilian clothes. Along the way, he met with a group of Loyalist couriers who were exhausted by their efforts to avoid Patriot patrols. The couriers were attempting to deliver a packet of letters to the Loyalist contact in Albany. Harris told them he was heading in that direction and would be happy to deliver the packet for them. The Loyalist couriers gladly accepted his offer. Harris departed with the packet but instead of Albany, he took the letters to the headquarters of General Schuyler.

Without ruining the seals, the Colonists opened the letters from Brigadier General Watson Powell to Colonel Barry St. Leger which gave details of the planned attack by St. Leger on Fort Stanwix. The second letter provided all the details of the three-pronged attack planned by the British. Burgoyne would invade from Canada, St. Leger would advance from the west of Oswego, and General Howe would come up from New York.

General Schuyler recognized the importance of the courier connection and set a plan into motion. He established Mr. John Fish as Harris's contact with the Loyalists, and simultaneously sent copies of the intercepted letters to Washington. At the same time, he sent the information regarding the British attack on Fort Stanwix to General Nicholas Herkimer and Colonel Peter Gansevoort stating, "A report prevails that Sir. John Johnson intends to attack your post. You will therefore put yourself in the best posture for defense. I have written General Herkimer to support you with militia, in case you should be attacked. Give him therefore the most early intelligence if any enemy should approach you."

General Washington responded to the intercepted letter by congratulating General Schuyler for the victory of the French over the Royal Navy (the sea battle off the coast of Rhode Island did not happen due to stormy weather). Washington also informed Schuyler that he was sending Brigadier General John Stark and several regiments north to invade Canada. This was a ruse as the letter was intended to be intercepted by the British and possibly keep Burgoyne from heading south. It is not known if the plot was successful or not.

Siege of Fort Stanwix

The result was that Fort Stanwix was not surprised by the British attack—possibly due to Moses Harris. On the morning of July 8, 1777, a "deserter" entered the camp of a British detachment under the command of Lieutenant Colonel John Hill. The detachment was tasked to pursue the Rebel military who had escaped from Fort Ticonderoga and were heading to Fort Anne. The deserter told Colonel Hill that the fort was manned by over 1,000 troops (in fact there were less than 400), far more than in Colonel Hill's detachment. The deserter then disappeared.

A skirmish soon ensued between the two forces, but was abruptly cut short when the Patriots heard Indian war whoops coming from the north. In fact, the war whoops were the brainstorm of a British officer named John Money, Burgoyne's assistant quartermaster. He was leading a group of Indians who proved reluctant to fight the Patriots. Money decided to use deceptive tactics as he began to shout war whoops implying that the Indians were about to attack—they were not, it was all for effect. The ruse worked as the Patriots retreated, and the battle was over.

Colonel Barry St. Leger arrived in Oswego on July 27, 1777, and began to draw up his plan of attack for Fort Stanwix. Once again Silas Towne proved to be an intelligence asset for the Colonists. He hid in the woods within earshot of St. Leger's war council and heard St. Leger's plan of attack for Fort Stanwix which he then reported to the Patriots.

When the British Army arrived at Fort Stanwix in early August 1777, Colonel St. Leger decided to try a tried-and-true deception technique. He ordered his troops to march in front of the fort, attempting to convince those inside of his superior strength. In previous cases, the fort would be surrendered. This time, however, it did not work in Colonel St. Leger's favor.

On August 6, 1777, at the battle of Oriskany, St. Leger deployed Major Stephen Watt's troops to support his efforts. As the troops approached the battle, Major Watt ordered his men to turn their coats inside out, which would hide their distinctive regimental green color. The reverse color was more like a traditional light beige similar to hunting coats worn by the militia. The tactic almost worked, however, Captain Gardner of the Patriots recognized one of the Tories and the ruse was over.

In August 1777, a Patriot named Lieutenant Colonel Brooks suggested a plan to General Arnold that could lift the siege of Fort Stanwix. He recommended that they tell a captured British soldier named Holds that they would execute his brother who had also been captured if he did not deliver a message to St. Leger. The message was an embellished report of the number of troops Benedict Arnold was leading to attack the British at Fort Stanwix. The message also stated that a number of Oneida Indians were to arrive at St. Leger's camp and to confirm the information was given to St. Leger. Maybe a coincidence, but St. Leger broke the siege of Fort Stanwix on August 28, 1777—the date he received the message.

General Stark's Raid

In mid-August 1777, General John Stark and his New Hampshire militia men aided General Schuyler in an attempt to counter the British, who were believed to be mounting an attack on eastern New York and Vermont in search of supplies. Stark and his men were in Manchester, Vermont, awaiting word of the British destination. On August 13, 1777, a woman rode a horse into Stark's camp with news that hostile Indians were causing terror in her town. She had come herself as it was not safe for a man to be on the road.

Stark immediately ordered about two-hundred men to stop the supposed marauders and gather intelligence. The detachment soon learned that the Indians were in fact clearing the way for a larger force that was marching toward Bennington. Couriers were immediately dispatched to Manchester to forward the troops quickly to support Stark. The early warning supplied by the unknown woman led to an important victory for the Americans in the battle of Bennington.

⁕

Arguably the most important Patriot agent in the Northern Department was Alexander Bryan, an innkeeper in Saratoga Springs. Both Loyalists and Patriots frequented his inn. General Gates knew of him and his strong feelings for the Patriot's cause, and with this in mind, asked Bryan to perform a mission for him. Gates asked him to enter the British camp near Fort Edward and stay there until he learned the details of Burgoyne's plan to advance through Mohawk Valley. Bryan accepted the challenge and was soon in the British camp where he was successful in learning about Burgoyne's plan.

Early September 1777, Bryan was discovered by the British but managed to escape on horseback. He eluded the patrol and informed General Gates that the British were planning to cross the Hudson at Stillwater and surprise the Patriots by surrounding them. The timeliness of the information was crucial because it gave the Patriots two days to prepare for the attack, which came on September 17, 1777. Alexander Bryan is truly one of the heroes of the battle of Saratoga. In addition, Bryan pointed out the importance of the Bemis Heights to General Gates. By placing troops on the Heights, he could prevent Burgoyne's army access to the only road south to New York City.

SUMMARY

While all of these examples do not show a high level of sophistication in intelligence gathering and deception, they do show that while intelligence gathering in the Northern Department was not a highly organized network (such as the Culper Ring), in its own way it did provide valuable information to assist the American cause.

It should be noted that while the local Indians were employed by both sides for intelligence gathering, the British were much more successful in working with the Indians than the Americans. The British promised the Indians that they would not settle on their lands.

While the Northern Department consisted of only a portion of New York State, it played a major role in the American Revolution with the victory at the battle of Saratoga—all without an organized intelligence network. It was all individually initiated. Even in Alexander Bryan's mission at Saratoga, while Schuyler asked Bryan to undertake, it was Bryan's innate intelligence and bravery that made it successful.

Many of the techniques employed by the intelligence operatives in the Northern Department had been employed for centuries by spies but somehow they still seemed to work in the American Revolution. They were what today we call "human intelligence," but unlike today they were not trained agents but rather exceptional people who were willing to take a risk in support of their country. The Northern Department remained in existence until January 15, 1783, when the war with the British came to an end.

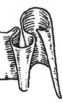

a person of interest
in the northern department

ALEXANDER BRYAN

I N 1777, ALEXANDER BRYAN WAS A 44-YEAR-OLD INNKEEPER IN the vicinity of Saratoga Springs. He was described as "a person endowed with great physical powers of endurance; well acquainted with the country; shrewd, discreet, and reticent, gifted with a fine address and presence, and, considering the meager educational advantages of the time, possessed of much more than ordinary intelligence."

His inn was located along a main road and was frequently used by both British and American soldiers—at separate times, of course. Bryan was friendly to all and both sides considered him to be an ally for their cause.

On August 19, 1777, General Horatio Gates arrived at Stillwater in desperate need of information regarding Burgoyne's army and his intentions. But acquiring this information required a spy. Gates went to the local Committee of Safety seeking a potential candidate to undertake the mission, and the unanimous selection of the committee was Alexander Bryan.

When General Gates met with Bryan, he detailed the importance of the mission and what it entailed. Bryan accepted the task with one reservation: his son was dying and his daughter-in-law was about to deliver another baby after a difficult pregnancy. Gates assured Bryan that he would send a medical team to provide whatever medical attention was needed. With this assurance, Bryan undertook the mission.

To alleviate suspicions, Bryan took a circuitous route and arrived at the enemy encampment near Fort Edwards, where he was welcomed as an old friend. As he wandered through the camp, he was able to acquire intelligence that would be helpful to General Gates. Realizing the importance of what he had learned, in the early morning hours of September 15, 1777, Bryan left the British encampment and headed back to Gates' headquarters. What he did not know is that the British had become suspicious of him and his departure from their camp was noted and a chase began. Finally, to elude the British party, Bryan abandoned his horse and jumped in a shallow creek. He submerged his body, breathing thorough a reed and remained there until the chase party returned to camp.

Bryan informed Gates that Burgoyne was planning to cross the Hudson River and mount a surprise attack on the Americans from there. Gates was delighted to have this information. Based on Bryan's report, Gates decided to fortify the Bemis Heights area. Within days, the first battle, known as the battle of Freeman Farm, took place and then on October 7, 1777, the battle of Saratoga occurred. In both battles, Bemis Heights, the area highlighted to General Gates by Alexander Bryan played an important part. Bemis Heights overlooked the only road Burgoyne could traverse on his way to New York City.

When Bryan returned to his home, he found that General Gates had not kept his promise about medical attention for his family during his absence. None had been forthcoming. He found that his son had died and his daughter-in-law had delivered a premature child. To make matters worse, none of the after-action reports written by General Gates even mentioned Alexander Bryan. He was given no credit for his successful mission.

When he died on April 9, 1825, he was buried in the Gideon Putnam Burial Grounds in Saratoga Springs. His marker finally gives him the credit he so much deserved for his Revolutionary War spying efforts. It reads:

In memory of Alexander Bryan, who died April 9, 1825 at age 92. The first permanent settler, and the first to keep a public-house, here for visitors. An unpaid patriot who, alone and at great peril, gave the first and only information of Burgoyne's intended advance on Stillwater, which led to timely preparations for the Battle of September 19th, followed by the memorable victory of October 7, 1777.

CHAPTER

XII

The Highlands
Department

MAJOR EVENTS

1777
Battle of King's Ferry
Battle of Stoney Point
Battle of Forts Montgomery and Clinton

1778
Installation of great chain at West Point

1780
Benedict Arnold defects to British
Capture and execution of Major John André

ORIGINALLY PART OF THE NORTHERN DEPARTMENT, THE
Highlands Department became its own entity on November 12, 1776,
upon the request of General Washington. Recognizing the importance of the Hudson River to both the Americans and the British, the department was centered on the defenses of the Hudson River, about fifty miles
north of New York City. The Hudson River was a critical supply line for the
Americans between the northern colonies and those of the south. As early as

1775, Washington had come to realize that the overall strategy of the British was to attempt to cut the Colonies in half. The British force would move from Canada through the Hudson River Valley, where they would meet British forces from New York City. The mission of the Highlands Department was to prevent this from happening. The department also was to prevent the British naval vessels in New York Harbor from coming up stream to meet the British troops coming south.

The department's military activity focused entirely on the forts situated along the Hudson River, since possession of the forts meant free access to movement of ships up and down the Hudson River. In the fall of 1777, General Henry Clinton's army entered the Highlands area to capture the forts along the river so General Burgoyne's army, approaching from the north, would have easy access to the river. Since Burgoyne's army was defeated at Saratoga, Clinton's initiative was of no value. Not wanting to be isolated in the Highlands, Clinton removed his army from the area. A period of relative calm then existed in the Highlands until late 1779 and 1780, culminating in the Benedict Arnold defection.

The Highlands Department gained notoriety in September 1780 when General Benedict Arnold, the newly appointed commander of the fort at West Point, committed the treasonable act of fleeing from West Point and joining the British forces in New York. Arnold's attempt to surrender West Point to the British, thereby opening the Hudson River Valley for the movement of British troops, had failed.

The Highlands Department was the smallest of the departments with a specific, critical mission, but it was the only one where Washington reserved the right to interfere with the department commander (as he did when Clinton and his army headed north in the Highlands). There were nineteen commanders of the department throughout its existence.

Geography of the Highlands

The Hudson River Highlands is a fifteen-mile-wide ridged valley composed of granite and poor soil, making it sparsely settled in the 1700s. The river passing through the valley is tidal as far inland as Kingston and difficult to navigate near West Point because of three sharp turns in that area. The river normally runs in a north-south direction, with the exception of at West Point, where the three sharp curves—one at West Point, one at Anthony's Nest, and one at Dunderberg—made ships passing through this area vulnerable to shore batteries.

The geography of the Hudson River Valley dictated that forts be placed on high grounds along the river's south side. Forts were built at Fort Clinton, Fort Montgomery, Fort Lafayette, Stoney Point, and West Point. *(See map below)*

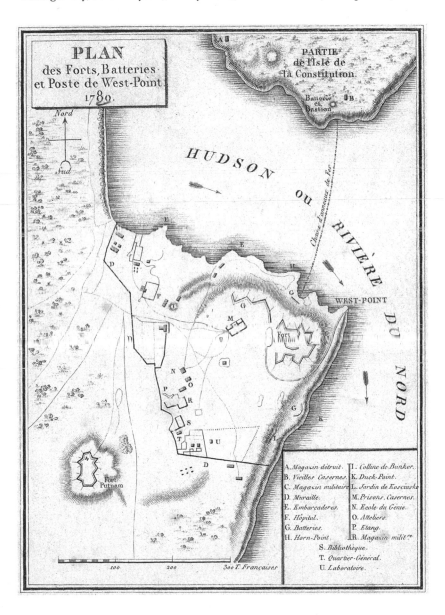

INTELLIGENCE OPERATIONS

Due to the sparse population in the Highlands area, limited intelligence came from there. As a result, General Washington was dependent on the Culper Ring network on Long Island and other spies in the New York City area for his information. Despite limited activity, successes still occurred from time to time. One in particular occurred while the area was still part of the Northern Department. On February 15, 1777, the New York State Committee on Conspiracies was informed about the proposed movement of Burgoyne's army through the Hudson Valley to connect with Clinton's army. This information was in American hands thirteen days before the proposal was made to the British king. Thus when the Highland Department was formed, they had a clear understanding of what their intelligence requirements would be.

The British were also short on intelligence for the area. In fact, the British didn't know about the chain placed across the Hudson River at West Point until Benedict Arnold informed them after his desertion. Their best source of intelligence came from Tory Colonel Beverly Robinson, whose estate was in the area of West Point.

General Washington did, however, receive some intelligence on the activities of the Highlands as shown in the following letter to William Livingston Sr. on October 8, 1777:

> *Sir: I yesterday received certain intelligence, that the enemy had proceeded up Hudson's River from New York, and landed a body of men at Verplanck's Point, a few miles below Peekskill ... Should any disaster happen, it is to foresee the most unhappy consequences. The loss of the Highland passes would be likely to involve the reduction of the forts. This would open the navigation of the river, and enable the enemy, with facility, to throw their force into Albany, get into the rear of General Gates, and either oblige him to retreat, or put him between two fires.*

While there was always a commanding general for the Highlands, Washington kept a close eye on the department and assumed command when necessary (as he did in 1779 prior to the battle of Stoney Point). Needing current intelligence on the status of the fort at Stoney Point and King's Ferry, he employed some of his most effective intelligence-gathering techniques. First, he sent a group of women posing as Loyalists (whom he called "half-Tory") to infiltrate the enemy lines to gather intelligence for his use. They reported that Clinton was well-dug in and fortified at King's Ferry and in a position of strength with no apparent weaknesses. Not finding the report complete, Washington turned to another ploy. He sent Captain Allan McLane, who was a trusted intelligence officer, into the enemy camp under a flag of truce. McLane was adept at looking at a situation and quickly assessing the terrain and potential weak points, and in this case he did just that. The British had failed to complete the defenses around a large rock on the inner line—a weakness.

One of the more ingenious intelligence coups involved placing a chain across the Hudson River at West Point. This deceptive intelligence ruse was accomplished by a supposed group of amateurs. The links of the chain were made by the Sterling Iron Works in Warwick, Orange County, and then were crated and shipped to Windsor, New York, just north of West Point—beyond observation of the British. When connected, the links were sent floating down the Hudson on logs, again out of view from the British. While the British knew about the obstacles across the lower Hudson River, they were unaware of the chain at West Point until Benedict Arnold deserted and told them of its existence. The chain's effectiveness was never tested by the British.

THE TREASON OF BENEDICT ARNOLD

The treacherous actions of Benedict Arnold are well-known in the annals of American history. But why did he desert the American cause? When examining the events leading up to his desertion, a series of intelligence failures and a streak of luck (both good and bad) provide the answer. The following specifics provide a case in point.

IN PHILADELPHIA:
Arnold's lust for money became apparent when he got involved in various nefarious financial deals in Philadelphia.

Courtmartialed in December 1778, based on his mismanagement of command in Philadelphia. Found innocent, but reprimanded by Washington.

Winter 1778, Washington offered Arnold command of the left wing of the Continental Army. Arnold declined, claiming his battle wound still needed to heal. Washington was puzzled by his decision as the left wing command was a coveted position. Arnold may well have already been planning his defection.

Possibly as early as May 1780, Arnold was corresponding with the British, offering West Point as the valuable asset he could deliver. (His messages were always enciphered using a dictionary code.)

Arnold sent messages to British Major John André by messengers (one named Joseph Stansbury was known to be against armed conflict with the British). Arnold used an alias to hide his identity.

Arnold was supplying the British with intelligence information from a variety of sources including Washington himself. For example, he learned of the landing of the French force in Rhode Island while having dinner with Washington. The information quickly made its way to the British in New York. The information made General Clinton break off his offensive in the south and return to New York leaving Cornwallis in charge in the south.

Unknown to Washington's intelligence operation, Arnold began divesting himself of his American holdings and sent the money to a bank in England.

The Culper Ring began to pick up rumors of an American general coming over to the British side, but no names were detected.

The British had developed a list of potential American generals who might defect. Benedict Arnold was not on the list.

AT WEST POINT:
On June 29, 1780, Washington finally named Arnold to be the commander of the fort at West Point, satisfying Arnold's motive.

On July 15, 1780, Arnold states his terms for going over to the British side in the following letter. The main focal point of the proposal is the turning over of West Point to the British, thereby opening the Hudson River to the British for north/south movements.

> *July 15, 1780*
> *Benedict Arnold to John André*
> [Enclosed in a cover addressed to Mr. Anderson (André's pseudonym)]
> *Two days since I received a letter without date or Signature, informing*

me that Sir. Henry was obliged to me for intelligence communicated, and that he placed a full confidence in the Sincerity of my intentions, etc. etc. On the 13th Instant I addressed a letter to you expressing my Sentiments and expectations, viz, that the following Preliminaries be settled previous to cooperating. First, that Sir Henry secure to me my property, valued at ten thousand pounds Sterling, to be paid to me or my Heirs in case of Loss; and, as soon as that happens (strike out) shall happen, hundred pounds per annum to be secured to me for life, in lieu of the pay and emoluments I give up, for my Services as they shall deserve - If I point out a plan of cooperation by which Sir. Henry shall possess himself of West Point, the Garrison, etc. etc. etc. twenty thousand pounds Sterling I think will be a cheap purchase for an object of so much importance. At the same time I request thousand pounds to be paid my Agent - I expect a full and explicit answer. The 20th I set off for West Point. A personal interview with an officer that you can confide in is absolutely necessary to plan matters. In the mean time I shall communicate to our mutual Friend Stansbury all the intelligence in my power, until I have the pleasure of your answer.

Moore July 15th (1780)
To the line of my letter of the 13th I did not add seven.

When Arnold took command of West Point on August 3, 1780, he immediately put his plan into action. Placing his troops in a vulnerable position, Arnold allowed the British an easy target to capture the fort. He also ignored routine maintenance of the chain across the river at West Point.

Even with all of the preparations in place, the British didn't take any action, which frustrated Arnold to no end. Eventually, arrangements were made for a face-to-face meeting with a British official for September 17, 1780.

As the British frigate carried John André to meet Arnold, it was fired upon when it entered the area and was forced to retreat.

On September 19, Culper Ring agents noticed that Clinton was gathering ships and troops for a military expedition, but they had no idea where that would be.

The Plot Unfolds

At last, on September 20, the British frigate Vulcan was able to deposit its passenger John André near Haverstraw, New York. André met with Arnold in the house of a Loyalist, Thomas Smith. Arnold gave André papers regarding West Point, which included a hand-drawn map, indicating the positions of the troops around West Point and the chain across the Hudson. (*See opposite page*)

The following morning, when André returned to his rendezvous spot with *The Vulcan*, the ship was gone. It had been fired on and had to move further up river, leaving André stranded. Realizing he would have to return to New York on foot, he went back to the Smith home. When Arnold learned of his dilemma, he provided him with an official pass under the name of John Anderson and gave him civilian clothes. Not suspected by anyone, André spent his first night in the company of a New York militia unit.

On September 23, the secret motives of Arnold and André became quite plain. Smith escorted André as far as Pine's Bridge over the Croton River. Later that day, André encountered two Rebel men, one wearing a Hessian coat and the other a British soldier's coat. Assuming they were British, André identified himself as a British officer who was carrying a valid pass from General Benedict Arnold. When searched, the men discovered the papers he was carrying back to New York and André was arrested. The Rebels escorted André to their commander, Colonel John Jameson, who was a little more than perplexed by the events at hand. He sent a letter to Arnold asking for instruction of what he should do with André, and also dispatched a courier to Washington in Connecticut.

On September 24, Jameson's letter reached Arnold when he was expecting Washington to join him for breakfast. Immediately realizing the plot had failed, Arnold had no choice but to flee. Luckily for him, *The Vulture* was still in the area and it became his escape route. When Washington arrived at West Point, he only found Arnold's wife, Peggy.

Clinton's military goal of capturing West Point had collapsed as did the British dream of opening up the Hudson River for access to Canada. Major John André was tried as a spy, found guilty, and sentenced to be hanged. Before the hanging, with Washington's permission, André wrote a letter to Clinton as follows:

BENEDICT ARNOLD'S MAP OF WEST POINT

Tapaan, September 29th, 1780

Sir:

Your Excellency is doubtless already apprized of the manner in which I was taken and possibly of the serious light in which my Conduct is Considered and the rigorous determination that is impending.

Under these Circumstances I have obtained General Washington's permission to send you this Letter, the object of which is to remove from your Breast any Suspicion that I could imagine that I was bound by your Excellencys Orders to expose myself to what has happened. The Events of coming within an Enemys posts and of Changing my dress which led me to my present Situation were contrary to my own Intentions as they were to your Orders; and the circuitous route which I took to return was imposed (perhaps unavoidably) without alternative upon me.

I am perfectly and tranquil in mind and prepared for any Fate to which an honest Zeal for my Kings Service may have devoted me.

In addressing myself to your Excellency on this Occasion, the force of all my Obligations to you and of the Attachment and Gratitude I bear you, recurrs to me. With all the Warmth of my heart I give you thanks for your Excellencys profuse kindness to me, and I send you the most earnest Wishes for your Welfare which a faithfull affectionate and respectfull Attendant can frame.

I have a Mother and Three Sisters to whom the value of my Commission would be an object as the loss of Granada has much affected their income. It is needless to be more explicit on this Subject; I am persuaded of your Excellencys Goodness. I receive the greatest Attention from his Excellency General Washington and from every person under whose charge I happened to be placed. I have the honor to be with the most respectfull Attachment.

Your Excellencys
Most obedient and most humble Servant
John André Adj Gen
His Excellency
Sir Henry Clinton K.B.

Washington proposed to General Clinton that they have a prisoner exchange, André for Arnold, but Clinton refused and on October 2 André was hanged.

Arnold's plot almost succeeded despite the many red flags that occurred along the way. Many questions remain unanswered. Why was it unknown to anyone that Arnold was disposing of all his property in America, and if it was known, why was it not questioned? Why did no one question why Arnold would turn down the command of the left wing of the Continental Army—a prime assignment? And why did the comments of Colonel John Brown about Arnold, written in 1777, stating that "Money is this man's god—and to get enough of it he would sacrifice his country" go unheeded? Some can be explained by the well-known fact that Washington was a close friend of Arnold's and apparently was blinded to his faults. But Arnold's treason remains an enigma to this day.

Though the Continental Army suffered a great loss when General Arnold defected, at least he was replaceable. As for the British, Clinton lost his best intelligence agent. It also meant that the Americans retained control of the Hudson River, which was a severe blow to the overall British strategy.

Once Arnold's treasons were exposed and he had successfully defected to the British, Washington became obsessed with the idea of kidnapping and trying him for treason. He even recruited a Sergeant John Champe to perform such a task. The plan came close to accomplishing its goal, but in the end Arnold unwittingly escaped the kidnapping.

SUMMARY

Had it not been for Benedict Arnold's treasonable action at West Point, the Highlands Department would rarely be mentioned in studies of the American Revolutionary War as very few military engagements took place there. The department's role was predominately of a preventative nature—to keep the Hudson River and the Highlands out of British control.

Despite Washington's involvement in the other colonies, he maintained a close eye on the Highlands as the British could have cut the Colonies in half by taking control of the Hudson River Valley. A little paranoid that this may come to fruition, Washington changed commanding generals for the Highlands nineteen times to ensure dependable and competent leadership.

It is ironic that while Washington was well aware of the strategic value of the Hudson River Valley he was not able to establish an intelligence network in the area. The Culper Ring located in New York City and Long Island was targeted against only the New York City end of the Burgoyne plan. There was no such network for the Burgoyne movement in the Highlands. It depended entirely on individual Patriot agents.

The area played a major role in the strategic planning for both sides, but it became relevant only when General Burgoyne started his movement down from Canada intent on transiting the Hudson River to New York. That move ended at the battle of Saratoga, which was won by the Northern Department.

～

a person of interest
in the highlands department

SERGEANT MAJOR JOHN CHAMPE

HAD IT NOT BEEN FOR THE EVENTS OF SEPTEMBER 25, 1780, Sergeant Major John Champe would be just another Revolutionary War soldier. But when General Benedict Arnold fled to the safety of a British ship, Champe's role changed dramatically.

George Washington had been warned by an American spy in Philadelphia named John Vanderhovan that there was a strong possibility that an American general was about to defect to the British, but no name was given. Washington had suspicions about Major General Arthur St. Clair; however, he did not suspect one of his favorite generals, Benedict Arnold, to be guilty of treason. Therefore, he was badly shaken when the events of September 25, 1780, transpired. It became Washington's obsession to make an example out of Arnold. And this is where Sergeant Champe enters the picture.

After Washington's proposed exchange of Major John André for Benedict Arnold failed, Washington became adamant that he wanted Arnold taken alive. With this in mind he developed a plan to kidnap Arnold and bring him back to the American side for trial. Washington needed an American agent to penetrate the British lines, and turned to Major Henry Lee, commander of a corps of Light Dragoons, to recruit a candidate.

Lee had been on several intelligence missions for Washington, and would know the type of individual required for the Arnold mission. He immediately thought of the 23-year-old sergeant major in his corps, John Champe. Lee described Champe as "rather above common size—full of bone and muscle, with a saturnine countenance in mood, grave, thoughtful, and tacit, of tried courage and inflexible perseverance." An ideal choice for the mission according to Major Lee.

Once Champe agreed, Lee briefed him on the specifics of the mission. He was to familiarize himself with the movements of Benedict Arnold, and with the help of one or two associates, kidnap the general. Under no circumstances was he to kill the general. As a secondary mission, he was to ascertain whether General St. Clair was, in fact, also a traitor to the American cause.

Champe would not be completely alone on this mission. He would need to be in constant communication with the American army, so Washington assigned Mr. Baldwin of New Jersey to be his contact. For this service, Mr. Baldwin was to be paid one-hundred guineas, five-hundred acres of land, and three slaves if the mission succeeded.

Like many before him, Champe had reservations about becoming a deserter. Being so labeled, he could not be promoted to ensign, which was a personal goal of his. Lee assured him that General Washington, who knew about the mission, would protect his reputation when he returned. In addition, Champe was told that when and how he would desert would be left to him to decide. Lee did not want to know in advance, so his look of surprise when he learned of the desertion would provide good cover.

Once the agreement terms were made, Lee gave Champe two letters addressed to associates in New York City who would help him complete his mission. They would provide finances for the mission as well as secure a boat to bring Arnold back to New Jersey.

Champe observed the camp life routine to settle on the best time to "desert," and finally one night in late September 1780, he made his break. The Dragoon patrol spotted him and reported the incident to the officer of the day. Eventually they realized the deserter was Sergeant Major Champe. Major Lee was awakened, and once advised of the incident, immediately began delaying tactics to allow Champe to make his getaway—and with success. Aware of his pursuers, Champe changed his course from Paulus Point to a British frigate moored near Bergen, New Jersey. Reaching the shore line, he swam out to a British boat that rescued him and took him aboard. The rescue was reported to Lee by the pursuers, signaling the start of the mission.

Champe told the captain of the ship that he wanted the safety of New York City, and so he was sent into New York a few days later with a letter from the captain describing the events. In New York, he was a person of interest to Clinton and his staff. As a senior non-commissioned soldier from a well-known unit of the Rebel army, he was a valuable source of intelligence. In his interrogation, Champe stated that many in the Rebel army admired what Benedict Arnold had done and could easily be convinced to do the same if so encouraged by the British. When asked about the fate of Major André, Champe implied that he had no direct knowledge of his current status, but felt there was a chance his life would be spared.

Realizing that at that time Benedict Arnold was recruiting for his American Legion, Clinton sent Champe on to Benedict Arnold. At the meeting between Arnold and Champe, Arnold was impressed with Champe to the point that he offered him a position in the American Legion at the same rank as he held in the

Continental Army. Champe refused the offer stating he wanted nothing more to do with war.

The sequence of events that followed are interesting as they show how easy it was for Champe to keep both Washington and Lee informed as to his progress in his mission. The letters moved quickly, and the system provided a secure channel of communications between Champe and the Continental Army.

Within five days of his arrival in New York City, Champe met with his two compatriots for the mission, one of whom was Mr. Baldwin but the other remains unidentified. Champe gave them both the letters he had carried with him that described the mission. He also gave Mr. Baldwin a letter he had written to inform Lee of the status of his mission. That letter was duly delivered and a response from Lee soon was returned to Champe.

The correspondence between Champe and Major Lee was made possible by an efficient and secure channel for communications:

- The day after his meeting with Arnold, Champe wrote a letter to Major Lee describing all that had happened and Lee replied that General Washington told him to press on.

- The next letter to Lee summarized the events including Arnold's offer to have him join his American Legion. In the same letter, Champe indicated that the suspicion of the loyalty of General St. Clair was a rumor started by the enemy camp.

- Following the execution of Major John André, a letter was sent to Champe informing him of the execution, making a prisoner exchange with the British impossible. Now the only way to grab Arnold fell to Champe.

Champe wrote in return that he understood the importance of his mission. He also sent documents that proved the loyalty of General St. Clair. These were shown to Washington, who responded with the following letter to Major Lee:

October 13, 1780

Dear Sir; I am very glad your letter, of this date, has given strength to my conviction of the innocence of the gentleman who was the subject of your inquiry.

I want to see you on a particular piece of business. If this day is fair, and nothing of consequence intervenes, I will be at the marquis's quarters by ten o'clock

to-morrow. If this should not happen, I shall be glad to see you at head quarters.
I am, dear sir, your obedient servant.

G. Washington

On October 19, Champe updated Lee on his plan to capture Arnold and also requested more funding for his mission. Washington's reply to Lee states:

Headquarters, October 20, 1780

Dear Sir, The plan proposed for taking A_____d (the outlines of which are communicated in your letter, which was this moment put into my hands, without date,) has every mark of a good one. I therefore agree to the promised rewards; and have such entire confidence in your management of the business, as to give it my fullest approbation; and leave the whole to the guidance of your own judgment, with this express stipulation and pointed injunction, that he (A____d) is brought to me alive.

No circumstances whatever shall obtain my consent to his being put to death. The idea which would accompany such an event, would be, that ruffians had been hired to assassinate him. My aim is to make a public example of him; and this should be strongly impressed upon those who are employed to bring him off. The sergeant must be very circumspect; too much zeal may create suspicion, - and too much precipitancy may defeat the project. The most inviolable secrecy must be observed on all hands. I send you five guineas; but I am not satisfied of the propriety of the sergeant's appearing with much specie. This circumstance may also lead to suspicion, as it is but too well known to the enemy that we do not abound in this article.

The interviews between the party in and out of the city should be managed with much caution and seeming indifference; or else the frequency of their meetings, etc. may betray the design, and involve bad consequences; but I am persuaded you will place every matter in a proper point of view to the conductors of this interesting business, and therefore I shall only add, that, I am, dear sir, etc. & etc.

George Washington

It is not known how much of Washington's letter was shared with Champe, but he now knew he had a go-ahead with his plan. What he probably did not know was Washington's concern about his joining the British Army, whereby potentially he could be fighting against his own countrymen. Ten days later, Champe wrote his last letter to Lee detailing his plan and informing Lee that the plan to abduct Arnold was scheduled for December 11, 1780.

Plan to kidnap Arnold

The plan was simple yet complex—simple in design but complex as it was very dependent upon the timing. By enlisting in Arnold's American Legion as a master sergeant, Champe had unlimited access to Arnold and could observe his normal routine, particularly at his home. Arnold would normally return to his house about midnight and stroll through the garden (probably to use the facilities at the end of the garden), which was a perfect area to abduct him.

With this in mind, Champe had previously loosened several of the pickets from the fence that separated the garden from an alley. Once kidnapped, this would allow Arnold to be passed out through the fence and taken down the alley. The intent was to take Arnold down to the wharf, where a whaler boat would be ready to take him to Lee on the New Jersey shore. If stopped on the way to the whaler, they would respond they were taking a drunken soldier to the guard house on the wharf.

On the morning of December 12, 1780, Lee's Dragoons waited on the Jersey shore for the arrival of a boat carrying a unique cargo. It never appeared, however, and when Lee informed Washington, it was assumed that Champe had been found out and captured. Within a few days, Lee was able to figure out what happened from Champe's accomplice.

The day before the abduction was to take place, Arnold moved his headquarters to a new location. This move was in preparation for the deployment of his American Legion via ships on an expedition in Virginia. Since his Legion was made up primarily of American deserters a close watch was maintained to prevent more desertions. On December 11, 1780, Champe and all the troops were put on British galleys. All was lost for Champe and his plan.

Champe's return to Washington's command

Champe was in the American Legion throughout Arnold's expedition in Virginia, and it was not until May 1781 that he escaped and returned to the Continental Army, where he found his way to now Lieutenant Colonel Lee and General Nathanael Greene. After meeting with General Washington, he was provided with a discharge and released from the army—all because of his enlistment in the British Army which was absolutely forbidden by George Washington, and he would not waiver even in the case of Champe.

Master Sergeant John Champe accepted his fate and made no effort to re-enlist in the army, nor did he seek recognition for the special mission he undertook at the request of General Washington. Had he been able to complete his mission, General Benedict Arnold's fate would have been quite different and the name of Master Sergeant John Champe would be recognized as one of the real heroes of the Revolutionary War.

———

The Champe story in itself is noteworthy, but it also provides interesting insights into Washington's attitude concerning intelligence. Washington's delegation of authority in intelligence matters is quite clear in the Champe case. Washington selected one of his trusted officers to handle the case and did not interfere in his handling of the mission, even accepting the risk of such missions and the fallout that ensued. Champe is assumed to be caught—end of story. And secondly, it is interesting to note the ease in which communications were maintained between Lee and Champe. Washington was unforgiving of the fact that Champe had willingly enlisted in Arnold's American Legion—a unit of the enemy—and in fact fought against the Colonial militia in Virginia. This fact alone disallowed him from recognizing Champe for his efforts.

CHAPTER

XIII

The Western Department

MILITARY CAMPAIGNS

1778
General Edward Hand Expedition
Colonel George R. Clark Expeditions

1779
Colonel George R. Clark Expeditions

1781
Colonel Daniel Brodhead Expedition

1782
Lt. Colonel David Williamson Expedition
Gnadenhutten Massacre
Colonel William Crawford Expedition
Frequent Indian raids on settlers and settlements throughout period

THE WESTERN FRONTIER JUST PRIOR TO THE REVOLUTIONARY War was loosely perceived to be any area west of the Appalachian Mountains. The area was controlled by two forts, Fort Pitt near Pittsburgh and Fort Detroit in Michigan. Built in 1758 by the British, Fort Pitt

was given to the Colonists in 1772, and later, on April 10, 1777, it served as the department headquarters when the Western Department was formed. The importance of Fort Pitt can be traced to the 1760s and the population growth during that time period. In 1760, the population in the area amounted to 147 settlers; however, by 1765 the population had grown to 7,000. It had become a major gateway to the western territories for both the settlers and the military.

Fort Detroit has a different lineage. Fort Pontchartrain du Detroit was originally built in 1701 by the French, and served as a connection between the Indian tribes and the fur traders. The French lost control of Fort Detroit in November 1760, as a result of the French and Indian War when the British assumed control of Detroit. It became the most western of the outposts of the time, and the British quickly began to use the location for intelligence purposes. The French, being mainly fur traders, had developed a strong relationship with the local Indian populations, which made the British highly suspicious of them for two reasons in the mid-1770s when the Revolution began. First, the relationship between the French and Indians might make it difficult for the British to develop friendships with the tribes, and second, the French themselves were supportive of the Colonial drive for independence.

British Strategy

Early intelligence gathering by individuals was a random aspect for both the British and the American forces in the west prior to the spring of 1777; the area was not the main focus of the military campaigns. Then a major change occurred for the British. When General Burgoyne returned to England from Canada, he was dissatisfied with the conduct of the war in the west so he created a new tactic. On February 28, 1777, he presented *Thoughts for Conducting The War on the Side of Canada* to the Secretary of State for American Affairs, Lord George Germain. Burgoyne's strategy called for increased activity in the west to divert from the activity in the east. The British would utilize Indian tribes to create problems for the Colonies. All of these arrangements were to be facilitated through Fort Detroit. In March 1777, King George III gave his stamp of approval, and Burgoyne returned to America to implement his strategy, which recast the war in the west into a more organized and structured campaign.

American Response

The American reaction to the increased activity in the western area was the establishment of the Western Department in April 1777, with General Edward Hand in command. The new department's boundaries were west and northwest of Virginia and Pennsylvania, west from Pittsburgh to the Illinois country, and north to the southern peninsula of Michigan.

Much of the territory considered as the Western Department, such as Ohio, Indiana, Illinois, and Michigan (particularly Fort Detroit), was actually in the Province of Quebec. While the American retreat in 1776 ended military activity in the eastern part of Canada, it merely shifted to the western area of the Province of Quebec.

The Indian Participation

The Indian tribes in the Ohio Valley were easily swayed to the British cause as a means of preventing further white man settlements in the valley. And they had good reason. A British Proclamation of 1763 forbade British colonists from settling west of the Appalachian Mountains. Settlers objected, and in 1768, two new treaties were negotiated with the American Indians. The Treaty of Fort Stanwix and the Treaty of Hard Labor, signed in the town of Hard Labor, South Carolina, resulted in opening the Ohio Valley for settlement once again. However, the Shawnees, Mingos, Delawares, and Wyandots, all who lived in the Ohio Valley, had not been consulted about the treaties and problems arose. This contentious atmosphere was what the British hoped to exploit in their western campaign.

Initially, the British employed propaganda to encourage the Indians to join their side in the conflict. They spread word among the Indian tribes about the many defeats of the Colonial army (some real and some fabricated), and even convinced many of the tribes that General Washington had died on the battlefield. They often used old newspapers to further prove their point. Since the Indians had no other source of obtaining accurate accounts of what was happening in the eastern campaign, the British propaganda efforts were effective.

The Rebel side also used propaganda as a weapon with the Indians. Two Moravian preachers, who lived with the Christian Delaware Indians, David Zeisberger and Johann Heckewelder, were effective in agitating the Indians against the British. They used the Christian Delaware Indians to spread the word to the other tribes in the area.

INTELLIGENCE DEVELOPMENTS

With that background, it is obvious that after 1777 major changes occurred in the west, including the collection and use of intelligence. While still relatively unsophisticated, spying and the reporting of intelligence became an essential part of the campaign. British intelligence gathered and reported to Fort Detroit (Major Arent Schuyler de Peyster) was forwarded on a routine basis to the commanding general of Fort St. John in Niagara, New York (Colonel Mason Bolton), then forwarded on to the governor of Canada in Quebec (Sir Frederick Haldimand) who forwarded them on to higher authorities as required. Most of the intelligence reports were of the strategic nature and not tactical. Haldimand established a system of "ledger books" wherein these reports were entered depending on subject. This today would be said to provide "continuity" on a subject.

However, the British did recognize the high probability that couriered correspondence may not be delivered to the intended person. A quote from the journal of Henry Hamilton indicates their concern regarding deliveries and their method to counter it from happening to them:

> *August 8th (1777) this intelligence was communicated to the commanding officer at Niagara, (Lieut. Colonel Bolton) by letters, one sent by land by a Savage, who was but 9 Days going, another in a batteau, by Lieutenant Chevalier Chabert. By these messengers the letters for the Commander in chief at Quebec got safe to Niagara.*

And what type of intelligence was contained in this correspondence? An extract from a letter written in Detroit on May 28, 1779, by Captain D. Brehm serves as a good example:

The Rebells have five Forts, from Fort Pitt towards this place, one at Beaver Creek about 27 miles from said Fort it is called Fort McIntosh 2nd at Kentucky about 30 miles above the Falls of the Ohio 3rd on the Island near the Falls 4th below the Falls and the 5th at Tuscawiawas, called Fort Laurance. The Wabash Indians expect cannon ammunition men and provisions to assist and support them in driving the Rebells from Vincenne and the Illinois. The Chanees Delaware Mingoes and Sundusky Indians expect the same to dislodge the Rebells from the above mentioned five Posts—Captn Larnould thinks that 5 or 600 men with small cannon or Field pieces joined by the Indians would go a great length to satisfy them, providing there was provisions enough to support them & their familys till they were enabled again to plant their lands which many have left, besides 5 or 600 men for the defence of the Posts he says that the arrival of the 200 men he were reinforced by has made a great alteration in the Inhabitants & even among the Indians, the former before that became incolent and almost daring.

The intelligence gathered by Colonialist agents was sent to Fort Pitt for the use of the commander of the Western Department. Only rarely, when of value outside of the Western Department, was the intelligence forwarded on to General Washington.

Prior to 1778, the intelligence efforts in the west for both combatants centered on solidifying alliances with the various Indian tribes, but the mission changed due to an action that created a snowball effect. When the British instigated the Indians to raid the Colonists more frequently, the Continental Congress was forced to respond. The Congress directed two regiments to be sent to the western theater, increasing the intelligence needs for both the British and the Americans. Further, the raids into the Ohio country by Rebel leaders such as Colonel George Rogers Clark and General Edward Hand created a perceived threat to Fort Detroit, which increased the need for current intelligence for the British. For the Rebels, the increased Indian raids on settlements and a perceived threat against Fort Pitt drove their intelligence needs. Both sides became embroiled in an ever-increasing demand for intelligence.

The expedition of Colonel Clark in 1778-1779 provides an excellent case study of how intelligence was gained and used in the Western Department. In

1778, the French were aligned with the British through Lieutenant Governor Hamilton at Fort Detroit, and they had the French villages of Cahokia, Bellefontaine, Kaskaskia, and Vincennes, all of which posed a threat to the new settlers in the Kentucky area (at that time still a part of Virginia). When Colonel Clark became aware of the situation, he devised a plan to take the French villages to lessen the threat posed to the Kentucky settlers. Colonel Clark suggested that would ensure that the Mississippi River would remain open for movement of ships, which carried supplies for the Continental Army. The following chronology of his actions yields a rare insight into the use of intelligence in the Revolutionary War:

SUMMER 1778—Lacking current information about the area, Colonel Clark sent two scouts, Ben Lyon and Samuel Moore, to scout the area's defenses and ascertain the attitude of the local citizenry. They returned and reported to Clark that the defenses were weak and the citizens, while loyal to the French, did not have the same feelings for the British. With this intelligence in hand, Clark approached the governor of Virginia, Patrick Henry, who approved his proposed plan. Overtly the plan was to protect the settlers in Kentucky, and covertly to capture the British Fort Gage at Kaskaskia and Fort Detroit in the Illinois territory.

JUNE 26, 1778—Hoping for the element of surprise, Clark wasted no time and set out from Virginia with about two-hundred militia troops, arriving at Kaskaskia on July 4, 1778. The element of surprise worked and Fort Gage fell without a fight.

JULY 1778—Clark soon came to realize that the French troops, as well as the French citizens in the area, had no idea of the French/American alliance signed just one month earlier in Paris. He began a propaganda effort to inform all the French settlers in the area about the new alliance in order to persuade them to align with his force, and on July 20, the French troops of Fort Sackville at Vincennes swore allegiance to the Americans and the fort was occupied by Clark's troops.

JULY 1778—The American detachment (led by Captain Joseph Brown) departed Sackville at Vincennes leaving only three men and fifty Frenchmen to protect the fort.

AUGUST 1778—The British learned that Fort Sackville fell, and began preparations to recapture the fort. Their force of approximately 175 troops departed Fort Detroit on October 17, 1778.

DECEMBER 17, 1778—The British arrived at Vincennes and retook the fort without a shot being fired.

DECEMBER 1778—Clark desperately needed supplies to survive the winter. He was successful in getting a courier to Oliver Pollock, an American representative in New Orleans, requesting supplies. With the assistance of Bernardo de Gàlvez, the governor of New Orleans, a shipment of supplies was sent up the Mississippi River to Clark.

JANUARY 29, 1779—Colonel Francis Vigo, a Spanish trader, arrived at Kaskaskia and informed Clark about the fall of Vincennes. This new intelligence made Clark realize that the British were probably planning a spring offensive against Clark and his force—an offensive he would lose. Realizing he would need to precede the British attack, Clark decided that he would have to launch a winter offensive to catch the British off-guard. Winter offensives were rare, but presented an opportunity for victory. Clark placed an order for supplies amounting to $1,432, hoping that he would have the supplies in hand before a spring offensive could be mounted.

FEBRUARY 4, 1779—Clark dispatched the row galley Whiling down the Mississippi, up the Ohio, and north up the Wabash to anchor near Vincennes. There the galley would block any chance the British had at retreating, but also would serve as a supply ship for the American troops.

FEBRUARY 5, 1779—Lieutenant Colonel Clark and 172 troops (of which about 50 were French) departed on a 180-mile trek to Vincennes. The winter had not been severe, but heavy rains made the trek slow and tedious.

FEBRUARY 20, 1779—They captured five hunters who provided Clark with valuable intelligence. The movement of his force had been undetected, and the townspeople of Vincennes were very sympathetic to the Americans due to the harsh treatment received from Lieutenant Colonel Hamilton.

FEBRUARY 23, 1779—Clark's small force was located within sight of Vincennes and Fort Sackville on Horse Shoe Plain. They captured a French hunter who provided current intelligence on the lack of preparedness at the fort, how it was defended, and conditions in the town. Based on this intelligence, Clark decided to have the French hunter return to Vincennes that same day with a communiqué from Clark to the townspeople (positive propaganda). The communiqué was read in the town square and included instructions for the people to remain in their houses when Clark's forces arrived. Clark also intimated to the hunter that his force consisted of nearly 1,000 in number. The hunter did as Clark instructed with no reaction from the fort. Lieutenant Colonel Hamilton believed that the idea of a winter offensive seemed too farfetched.

FEBRUARY 23, 1779—Clark broke his men into two battalions marching toward Vincennes, one led by Clark and the other led by Captain Bowman. Arriving just out of sight of the fort, he used an ancient ploy of deception. Using a group of small ridgelines to hide the actual troops, he had them march along with banners flying and drums beating. Once they passed, the troops doubled-back and once again "passed in review," giving the impression that there were about 1,000 men in the opposing force. A British surgeon, who escaped from the town and returned to the fort, told Hamilton that the entire town was surrounded by Clark's force of over 500 men. The report was further accentuated by the commencement of firing on the fort by Clark's force.

Later that night Clark achieved another intelligence coup, when his troops captured two deserters from a British patrol in the town. When questioned, the two captives provided Clark with the positions of the other patrols. With these patrols eliminated, alerting friendly Indians to aid the British would be nearly impossible.

FEBRUARY 24, 1779—Lieutenant Colonel Hamilton, believing he was surrounded by 500 to 1,000 men, finally agreed to surrender. Clark's use of one of the oldest tricks in the military arsenal had worked. The next morning, when Hamilton met Clark his first comment was, "Where is your army?" Clark indicated they were right in front of him. Hamilton is reported to have turned away with tears in his eyes. He had been outsmarted.

While not one of the major battles of the Revolutionary War, the battle of Vincennes did have far-reaching results for the Americans. It not only ensured that Kentucky settlers would not be in jeopardy of British attacks, but also ensured that the Mississippi River would remain open for the vital shipment of supplies to the Continental Army, so long as they controlled the forts in the area.

The success of Colonel Clark's mission was in no small manner due to his understanding of the value of good intelligence and how best to utilize the information it provided. Clark's techniques were not new, nor was there an established intelligence network—just a good commander who used all his assets.

BRITISH VS. AMERICAN INTELLIGENCE OPERATIONS IN THE WEST

While the British intelligence reporting from the West may have been more systematic than the American system, the actual collection of intelligence was predominately driven by individuals working on their own, serving as unofficial spymasters for the Indians. By examining these individuals, it will be easier to understand the intelligence operations of the British in the western campaign.

For both parties, the efforts to recruit agents were limited to a rather small talent pool. They were frontiersmen who worked as traders with the Indians and therefore had friendly relations and access with the tribal members. The loyalty of these Indian traders often depended upon who provided them with the most financial gain for their furs—Americans or British. Attributed to pure luck rather than skilled recruitment, both sides were able to acquire frontiersmen. Three men in particular stand out for the British efforts: Matthew Elliott, Simon Girty, and Alexander McKee. The Americans on the other hand profited from the effort of Moravian ministers, particularly Johann Heckewelder and David Zeisberger.

British Agents

MATTHEW ELLIOTT—Matthew Elliott came to this country as a 25-year-old illiterate immigrant from Ireland. Finding distaste for the more settled colonies, he migrated to the Western frontier by way of Fort Pitt. Moving into the Indian country, he soon found a home among the Shawnee Indians and established himself as an Indian trader.

Before long he had acquired a Shawnee wife, as well as a good working knowledge of the Shawnee language. He would travel to Fort Pitt when supplies were needed and then once again return to the Shawnee territory. His activities not only became of interest to the Rebels, but to the British at Fort Detroit as well.

In 1777, the British arrested Elliott on suspicion of being a Rebel spy based on his frequent trips to Fort Pitt that had raised suspicion. He was taken to Fort Detroit where he was interrogated by Lieutenant Governor Henry Hamilton and sent on to Quebec for further questioning. There he was found innocent of anti-British activity and was released, returning to his Shawnee base via New York and Fort Pitt.

At Fort Pitt in the spring of 1778, he met his old friends Simon Girty and Alexander McKee, also Indian traders. Both Girty and McKee spent the majority of their time among the Indian tribes and had fallen under suspicion at Fort Pitt of spying for the British, which was not true at that juncture. Elliott along with Girty and McKee decided to leave Fort Pitt and support the British in the west. When Elliott arrived at Fort Detroit, Lieutenant Governor Hamilton was more than a little surprised to learn that Elliott now supported his efforts with the Indians.

Fort Detroit employed Elliott as an assistant in the Indian Affairs Department with two roles. He was an excellent linguist and had mastered many of the Indian tongues, which made him valuable as an interpreter. He was greatly respected among the Indian tribes which also made him an effective propagandist with the tribes. Both of these talents were his main contribution. As he wended his way among the tribes he could not help but pick up information of value to the British. But unlike both Girty and McKee, Elliott did not function primarily in the role of a spymaster as his official role was in the Indian Affairs Department.

By the time the war ended, Elliott had become a major landowner in the Detroit area. In 1790, the British called him to work with the Indians against U.S. forces. He rejoined the Indian Department and worked with the Shawnees and other tribes as tensions mounted. He observed and reported on the Indian response to the invasion of General Harmar's army in 1790 as well as the disastrous campaign of St. Clair in 1791. In both cases, Elliott provided supplies and tactical support to the Indians. His efforts to preserve the Indian Territory came to naught in 1794, when he watched the Indian warriors suffer a major defeat at the battle of Fallen Timbers. The American victory at Fallen Timbers now gave the Americans control of the Northwest Territory.

Between the Revolutionary War and the War of 1812, Elliott served as a member of the House of Assembly for Upper Canada from 1800 to 1812. His empathy for the Indians in the western area remained a strong focus in his life.

Relations between the British and the Americans continued on an uneven course until 1808 when Elliott was again involved in Indian affairs. When war again broke out in 1812, Elliott assisted the Indians as they conducted raids in the Detroit area. Leading a force of over six hundred warriors, they successfully captured the Americans at Detroit and retook the British fort. The victory was short-lived, however, when the American forces retook Detroit, forcing the British to move up the Thames River into Canada in September 1813. Elliott was among the retreating group. He died in May 1817, and to his last day he remained a strong advocate on behalf of the Indian tribes in the western territory.

SIMON GIRTY—Girty was born near Harrisburg, PA, in 1741. His early life was marred by seeing his father killed by an Indian. Later at the age of 15, Girty, his three brothers, and his mother were captured by the Delaware Indian raiders. His mother and three brothers were made slaves of the Delaware Indians, and Simon was traded to the Seneca Indians with whom he lived until he was repatriated at the age of 18. While his time with the Indians could have had a very negative impact on him, in fact, he came to admire the lifestyle of the Indians and adopted many of the Indian ways. His knowledge of several Indian languages and a familiarity with their culture made him an asset for a white man.

He found his way to Fort Pitt, where he worked as an interpreter between the various Indian tribes and local fur traders. He became well-known to the Indian tribes, and the Indians and Colonists developed a mutual respect for him.

In 1778, he accepted the position as a recruiter of the Continental Army hoping to be made the captain of the company he had recruited. However, military authorities soon took his command away, feeling he was not fit for the task due to his frequent bouts of drunkenness and his general crude behavior. Girty became disenchanted and began to spend an increasing amount of time among the Indians. The uneasiness grew among the residents at the fort as the Indian attacks were becoming more and more prevalent. His allegiance became suspect. Embittered by the course of events, Girty decided to change his allegiance to the British, who were delighted to have such a man on their side. He was shortly joined by his brothers, George and James.

Simon Girty's value to the British cannot be over-estimated. He freely moved among Indian tribes and served as a liaison between the British at Fort Detroit and the Indian chiefs, convincing them to assist the British in carrying the war to the Colonies with frequent raiding parties. Even more importantly, he became a spymaster among the Indians. After tasking the Indian scouts as to what intelligence he required, they would depart on the mission. These reports provided the British with the current status of Indian support for the British cause. Since Girty could not read or write, his reports were dictated to someone who could. Once written, Girty would employ Indian couriers to get the information to Fort Detroit, which would sometimes forward new instructions back to Girty via the courier, and sometimes he himself would return to Fort Detroit.

One of his biggest intelligence coups came in May 1782, when Colonel William Crawford of the Continental Army led an all volunteer force into the Ohio territory attempting to capture Fort Detroit. The force planned to leave Mingo Bottom on May 25, 1782, and conduct a surprise attack on Sandusky. Girty, however, had found a captured Colonial soldier who revealed the Crawford mission even before it left Mingo Bottom. Girty quickly sent the intelligence on to Fort Detroit and immediately began to mobilize the Indians, which led to the disastrous Colonial losses at the battle of Sandusky and the ultimate death of Colonel Crawford.

Girty remained active throughout the war period and became known to the Colonial authorities as a vicious man who served the British as a traitor. In 1782, the Colonists offered an $800 reward for his capture or death. When the British left Fort Detroit in 1796, Simon Girty fled to Canada, where he lived for the next twenty-two years. He died completely blind in 1818. The motivation for Simon Girty's activities during the Revolutionary War was a deep sympathy for the American Indian. He believed that the Indians native rights to their lands were being trampled by the settlers. Girty had harbored neither loyalty nor disloyalty for either the British or American sides in the conflict.

ALEXANDER MCKEE—Alexander McKee stands in sharp contrast to most of the other frontier men of his time. He was an educated man, very literate, as well as an accomplished businessman, who served as a diplomat with the Indians for the British long before the Revolutionary War—all of which made him a coveted British asset when the war broke out.

McKee was born in 1735 to a prosperous fur trader and his Shawnee "wife." The boy was raised as a Shawnee by a woman who may or may not have been his mother. The child received a good education and enjoyed a relatively easy childhood. For his time period, he was a very well-educated "frontier man." He was a gifted linguist in many of the Indian dialects on the frontier.

In his early manhood, he served in the French and Indian War during which he was wounded. After the war he worked with George Croghan in the British Indian Department. McKee then took over the fur trade business he had inherited from his father. By 1770 he was well-known as both a businessman and a politician as he had become the Justice of the Peace for newly formed Bedford County. In fact in October 1770, George Washington dined with McKee at Fort Pitt on his return from the Ohio country. In all probability, they discussed land speculation as both men were active in that field. By this time McKee had become a very wealthy man with an estate north of Pittsburgh. Long friendly with the Indians, he took a Shawnee wife who bore him five children. McKee lived at Fort Pitt and his family remained in a Shawnee village not too distant from the fort.

In 1771, when Croghan left the British Indian Department he recommended McKee to replace him saying, "The Shawnees whom I well know would tell him anything they knew as they consider him as one of their own." His diplomatic skills, knowledge of the Indian languages, as well as his awareness of the political world he lived in made him the perfect choice for the job. The Indians respected him, but the British authorities—aware of his skills—were often perplexed and disturbed by his long periods of unexplained absences between reporting. However, in 1775, they did promote him to lieutenant colonel in the Indian Department.

As the war came closer, McKee faced a serious problem. He was a Loyalist but kept a very low profile in order to protect his vast land holdings. He remained in the Fort Pitt area, but spent considerable time with his family in their Shawnee village as well as visiting other Indian tribes. Consequently when the war broke out, the residents of Fort Pitt began to suspect McKee's true allegiance—and not without reason. The British had not forgotten about McKee. On February 29, 1776, the British Indian Department agent at Fort Niagara wrote to McKee ordering him to meet with him at Fort Niagara saying, "Your knowledge of Indian affairs, your hitherto undoubted zeal for his Majesty's service, and the duty you owe to your government makes your attendance absolutely necessary." The existence of the letter became known to the authorities at Fort Pitt, and when challenged McKee produced the letter, denying any prior knowledge or compliance with the request. He was placed on parole by the Committee of Safety, and he remained under suspicion.

The situation reached its head in 1777, when the Continental Congress appointed a committee, chaired by Richard Lee of Virginia, to investigate the activities of McKee. This led to General Edward Hand, on December 29, 1777, ordering McKee to report to the Congress' Board of War in York, PA, to account for his activities. McKee ignored the order, but realizing he was about to be unmasked, he began to sell his land holdings. Ordered a second time, he continued to ignore summons, blaming bad health. Finally in March 1778, General Hand sent a squad to arrest McKee only to find he was no longer in the area. Sensing the danger, he had, in fact, fled in the company of two fellow frontiersmen—Girty and Elliott. His escape was a jolt to the officials at Fort Pitt, one of whom stated from his knowledge of "Indian affairs and Influence among the different tribes, we fear (he) is capable of doing extensive mischief . . . . There is no doubt but this will excite alarms throughout the country." The lieutenant governor at Fort Detroit, Colonel Hamilton, on the other hand was delighted to hear of McKee's escape and awaited his arrival at Fort Detroit. He quickly advised his Indian advisor John Hay to put out the word that McKee and his group were to be given safe passage to Fort Detroit.

Upon his arrival at Fort Detroit, Hamilton quickly appointed McKee as a captain in the Indian Department and put him to work. McKee soon found himself involved in an unsuccessful raid in Kentucky. After the raid McKee spent the majority of his time among the Indians of the Ohio tribes, gathering intelligence, and persuading the Indians to remain loyal to the Crown. Whenever Hamilton called an

Indian conference, McKee was always there as an interpreter as well as a diplomat. He also on occasion served as the commander of the large Indian force, when they gathered to join the British, for an attack on the settlers. One such occasion was the battle of Blue Licks in August 1782. His main role was to control the Indians and to prevent undue savagery.

An account written by the Moravian Minister Heckewelder provides the details as to how effective McKee's efforts to sway the Indians were. The letter recounts events in April 1778 at the height of the Delaware Indian confrontation:

Accordingly, in the morning we made our resolution known to Col. Hand and Gibson, whose best wishes for our success, we were assured of and leaving our baggage behind, and turning a deaf ear to all entreaties of well meaning friends, who considered us lost, if we went, we crossed the Allegheny river, and on the third day, at eleven o'clock at night reached Gnadenhutten, after having several times narrowly escaped falling in with war parties . . . when arrived within a few miles of Gnadenhuttenk, we distinctly heard the beat of war drums, and on drawing near, the war songs sung to the beat of the drums, all which being in the direction of the town lay, naturally we concluded that the Christian Indians must have moved off, wherefore we proceeded with caution, less we should fall into the warrior's hands. However, the people being there, informed us, that those warriors we heard were Wyandots from Sandusky, who arrived last evening, and were encamped on the bluff, two miles below the town, on the opposite sides of the river, and who probably would the next day, travel along the path we had just come.

Fatigued as we were, after our journey, and without one hour of sound sleep, I was now requested by the inhabitants of the place, men and women, not to delay any time, but to proceed on to Gasehoehkink (near thirty miles distant) where all was a bustle and confusion, and many were preparing to go to fight the American people, in consequence of the advice given them by those deserters, before named (the McKee party who had told them, that the American people were embodying themselves at the time, for the purpose of killing every Indian they should meet with, such friend or foe, and further were told, that Captain White Eyes had been threatened to be killed, if he persisted in vindicating the character of the American people; many believing the stories told them by McKee and his associates, and had in consequence already shaved their heads, ready to lay the plume on, and turn to war, as soon as the ten days should be expired, and tomorrow being the ninth day, and no message having yet been arrived from the friends at Pittsburgh.(McKee's party had arrived at Goschachgunk on April 1) it was not April 6, only six days since Heckewelder's arrival, they now were preparing to go-and further that this place, Gnadenhutten, was now breaking up for its inhabitants to join the congregation at Liebtenau, those deserters having assured them, that they were a day safe from an attack by the Americans, while they remained here.

I would proceed on . . . Arriving by ten o'clock in the forenoon within sight of the town, a few yells were given by a person who had discovered us, intended to notify the inhabitants, that white man was coming, and which immediately drew the whole body of Indians into the street: but although I saluted them in passing them, not a single person returned the compliment, which as my conductor observed, was no good omen. Even Captain White Eyes, and the other chiefs, who always had befriended me, now stepped back when I reached out my hand to them. Yet as no one would reach out his hand to me, I inquired the cause when Captain White Eyes boldly stepping forward replied "that by what had been told them by those men (McKee and parry) they no longer had a single friend among the American people, if therefore this be so, they must consider every white man who came to them from that side, as an enemy who only came to them to deceive them, and put them off their guard for the purpose of giving the enemy an opportunity of taking them by surprise." I replied that imputation was unfounded and that, were I not their friend, they never would have seen me here. "Then (continued Captain White Eyes) you will tell us the truth with regard to what I state to you!"-assuring him of this, he in a strong tone asked me, "are the American armies all cut to pieces b y the English troops? Is George Washington killed? Is there no more congress, and have the English hung some of them, and taken the remainder to England to hang them there? Is the whole country beyond the Mountains in the possession of the English and are the few thousand Americans who have escaped them, now embodying themselves on this side of the mountains for the purpose of killing all the Indians in the country, even our women and children? Now do not deceive us, but speak the truth." (he added); is all this true what I have said to you?" I declared before the whole assembly that not one word of what he had just now told me was true, and holding out to him, as I had done before, the friendly speeches sent me for them, which he however as yet refused to accept . . . (These were letters sent by Morgan and forwarded from Gnadenhutten by a special messenger on the morning of Apl 6 . . .) A newspaper containing the capitulation of General Burgoyne's army, being found enclosed in the packet, captain White Eyes once more rose up and holding the paper unfolded with both hands, so that all could have a view of it, said "see my friends and relatives, this document containeth great events, not the song of a bird, but the truth?" Then stepping up, to me, he gave me his hand saying:"You are welcome with us Brother;" when everyone present, followed his example . . .

The above is just one example of the work of McKee as a propagandist. In this case his efforts came to naught. However, the example does clearly show why Alexander McKee was a much-hated man by the newly formed American government.

After the war, McKee petitioned the British government regarding his financial losses and McKee was granted an award of 3,000 pounds in 1788. He continued to work with the Indians of the Ohio Confederacy, and became the Deputy Superintendent General for Indian Affairs for Upper and Lower Canada in 1795.

His work with the Indians during the Revolutionary War was a major contributing factor in the conflicts of the Western Department with the Indians. His diplomacy, linguistic ability, and his political sense made his service invaluable for the British. And for the Indians, as a captain in the British Indian Department, they knew he spoke with authority.

FEMALE AGENTS—While it is known that Girty and his associates frequently used Indian women as couriers to take their intelligence reports from the wilds of the Western Department to the British fort at Detroit, the couriers were never identified. They apparently were very adept in their mission as their use continued throughout the war period. This department was not conducive to white females working as spies, the terrain was rough and white females in such an area would seem suspicious or be targeted by Indians.

American Agents

JOHANN GOTTLIEB ERNESTUS HECKEWELDER—Johann Heckewelder was a Monrovian reverend who served as a missionary to the
Indians in the western area of the Colonies. Like several of his fellow
missionaries he not only served to spread the gospel, but also served as
the "eyes and ears" for the government with the Christian Delaware
Indians. He also was supplying information to the command at Fort
Pitt, with reports sent regularly every ten days. He became a spymaster
using the friendly Christian Delaware Indians as his agents to collect
the data and then also used them as couriers.

JOHN MONTOUR, THE CHAMELEON—John Montour was a man
who served both sides during the Revolutionary War. He was born
in 1744, to a father of Iroquois and French descent and a mother
of the Delaware tribe. His father, a gifted linguist, frequently served
as an interpreter. His language skills were well-known to George
Washington. His father wanted John to be familiar with both the
Indian and white man's way of life. John attended Bafferton School at
William and Mary, and continued his education in Philadelphia. Like
his father, John Montour was a gifted linguist conversant in English,
Mingo, Delaware, and Wyandot.

By 1775, John was living on Montour Island in the Ohio River
south of Pittsburgh, where he and his father ran a trading post. He was
known to have worked with Simon Girty, an Indian trader with ties
to Lieutenant Governor Hamilton at Fort Detroit. That same year
Montour went to Detroit and presented Hamilton with a friendship
belt, which led to cooperation with the British in 1776 and 1777.
He was instrumental in persuading the Delaware, Mingo, and Wyandot Indians to support the British in the conflict. He had an informal
intelligence network providing information to Hamilton regarding the
Indian tribes in the area. Montour is frequently mentioned by Hamilton
in his correspondence back to Quebec. In the spring of 1777, Daniel
Sullivan was sent by the state of Virginia into the Ohio Valley on an
intelligence mission. He arrived in Detroit and was accused of being
an American spy by a Mingo. Montour, also in Detroit at the time,
confirmed the accusation to Hamilton and the man was imprisoned.

However, for some reason, Montour's attitude changed in early 1778, when Hamilton reported to Quebec that Montour had helped three prisoners from Virginia escape. The escapees were recaptured, sent on to Quebec and Montour was confined in Detroit. He was freed only after many pleas for his release from the Mingo and Wyandot chiefs. His imprisonment seems to have soured his feelings for the British and he returned to the Delaware tribe.

Once again he worked for the American cause and in the spring of 1779, Montour was able to convince the Wyandots to abandon the British and allow General Lachlan McIntosh's troops to cross their land on their way to Detroit. And by late 1779, he was a captain of a company of Delaware Indians and on their payroll.

Things changed yet again for Montour after he learned of the Gnadenhutten massacre, in which ninety Delaware Indians were killed by the Americans. Brigadier General William Irvine, commander of Fort Pitt, began to suspect Montour's allegiance as shown in the following letter:

(Irvine to Lincoln)
Fort Pitt, April 10, 1782

Sir: I wrote to you somedays since about a certain Montour, captain of Delaware Indians, I did not like to explain by him my reasons for sending him.

He seemed anxious to be either employed or go with his wife to the Indian country for a place of safety, as he termed it. The fact is I was suspicious of his fidelity, but he is so cunning that no hold could be laid on him. This, however, is the worst place he could possibly be in, if he meant to go off, being perfectly quainted with all the Indian country and at Detroit. He was in the British interest and service before he joined us. I suppose the best way to manage him will be to amuse him with expectation of being employed in service, perhaps, he might render service joined with the Oneidas. You will be better able to judge how he should be disposed of, when you see and converse with him. It must have been very ill-judged to give such a fellow a commission.

The letter was written at the same time that Montour was sent to Philadelphia, but he never went. He knew that if he responded to the request, he would not be able to return to assist the British with the Indians.

Instead he returned to the Delaware Indians in the lower Sandusky community and began working for the British once again. In November 1782, he and his brother brought four scalps and three young prisoners to the British authorities at Fort Niagara as a sign of continued friendship.

After 1782, Montour disappeared from the annals of history. His life, however, is an excellent example of how both sides used the American Indians in their intelligence efforts—they were a critical part. And to have a man such as John Montour, a gifted linguist and a man who had lived in both societies, working for you may explain why both sides were able to overlook his chameleon tactics.

DAVID ZEISBERGER—David Zeisberger was a Moravian preacher who was one of the first missionaries to enter the Ohio country. He established a community known as Schoenbrunn (Beautiful Stream) among the Delaware Indians. He then led six Moravian preachers who served as missionaries in the area, including Reverend Johann Heckewelder, who worked under his supervision in working with the Delaware Indians. In the summer of 1777, Zeisberger sent a letter to General Hand at Fort Pitt, warning him of an impending Indian attack on Wheeling. Such independent reporting by Zeisberger was done on occasion, but it was not the norm. The typical flow of intelligence meant that he'd gather information and report it to Heckewelder. His input would be merged with the information that had been collected by Heckwelder's other agents, and then a merged intelligence report would be forwarded to Fort Pitt.

Over time Zeisberger and his fellow Moravian preachers came under suspicion of spying. Finally in 1781, all of the six Moravian preachers were arrested and taken to Fort Detroit for trial. Heckewelder and Zeisberger were put on trial, found not guilty, paroled, and returned to the Delaware Indians.

It is highly probable that, in fact, the six Moravian preachers had their own spy ring operating in the Ohio country under the guidance of Heckewelder and Zeisberger. A diary entry of December 16, 1778, indicates their level of involvement. It reads:

> *Gelelmind came here with some Shawnee and Counsellor and we learned that the Wandot Half King and man Nations had accepted the Invitation to*

go to Tuscarawi and they have promised to speak with the General. We received news that a party of Mingo had gone to Fort Lawrence to get Scalps. Colonel Gibson had asked us to let him know when we heard about things like this, so we sent an express messenger to him with the news.

ADDITIONAL SPIES AND SCOUTS—In addition, many Colonists served the Continental Army as a "spy" or "Indian scout" during the war in the west. Some were members of the Continental Army, while others were local settlers or fur traders. Most of them served during a specific campaign or battle and not for the duration of the war. Some of their names and their areas of interest are listed below:

Detroit: James Cassedy, William Boslick, James Cochran, Laventure Wiggins, Israel Rutland (with Colonel Clarke), and John Edgar (with Colonel Clarke)

Kentucky: Joseph Kennedy (with Daniel Boone), John Ellis (with General Lewis), Abraham Cancey (with Captain Clement) and Moses Hitchling (with Captain Dikllard)

Ohio: Martin Wetzel (battle of Fort Pleasant), Henry Yoho, John Wetzel

Tennessee: John Sevier, Valentine Sevier (battle of Point Pleasant), Abraham Sevier (with Ensign Robert Sevier)

West Virginia: John Wetzel (with Rangers), Lewis Wetzel, and Martin Wetzel (Upper Ohio Valley)

The war in the west did not end with the Treaty of 1783. That treaty stated that all territory to the east of the Great Lakes and connecting rivers was thereby given to the United States. Great Britain retained possession, in fact, of the posts at Michilimackinac, Detroit, Niagara, Oswego, Oswegatchie, Point au Fer, and Dutchman's Post until the 1790s, when they were given up under the Jay Treaty. In that treaty the British ended their occupation of their posts located south of the Canadian border. Some of the British and American agents retired before the Jay Treaty and others remained active in their support of the Indians.

SUMMARY

There is no doubt that British and American intelligence gathering and reporting played a role in the Western Department during the Revolutionary War period. Much of the reporting was of the strategic type and not the timely tactical reporting, but it still was highly useful to the military commanders. Another tactic employed by both sides was the use of propaganda. Several agents were adept in this method to sway Indian tribes to their side in the conflict.

For the major participants collecting and reporting intelligence in the Western Department, their main drive was the protection of the Indian tribes and their territories. It was not out of allegiance to either the British or the American sides in the conflict.

For many Americans, the Revolutionary War occurred only in the thirteen original colonies, making names such as Paul Revere, the Culper Ring, and Nathan Hale memorable. The Western Department is generally ignored—but it should not be. While no major battles took place in the department, its mission was relevant. First, by the actions of the American agents in the area, Washington could keep abreast of possible Indian threats along the western borders of the Colonies. He need not deploy his sparse troops to counter such a threat. And second, by understanding what the British were promising the Indians if they won the war, Washington could, by positive propaganda, keep the eastern Indians on the side of the Colonies.

REVEREND JOHANN GOTTLIEB ERNESTUS HECKEWELDER

LIKE SEVERAL OF HIS FELLOW MISSIONARIES, HECKEWELDER served to spread the Christian Gospel, but also served as the eyes and ears of the government. For while the Moravian sect was pacifist in their beliefs, they looked upon their missionaries as "warriors" in the fight of good against evil.

Reverend Heckewelder's first mission in 1762 was to the Iroquois in the state of Pennsylvania. On this mission, he was accompanied by Reverend Frederick Post, who had a long history of assisting the government as required. Reverend Post taught his student well and once the Revolutionary War broke out, Heckewelder was quick to shift his allegiance from the British to the new Colonial government. He lived among the Delaware Indians in an area heavily populated by the Seneca and Wyandot Indian tribes, both of which were hostile to the Colonists. He was in enemy territory. He continued his work of converting the Delaware Indians, known as the Christian Delaware, while supplying information to the command at Fort Pitt—the reports normally were sent every ten days. He became a spymaster using the friendly Christian Delaware Indians as his agents to collect the data and then once collected used them as couriers.

His spy organization continued to function effectively in the territory, but did catch the attention of Simon Girty, who with his two compatriots, Matthew Elliott and Alexander McKee, sensed that too much information was being supplied to the commander at Fort Pitt. It was thought to be coming from the Moravian settlements, particularly Salem, the Heckewelder settlement. And Girty was correct as shown from a written statement by Colonel Daniel Brodhead, commander of Fort Pitt in 1779:

> I do certify that I have been acquainted with the Reverend John Heckewelder
> since the year 1778. That he resided on or near the Muskingum River Missionary
> from the United Brethren to the Delawares & other tribes of Indians during
> my command in The Western Department and discovered a decided and
> firm attachment to the cause Of the United States giving me every possible
> information or intelligence of the enemy's parties approaching our Settlements
> or posts, by which many of them were defeated and destroyed.

Finally in September 1781, the Indian Chief Hopocan (known to the white man as Captain Pipe since Hopocan is the Indian word for tobacco pipe) on orders from Fort Detroit began a three-month drive to close down all of the Moravian settlements in the West and in the process arrested both Heckewelder and his associate David Zeisberger and took them to Fort Detroit where they were put on trial for treason. In a twist of fate, the evidence on which Heckewelder and Zeisberger were tried came from the Indian Chief Hopocan who now testified on their behalf. His plea was impassioned and the two men were found innocent, but not entirely because of Hopocan's plea. Major Arent DePeyser knew that Hopocan was speaking for the entire Six Nations, a confederation of Indian tribes essential to the British Western campaign. DePeyser could not afford to alienate them. Therefore, the two men were found innocent and remanded to the custody of Hopocan for the remainder of the war.

Heckewelder immediately went back into action. By 1782, he was once again supplying intelligence to Fort Pitt in preparation for Washington's planned offensive through Ohio against Niagara. But some of the intelligence he provided was incorrect, and in fact, one case caused a massacre. He informed Fort Pitt that hostile Indians, who had settled in the vacated Moravian villages, were currently assisting in the violent raids against the settlers. This led to an expedition from Fort Pitt against the village of Gnadenhutten (*Tents of Grace*). What Heckewelder did not know, or report, was that a Christian Moravian tribe had returned to that village to harvest the corn they left behind. The Williamson militia arrived in the village and the resulting massacre caused the death of eighty-eight Moravian Indians, all of whom were innocent victims. Soon after the massacre, Heckewelder was arrested again by Simon Girty, who immediately blamed him for the massacre. He was once again taken to Fort Detroit, where he was held until the end of the war. Only years later did he admit that his faulty intelligence may have led to the horrible massacre. It was a matter of events occurring faster than intelligence reporting.

Heckewelder's intelligence work was undoubtedly known to General Washington, who on March 8, 1782, included the following in his instructions to General William Irvine: "To keep yourself informed of the situation at Detroit and the strength of the Enemy at that place." Again on March 22, 1782, General Washington, missing the intelligence work of Heckewelder advised Irvine "to make yourself acquainted with the nearest and best route from Fort Pitt to Niagara," and knowing of Heckewelder's arrest, he further advised Irvine to use Indians and traders to obtain the information, cautioning him to be discrete about it. He wrote: "In order to deceive those of whom you inquire, appear to be very solicitous to gain information respecting the distances etc. to Detroit. The other matter you may converse upon if curiosity was your only inducement." The other matter probably refers to the status of Heckewelder in Detroit.

Once freed, Heckewelder returned to Ohio to live. In 1792, Secretary of War Henry Knox named him as associate ambassador to assist General Rufus Putnam in negotiating peace with the Indians in the Ohio territory. That treaty was signed in September 1792. He again served as an associate ambassador to the Indians in 1793. His knowledge of the Indian language and their customs proved to be a definite asset in the negotiations. The Indians felt he could be trusted to protect their interests, which he did.

Later, John (Johann) Heckewelder wrote of his experiences. His first book was *Thirty Thousand Miles with John Heckewelder* and the second *History, Manners, and Customs of the Indian Nations Who Once Inhabited Pennsylvania and the Neighboring States*. The experiences of Johann Heckewelder also served as a model for James Fennimore Cooper when he wrote the famous novel *The Spy* (1821).

Reverend Johann Gottlieb Ernestus Heckewelder's service to his new country, predominately as a spymaster, has received little attention over the years. A man totally untrained in the ways of intelligence who somehow managed to contribute significantly to the new country he loved.

CHAPTER

XIV

The Virginia Campaign

Purpose

WASHINGTON'S PLANNING AND EXECUTION OF HIS CAMPAIGN against both Clinton and Cornwallis in Yorktown, Virginia, shows how he became the general in charge. He successfully integrated all aspects of command to achieve his goal. His basic problem was that his main army was located in White Plains, New York, and the enemy encampment was in southern Virginia, 419 miles away. How could he move his army south without the enemy knowing of his movement? He did it by a coordinated effort of his command to include logistics, transportation, and intelligence. The ingenuity of the execution of his Virginia campaign also gives a clear picture of how he viewed the role of the various geographic commands. The appearance of the Main Army in any one of the departments was a separate operation completely independent of the mission of that department. In this particular case General Nathanael Greene continued as the commander of the Southern Department even though his commander, General Washington, was also operating in the area.

Background

Ever since Washington's army was defeated in the battle of New York in 1776 and forced to retreat to New Jersey (in the Middle Department), he held the retaking of New York City as one of his top priorities; however, he had neither the troops required nor a sufficient source of supplies to launch such an attack. But in the spring of 1780, Washington's luck changed dramatically. The arrival of Rochambeau's French troops along with the strong departmental organization provided Washington with time to plan a grand offensive. That spring, Washington moved the Continental Army back into the Westchester County area of New York (in the Highlands Department) in preparation for a possible attack on New York City. His decision was partially based on the fact that 5,500 French troops under the command of General Rochambeau arrived at Newport, Rhode Island on July 11, 1780. While theoretically in the command area of the Eastern Department, the French forces were actually under the direct command of General Washington and remained in Rhode Island awaiting his orders. Eventually factors led to a change of plans from a campaign against New York City to a campaign against Cornwallis at Yorktown in Virginia as shown by the following chronology:

OCTOBER 4, 1777

In anticipation of the Alliance treaty being signed between the French and the American Colonists on February 6, 1778, Washington informed Congress of his plans for the combined French/American forces to attack New York City. Washington then wrote to the French Admiral, Count d'Estaing, whose fleet was in the West Indies stating, "New York is the first object upon which every other is dependent its capture likely to be a severe blow to the British."

APRIL 1780

Washington reported intelligence to Congress that he had received regarding the movement of British troops to the south. He looked upon this as good news as there would be fewer troops to defend New York City.

JULY 12, 1780

The long-awaited French squadron arrived at Newport, Rhode Island, with 5,500 troops under the command of Lieutenant General Jean-Baptiste-Donatien Rochambeau. In initial discussions with Washington, Rochambeau declined Washington's proposal of a joint attack on New York City believing it to be a tactical error—the war was now in the south. While the French were in Rhode Island, located in the command area of the Eastern Department, they were under the direct command of General Washington, not the commanding general of the Eastern Department.

JULY 17, 1780

Almost a year before Yorktown, a British spy in Connecticut reported the following to General Clinton: "That General report is that an attack on New York & Long Island is designed as soon as the French troops arrive in conjunction with the Continental troops. Mr. Washington is to have the Chief Command over all."

SEPTEMBER 20-22, 1780

Washington and Rochambeau met for the first time in Hartford, Connecticut, halfway between the two armies. Their discussions centered on what should be the target for their joint operation. Washington at first preferred New York, while Rochambeau preferred a Virginia campaign.

APRIL 28, 1781

General Clinton was advised that the French troops were actually "on their march to the North (i.e. Hudson River) and it is said were to take part with Continental troops at White Plains."

MAY 10, 1781

General Rochambeau arrived in Newport to take command of French troops. He received word that a major French fleet under Admiral Francois de Grasse "would be available for operations in North America" beginning in July or August.

MAY 21, 1781

Washington and Rochambeau met for a second time at Westfield, Connecticut, to discuss plans for a joint operation. Washington still focused on New York City, while Rochambeau preferred a focus on the Chesapeake Bay area. Rochambeau, among others, stressed that New York City was a small area of land surrounded by water, which made it relatively easy for the British navy to protect it and inflict heavy losses on the Colonial forces. They agreed to have Rochambeau contact French Admiral de Grasse, whose fleet was approaching the French West Indies, to assist the joint French/American planned campaign on New York City. Unknown to Washington, Rochambeau wrote a note to de Grasse, telling him not to come to New York, but to the Chesapeake Bay area.

MAY 1781

A female agent from New York City advised Washington to not have the French fleet come to New York as the British were waiting to destroy it.

MAY 29, 1781

A British spy named Moody captured Washington's dispatches of May 28–29 concerning the French/American plans for a joint operation against New York City. The plan had "a tolerable prospect of expelling or obliging them to withdraw some of their forces from the southward." Having been duped by Washington before, Clinton did not initially believe the report, but then accepted it as valid. It was not until four months later that Clinton realized he had been outsmarted again.

JUNE 10, 1781

Rochambeau forwarded a de Grasse message confirming the arrival of the French fleet in the West Indies and its availability to assist Washington in his endeavors. The French troops began to move out of Rhode Island to join Washington's force in Westchester County. The commander of the Eastern Department was advised of the move, but the movement was controlled strictly by Washington. The British were well aware of the troop movement and of the final destination.

JUNE 17, 1781

Instructions went out to all Colonial agents in New York City. They were to "inquire immediately" into the British troop strengths, deployments of artillery, and shipping.

JUNE 1781

Washington began to have second thoughts about an assault on New York City. Unaware of Rochambeau's note to de Grasse, he decided to send an aide to personally discuss the issue with de Grasse. The man selected was Captain Allan McLane.

JUNE 25, 1781

General Clinton, in an effort to fortify New York City in case of an attack, ordered Cornwallis to send some of the British troops to New York City.

EARLY JULY 1781

Captain McLane reached de Grasse's flagship and provided him with a status report. Soon thereafter, Admiral de Grasse decided to sail his fleet to the Chesapeake Bay area, not to New York City.

JULY 4, 1781

French troops joined Washington in Westchester County, New York (in the Highlands Department). Washington and Rochambeau make a personal reconnaissance of the defenses around Manhattan.

JULY 16, 1781

French fleet still anchored in West Indies.

JULY 27, 1781

General Louis Duportail, a French engineer, gave Washington his assessment for the success of an attack on New York City. He stated that the allies couldn't be successful due to insufficient forces.

JULY 30, 1781

Washington sent a dispatch to Lafayette stating "may find ourselves incompetent to the siege of New York"—indicating that he might be changing his mind about an attack on New York City.

AUGUST 1, 1781

Washington appeared to have taken the French engineer's comments to heart as in his diary he stated that he was "turning his views more seriously to an operation in the south."

AUGUST 9, 1781

Sergeant Daniel Bissell is selected personally by General Washington to enter New York City and ascertain troop levels, status of supplies, and deployments of troops. His reports are to be for Washington's eyes only.

AUGUST 14, 1781

Rochambeau received a letter from de Grasse stating that his fleet would leave the West Indies with twenty-nine ships and three French regiments (3,200 men) and head for the Chesapeake Bay and that he would be available from August 14 to October 29, 1781. When Washington heard the news, he decided not to attack New York but to go south to

Yorktown. The quick turn-around by Washington indicates the ability of the man to accept not only a new tactical situation but to adjust his plans accordingly. It should be noted that Clinton was made aware of the pending arrival of the French fleet.

At the same time Washington communicated with Lafayette, ordering him to keep Cornwallis pinned down at Yorktown as he put together his plan to go south (while Lafayette was physically located in the Southern Department all of his orders came directly from Washington). The "Fox," as Clinton called Washington, true to his name was creating a master plan of deception.

AUGUST 17, 1781

Responding to Washington's order, Lafayette sent soldier Charles Morgan into the Cornwallis camp with a specific mission. He was to convince Cornwallis and his staff that Lafayette had sufficient boats to cross the York River and pursue him if he tried to relocate his army. The information was bogus, but Cornwallis was sufficiently convinced that he remained in Yorktown. Again Cornwallis was duped.

MID-AUGUST 1781

As Washington's deception plan began to unfold, Washington himself played a part in keeping Clinton fixed on an attack on New York City. He met with a New York resident, well-known to be a British spy, and asked him a lot of questions, regarding:

- Water supply in the area
- Landing beaches on Long Island
- Terrain around Middletown, New Jersey, just west of Sandy Hook
- Condition of Sandy Hook itself

Washington explained to the man that he had no reason for this question, but he was fond of knowing the situation of different parts of the country, as in the course of war he might be unexpectedly called into that part of the country. He asked the conversation between the two men be kept secret. General Clinton had the information that same evening.

AUGUST 17, 1781

A French general personally carried a letter to de Grasse stating that a combined French/American army would meet his fleet at the Chesapeake

Bay. Washington selected 1,200 troops of his army to join the 5,500 French soldiers for the march to Virginia.

AUGUST 18, 1781

Washington ordered General Heath, commanding general of the Northern Department, to remain in the New York area and to continue harassing the British. He was assigned 4,000 regulars and 2,500 militia.

AUGUST 18, 1781

A German Jager officer, Lieutenant Colonel Ludwig von Wurmb, learned through his own spies that the Americans had established depots of food and forage across New Jersey. He also learned that a French officer had sent his American mistress to Trenton, New Jersey. From these reports he concluded that General Washington and the French would march across New Jersey and move southward. No British action was taken as a result of this report. It is also interesting to note that the Hessians had their own intelligence system.

AUGUST 21, 1781

The March southward began. General Heath was instructed to secure the King's Ferry area and the surrounding area to prevent enemy spies from observing the troop movement. It took six days for the 5,500 French and 1,200 American troops to cross the Hudson and enter New Jersey (Middle Department). As part of the deception plan the American troops dragged landing crafts along suitable for crossing the isthmus between New Jersey and Staten Island.

AUGUST 22, 1781

British agent "Squib" reported, "It is said that they will go against New York, but Circumstances induce me to believe they will go to the Chesapeak. Yes for God's sake be prepared at all points."

AUGUST 27, 1781

Washington learned that a British fleet under Hood had arrived at New York City and soon departed accompanied by Admiral Graves.

AUGUST 28, 1781

Another deception took place. An American courier headed for the huge encampment at Chatham strayed too close to British lines and was captured with dispatches for the camp commanders. The dispatches were written in the hand of Washington. However, the dispatches contained all false information, stating that the Americans were coming to New York City—thereby confusing the British. (Clinton had been taken in so often by the Fox that he was wary of the information in the dispatches.)

AUGUST 28, 1781

The combined forces arrived at Chatham, New Jersey, where an elaborate large encampment site had been created as part of Washington's deception plan. Events moved quickly since only fourteen days earlier Washington shifted his planned attack from New York City to Yorktown. And by the 28th a large encampment had been built at Chatham. The ovens were built by the French and also by Christopher Ludwick, "The General's Baker" and sometime spy. Clinton knew of the building of the ovens since August 22nd.

That same day two British spies, George Hamilton and Barnabas McMahon, reported to Clinton that 3,000 French troops had arrived at Pompton, New Jersey, on August 26 and General Benjamin Lincoln with 1,700 troops had arrived at the Aquack Bridge. General Washington and his guards were also at Pompton.

At Goshen, New York, they had counted the artillery and ammunition wagons and their place in the American column. And finally they reported that the American column had boats with them to attack Staten Island.

Washington had French soldiers in their bright-colored uniforms walk along the northern New Jersey shore where they could be seen by the British observers.

AUGUST 30, 1781

The French fleet under Admiral de Grasse, composed of 29 ships, arrived in the Chesapeake Bay area. While Clinton was aware of the French fleet, he had no idea exactly how many ships were in itt.

AUGUST 30, 1781

Two unidentified British agents reported that the French 1st and 2nd Divisions were at Old Whippy, ten miles from Morristown, New Jersey. The destination of these troops was Chatham, New Jersey. In addition, they reported that General Lincoln and his troops were marching toward

Springfield, New Jersey. Their reports also provided a description of all the artillery moving with the army and the fact that both the French and the American troops had boats with them. Their reporting also included such details as the name of the house where Washington dined on his journey to Chatham, the Order of Battle for both the American and the French forces, as well as the stockpiling of forage at Trenton and Princeton, New Jersey.

That same day Washington's forces reached Princeton, New Jersey. Two columns of the French/American troops merged into one column and proceeded on September 1 to cross the Delaware River—the deception was now exposed.

SEPTEMBER 2, 1781

Clinton realized that Washington and his combined force were headed southward and he was trapped. He was still required to keep troops in New York City in case of an attack, but he did not have time to deploy troops to assist the British forces at Yorktown. Clinton had again been duped by the Fox. Clinton wrote in his diary the following: "By intelligence which I have just this day received would seem that Mr. Washington is moving an army southward with an appearance of haste and gives out that he expects the cooperation of a considerable French armament." That same day Washington's army passed through Philadelphia (Middle Department) which was duly reported to Clinton in New York.

SEPTEMBER 4, 1781

Reports warned Clinton that de Grasse was landing troops to reinforce Lafayette south of the James River, and that Washington's army was approaching the Elk River in Maryland.

SEPTEMBER 5, 1781

Nine vessels of the British fleet under the command of Admiral Thomas Graves arrived in the Chesapeake Bay area and engaged the French fleet. The British were soundly defeated and the French navy now had complete control of the Chesapeake Bay area.

One of the probable reasons for the British naval defeat was the intelligence of James Rivington, the Tory editor of the Royal Gazette in New York City and also an American spy. In 1781, he had acquired the Royal Navy signal book which he dutifully passed to the French Admiral de Grasse. After the war Washington was reported to have given Rivington a bag of gold for his service. (The French had brought gold with them to pay for such services.)

SEPTEMBER 6, 1781
Washington and his army arrived at Head of Elk, Maryland (Southern Department).

SEPTEMBER 8, 1791
The French fleet arrived at Head of Elk, Maryland.

SEPTEMBER 11, 1781
American spy J. Jag made three trips into New York City to evaluate the status there. These reports were forwarded to Washington. The reports indicated Clinton and his troops remained in New York.

SEPTEMBER 11, 1781
De Grasse established a blockade position at the mouth of the Chesapeake Bay. British Admiral Graves did not challenge the blockade.

SEPTEMBER 12, 1781
Washington met with de Grasse on his flagship. De Grasse informed him that he could remain in the area until the end of September.

SEPTEMBER 15, 1781
The battle of the Chesapeake. The French fleet decisively routed the British fleet. The French then blockaded the entrance to the Chesapeake Bay as well as the area around Yorktown thereby preventing the British from re-supplying Cornwallis.

SEPTEMBER 1781
Clinton, now aware that a French man-of-war had blocked all access to the British fleet, waivered about approaching the rear of Washington's army over land. He remained in New York under the watchful eye of several American spies.

SEPTEMBER 21, 1781
James Lovell, an American code breaker, sent Washington a copy of the British cipher system that would allow Washington to decipher British dispatches successfully.

SEPTEMBER 26, 1781
The combined French and American troops concentrated at Williamsburg, Virginia.

SEPTEMBER 28, 1781
Allied American/French forces took up siege positions.

SEPTEMBER/OCTOBER 1781
Due to the intelligence efforts of James Armistead, Private Charles Morgan, and the code-breaking efforts of James Lovell, Washington and Lafayette were kept informed of the status of Cornwallis' army.

OCTOBER 4, 1781
Washington sent the following letter to the code breaker, James Lovell: "I am much obliged by the Communications you have been pleased to make me in your Favr. of 21st ultra. My Secretary has taken a copy of the Cyphers, and by help of one of the Alphabets has been able to decypher one paragraph of a letter lately intercepted going from L[or]d Cornwallis to Sir H[enr]y Clinton."

EARLY OCTOBER 1781
An intercepted cipher letter from British Admiral Graves to Cornwallis was deciphered by James Lovell. The message stated that the British fleet was unable to re-supply the British forces until the French fleet ended their blockade of the port. Washington now knew that he had the British forces trapped.

OCTOBER 19, 1781
The British surrendered. Washington had once again proved himself to be a master of deception.

NOVEMBER 5, 1781
The French fleet, having accomplished their mission, departed for the French West Indies.

CONCLUSIONS

The battle of Yorktown was not a random confrontation of two armies. It was a carefully planned and well-executed maneuver employing all the talents of Washington with the assistance of Rochambeau. Once Rochambeau persuaded Washington in late July that their combined forces should be used against the British in the south and not against New York, the plan developed quickly. By the middle of August, the plan was put into operation.

By using all his assets at hand, Washington was able to develop a complicated plan in a very timely basis. He knew that his military structure of independent military departments could be relied on to handle their parts in the operation.

Washington also knew that he had valuable intelligence assets providing him with timely information in two areas of interest: first, the Culper Ring which kept track of British troops in New York; and second, the departments had their own intelligence agents providing local information as the troops moved through their areas. He also skillfully employed one of his favorite tactics—the art of deception. Using this technique he was able to get his troops to Head of Elk in Maryland before the British knew of his movements. By that time it was too late for the British to move their troops out of New York to counter the Continental Army.

But the real coup was the successful decryption of a British admiral's message stating he could not re-supply Cornwallis until the French navy lifted their blockade of the port. With this intelligence, Washington knew he had the British trapped.

It was a masterful success—a very complicated plan with many moving parts that all had to connect to make it a successful operation. And it was accomplished in just over a one-month period. It stands as an excellent example of the value of up-to-date information and the intelligent use of that information by a military leader.

The Fox had finally beaten the Hound, and the hunt was over.

CHAPTER

XV

Technology During the Revolutionary War

WHEN THE AMERICAN REVOLUTION BROKE OUT IN 1775, military weapon technology had advanced little since the invention of the musket. There were no secret weapons with which to surprise the enemy. Even the first rifle, a breech-loading flintlock, which was invented by a young British soldier, Patrick Ferguson, saw very limited use. The same was true in the area of medical services. Dr. Jenner had not as yet invented the smallpox vaccination which could have saved many civilian and military lives.

However, directly relating to espionage and spying activities there were two specific areas in which inventions came to light: one focused on the waterways, particularly the major ports as the British forces were very dependent on supply shipments from England; and the second focused on securing messages and their delivery to the designated person.

SMALLPOX INOCULATION

In 1774, smallpox arrived in America from Europe and caused an epidemic among the civilian population in the Colonies. An ancient system of inoculating with live vaccine which could, in fact, bring on the disease was the only option. Once the war began the smallpox epidemic quickly spread in the military forces. It was initially suspected as being caused by the British sending smallpox victims into towns and military encampments in hopes of spreading the disease. At first denied by the enemy, but eventually admitted to by the British—it was an early form of biological warfare. The epidemic spread so fast that Washington worried about the impact on his fighting force.

His concern was that infected soldiers had to be quarantined, thereby reducing the size of his small army. He initially resisted inoculating the soldiers since the live virus inoculation meant that inoculated soldiers had to be isolated for up to two weeks to ensure they did not contract the disease, potentially again reducing the size of his available army. Finally during the winter encampment at Morristown, New Jersey, Washington made the decision to have the entire army inoculated in time for the spring campaign. It proved to be a positive decision.

FRANKLIN'S BOAT

A man of many talents, Benjamin Franklin may have unwittingly developed an idea for a new boat in 1776 while onboard a ship heading to France. That boat was known as the "Jet" boat. It could have been a great asset to the couriers in the New York area as they ferried messages across Long Island Sound between Long Island and Connecticut. The design was a simple one: water would be drawn into the boat using a pump and then forced through a nozzle out the stern of the boat, thereby providing a propelling force.

There are no records to indicate that a working model of the boat was ever created, but Franklin does refer to it in a letter discussing boat designs. However, the potential for quick movement of communications across water was envisaged by Franklin.

DAVID BUSHNELL'S "THE TURTLE"

There was one marine invention that was used by the Americans against the British navy during the Revolutionary War. It was the invention of a young 33-year-old recent graduate of Yale University in Connecticut, David Bushnell. Bushnell wanted to design a method of attaching a mine to the hull of a ship and then detonating it with a timing device—so he designed the first successful submarine that came to be known as the "Turtle." It was a tortoise-shaped, iron-plated vessel capable of holding one person with enough oxygen for an hour-and-a-half mission. The torpedo was carried outside the vessel and could be released by an internal lever once attached to the target ship. Not only was the design of the

Turtle unique, but it also represented the first use of the screw propeller, which later replaced wind as the propellant for a ship.

The *Turtle* was made of oak with dimensions of five and a half feet wide and seven feet tall. Propulsion was by oars at a speed of about three miles an hour. Equipment onboard included a barometer to check depths, a pump, as well as a second set of oars to raise and lower the vessel. The barometer was a glass tube eighteen inches long with a one-inch diameter standing upright. The upper end was closed and the lower end screwed into a brass pipe through which sea water flowed into the tube. A cork rose in the tube when the *Turtle* submerged and dropped when it surfaced.

It was soon discovered that candles could not be used to illuminate the dials as they consumed too much of the oxygen in the *Turtle*. In an attempt to solve the problem, Bushnell's friend in Connecticut, Dr. Benjamin Gale, wrote to Congressman Silas Deane in Philadelphia asking him to contact Benjamin Franklin to find out if he knew of any kind of phosphorus that might give off a light while not consuming air. There is no record of a reply from Franklin; however, the problem was solved when Bushnell thought of using the phosphorescent weed called foxfire.

Bushnell also invented the mine device to be used with the *Turtle*. The device was egg-shaped and made from two pieces of solid oak hollowed out to hold 150 pounds of gunpowder. It was secured to the back of the *Turtle* with two iron rods that passed through two matching holes in the back of the *Turtle's* cockpit. Using a bolt arrangement the mine could be detached from inside the *Turtle*. It was attached to the tip of the auger by a rope. The auger would pierce the wooden hull of the ship and the mine detonated. For the trigger mechanism Bushnell developed a sturdy clock mechanism with an arm that snapped the trigger of a modified flintlock gun at a preset time thereby setting off the gunpowder.

The *Turtle* was constructed in Old Saybrook, Connecticut, in 1775. The *Turtle's* first sea trial was held in the Connecticut River and revealed several problems with the vessel, two of which were the failures of the ballast pump and internal lighting. Finally in 1776, the problems were corrected and the vessel was ready to be deployed. Initially the *Turtle* was designed to combat the British vessels in Boston Harbor; however, by the time it could be deployed the British had stopped their blockade of Boston Harbor and their ships had been relocated to Nova Scotia.

The next target chosen was the British fleet in the harbor of New York City. The *Turtle* was transported on a sloop in 1776, ready for action. Bushnell himself was not physically strong enough to handle the vessel so a volunteer was required. General Washington solicited his troops and Ezra Lee, a 45-year-old sergeant from Lyme, Connecticut, volunteered for the mission. After two months of training, he was ready for the first mission.

The first mission in New York Harbor was against the British ship *The Eagle*. Lee successfully maneuvered his vessel close to *The Eagle* where he submerged and went under the bottom of the British ship. After his first attempt to attach a torpedo to the hull of the ship was unsuccessful, he was forced to surface for air. He made a second attempt but again was unsuccessful. The mission was hampered by the fact that *The Eagle* had a metal plate along the hull making it impossible to attach a torpedo. Discovered by the British, Lee released a 250-pound time-operated torpedo. The explosion of the torpedo so startled the British navy, that they immediately raised their anchors and moved their ships to the safer waters of New York Bay.

Two subsequent missions of the *Turtle* were also unsuccessful due largely to the tides and currents of New York Harbor. The *Turtle* could not be maneuvered into position. Realizing the tricky currents of New York Harbor, Bushnell then decided to move the *Turtle* back to Connecticut where more favorable conditions existed. The Turtle was loaded onto a sloop with hope of bypassing the British into Long Island Sound and returning to Connecticut. However, the British did attack the sloop and it subsequently sank along with its precious cargo—the *Turtle*.

Today a model of Bushnell's *Turtle* can be seen on display in the Submarine Force Museum, Groton, Connecticut.

Later, Bushnell created underwater mines that could be used against the Royal navy. The mines were barrel-shaped and suspended just below the water line. The mines would explode if the springboard metal rods protruding from them made contact with an object in the water. (This is the same technology used by modern mines.) To make the mines more effective, he fastened two of the barrels with a rope between them. When the rope hit the hull of a ship, the mines would swing against the ship and explode.

Anxious to test his latest invention, in December 1777, Bushnell released twenty of the mines in the Delaware River close to Philadelphia which was under British control. The first mines killed two boys who got too curious about the barrels, and again in January 1778, barrels exploded near a barge killing four and wounding several others. The explosion caused by the barge alarmed Philadelphia. Citizens and soldiers alike didn't know if the city was under attack. Troops were assembled and cannons rolled out. Rumors flew that the barrels contained Rebel soldiers to retake Philadelphia. The British soldiers fired at the barrels as they floated by. This mine fiasco came to be known as the Battle of the Barrels.

For his efforts with the *Turtle*, Sergeant Ezra Lee was commissioned a lieutenant by General Washington. He served throughout the entire war, often in Washington's Secret Service and seeing combat in the battles of Trenton, Brandywine, and Monmouth. Both Bushnell and Lee were to become original members of the Society of the Cincinnati formed in May 1783.

David Bushnell served in the Continental Army for the duration of the war. He later went to France but returned to the United States settling in Georgia where he was the head of a school. He finally moved to Warrenton, Georgia, where he practiced medicine until his death in 1824.

Known as the father of the submarine, it is appropriate that a U.S. Navy submarine tender was commissioned and named the *David Bushnell* in 1915. The ship met its demise in the Pacific Ocean atomic bomb test at Bikini Atoll in 1946.

COMMUNICATION DECEPTIONS

The securing and delivery of communications was a serious problem for all parties in the Revolutionary War. There was only one way to deliver a message over distance and that was by courier, which was always a risky business. The sides were similar in that they both employed codes and ciphers (discussed in Codes and Ciphers chapter, page 231) but their techniques to ensure delivery varied.

Clinton's Silver Bullet

One example of British ingenuity centers on Sir Henry Clinton and his efforts to communicate with General Burgoyne in October 1777, prior to the surrender at Saratoga. Clinton's message was written on thin silk and then placed in a small silver bullet (about the size of a rifle bullet). The bullet consisted of two halves that were secured together. Silver was used as it was easy to swallow in cases of emergency and the silver would not corrode and cause injury.

With the message secured inside, the Clinton bullet was given to Lieutenant Daniel Taylor to carry to Burgoyne. Early en route, Lieutenant Taylor was captured and immediately swallowed the silver bullet in front of his captors. A doctor was called who provided "a strong emetic, calculated to work either way." It worked via the throat, but Lieutenant Taylor quickly swallowed it again. The second time it was vomited up and the message was revealed. Lieutenant Taylor was court-martialed and hanged on October 16, 1777. How many silver bullets actually existed is unknown as are any details regarding successful use of the bullet to avoid detection. The "Taylor Silver Bullet" and the Clinton letter are in the collection of the museum at Fort Ticonderoga, New York.

Invisible Ink

Invisible ink had been in use long before the Revolutionary War. But had somewhat fallen out of favor since its use had become commonplace. All of the earlier invisible inks became visible simply by placing the paper near a heat source. This fact was so well-known that British General Sir Henry Clinton would not use invisible ink but resorted instead to enciphering his messages. However, the Continental Army received a technological boost from a unique source—an American doctor and chemist, Dr. James Jay, who was living in London at the time. He was the brother of John Jay, the American revolutionist.

In 1775, Dr. Jay, who had been knighted by King George III in 1763, began to use his skills as a chemist to develop a new form of invisible ink for the use of the Continental Army in America. His goal was to develop an ink that would not appear through the heat process and thereby make it very secure. After many experiments Dr. Jay succeeded in his task and sent some of the fluids to his brother John in America.

The new ink which Dr. Jay called "sympathetic ink," consisted of one fluid for writing (known as an agent) and one fluid to bring the invisible text to light (known as the reagent). Dr. Jay's exact ingredients are unknown; however, there is one sympathetic ink of the period (similar to that of Dr. Jay) for which the ingredients are known. It consisted of gallic acid combined with acacia. Both of these ingredients were in rare supply at the time, making duplication of the ink difficult. Together they did produce the proper color when used with a reagent which could have been ferrate sulphate dissolved in distilled water. It was recommended that fresh white paper be used to write upon. To reveal the text, the paper was brushed with the reagent using a very fine hair brush—too heavy of an application would blur the letters.

General Washington disbursed the liquids sparingly. If he used the ink in a letter to a person known not to have the reagent he would send it separately from the letter but never together. One courier would carry the letter and the other the reagent liquid. The following excerpt from a letter from General Washington to Major Talmadge, a prime agent in New York, indicates his concern lest the knowledge of the ink be exposed:

July 25, 1779:
Sir

All the white ink I now have - indeed all that there is any prospect of getting soon - is sent in phial no. 1 by Col. Webb. The liquid in no.2 is the counterpart, and brings to light what is wrote by the first, by wetting the paper with a fine hair brush. These you will send to C. – Jr. As soon as possible, and I beg that no mention may ever be made of your having received such liquids from me, or any one else. In all cases and at all times, this prudence & circumspection is necessary; but it is indispensably so now.

Washington also provided a means whereby letters containing the sympathetic ink would be recognized. His instructions to the agents were:

He may write a familiar letter on domestic affairs, or on some little matter of business, to his friend at Setauket or elsewhere, interlining with the stain his secret intelligence, or writing it on the opposite blank side of the letter. But that his friend may know how to distinguish these from letters addressed solely to himself, he may always leave such as contain secret information without date or place (date it with the stain) or fold them up in a particular manner, which may be concerted between the parties. This last appears to be the best mark of the two. The first mentioned model, however, appears to me the one least liable to detection.

There are no indications that the British ever learned of the existence of the sympathetic ink during the course of the war. But later in the war the British had their own sympathetic ink as indicated by Major André's instructions to his agents. He instructed them to place an "F" for fire or an "A" for acid at the top of the letter so that the recipient would know to use heat or chemicals to produce the hidden text. Neither side was successful in uncovering the message if chemicals were used.

SUMMARY

Unlike the later wars, technology did not play a major role for either side in the Revolutionary War. The intelligence world remained rooted in the human spy.

The technology with the greatest impact on the Revolutionary War is not one of mechanical advances, such as the Bushnell submarine or the Franklin boat, but in fact is in the area of medicine—the inoculation for smallpox. The disease was a major cause of the loss of manpower for the Colonial army, which had no men to spare. Washington's decision to inoculate his entire army ensured him that his army would not be depleted by the dread disease.

In addition, George Washington was well aware of the threat of biological warfare. He had received several intelligence reports regarding the British sending smallpox victims into Rebel towns and military encampments to spread small-pox—which, in fact, they did. And today one of our national intelligence require-ments is the use of biological weapons—the scourge is still with us.

Both sides were concerned not only with the enciphering of communications but also the delivery systems used. General Clinton's silver bullet and couriers had been replaced within seventy years by the telegraph and later the radio. However, the transmittal of data remains a prime interest to both civilian and military users today.

From the engineering side the technical advances, while of interest from the historical aspects, had very little impact on the Revolutionary War. Franklin's design for a "jet boat" remained just a visionary idea. And for the Bushnell sub-marine, although it had potential, the British had received intelligence reports on the progress of the project and had taken actions to prevent such an attack. For example, British ships were refitted with metal keels to prevent mines from adhering to their wooden bottoms.

However, from these rudimentary efforts one can see several of the areas of interest to today's military. For example, from Bushnell's *Turtle* to a nuclear submarine, the emphasis for increased speed for boats, and the ever-constant threat of biological warfare. The seeds had been sown.

~~~

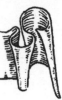

a person of interest
in american technology

AN UNKNOWN INNKEEPER

DAVID BUSHNELL, THE INVENTOR OF THE WORLD'S FIRST submarine, the *Turtle*, lived in Old Saybrook, Connecticut. Throughout the development of the *Turtle*, Bushnell corresponded with an old friend, Dr. Benjamin Gates, about the progress of his project. Dr. Gates lived in the town of Killingworth, Connecticut.

The owner of a tavern in Killingworth also served as the postmaster for the town. What the townfolks did not know was that he was a strong Loyalist and a member of a spy ring established by William Trone, the governor of New York. His job was to open suspicious mail, make copies for delivery to Governor Trone, and then send the mail on. The innkeeper was never suspected for his nefarious deeds and was successful in keeping the British advised of the status of the "underwater machine" being developed in Old Saybrook. On November 1, 1775, Governor Trone, based on the innkeeper's input, advised Vice Admiral Sullivan in Boston that Bushnell had completed his work on the "underwater machine" and intended to deploy it against the Royal navy in Boston Harbor. Initially the navy did not take the threat seriously, but later did alert all seamen to be on the lookout.

Thanks to an unknown innkeeper in Killingworth, Connecticut, the element of surprise was lost for the *Turtle*.

Codes and Ciphers

ALTHOUGH THE BRITISH HAD USED CODES AND CIPHERS FOR centuries, in early 1775 General Gage, the British commander in America, had no means of sending secret correspondence. He had no codes or ciphers, and no one on his staff knew how to create them. Aware of the rising tension in the Colonies and the need for protecting his communications, General Gage asked General Guy Carleton, the commanding general in Canada, to provide him with a method of enciphering messages, which was a single substitution system that may have also been used by the American traitor Dr. Benjamin Church in 1776.

When General Henry Clinton arrived and assumed command, he brought staff members who claimed to be conversant with ciphers, but were not sufficiently trained. For example, an enciphered message from an American general fell into Clinton's hands. He immediately sent it off to London to be deciphered and at the same time gave it to two of his officers. Clinton acted on their decipherment which resulted in disaster. The decipherment turned out to be incorrect.

Unlike the British Army, the Continental Army had codes and ciphers even before the conflict broke out. George Washington was well aware of the value of codes and ciphers, and even personally trained his staff members in how to use the various systems.

Both sides used basically the same types of systems because English was the common language. The systems had variants, but basically consisted of one of the following:

- Simple mono-alphabetic substitution
- Mono-alphabetic substitution with variants
- Transposition ciphers
- Dictionary ciphers
- Book ciphers
- Alphabetic one part codes

Following is an explanation of the various systems used by both sides.

SIMPLE AND MONO-ALPHABETIC SUBSTITUTION

British

When General Gage returned to America as the commander-in-chief of the British forces in 1774, he didn't have a working knowledge of codes or ciphers for secure communications. To alter the situation, he borrowed the cipher systems of the governor of Canada. The simple substitution used Latin, Greek, or other symbols for the individual letters of the English language. The system was given to the famous American traitor Dr. Benjamin Church to secure the communications between the two men. Dr. Church used this system for the famous letter that fell into the Colonial's hands and ultimately led to his arrest.

After General Howe replaced General Gage, he instituted a new cipher system similar to the previous simple substitution system, but included a new "wrinkle"—by prearrangement the substitution values would change after a designated line, i.e. line 10, line 14. A variant of this system was to change the cipher equivalents for each paragraph.

	A	B	C	D	E	F	G	H	I	J	K	L	M	N	O	P	Q	R	S	T	U	V	W	X		Y	Z
Line 1	19	9	17	13	16	7	12	8	14	15	26	4	18	21	3	2	10	11	5	24	20	1	25	23		22	6
Line 10	23	22	6	19	9	17	13	16	7	12	8	14	15	26	4	18	21	3	2	10	11	5	24	20		1	25
Line 14	5	24	29	1	25	23	22	6	19	9	17	13	16	7	12	8	14	15	26	4	18	21	3	2		10	11

This system was used by both sides throughout the war with little to no change. A historic letter between Clinton and Cornwallis was found under a rock near Little Egg Harbor and deciphered by Colonial James Lovell. The message read:

> *My Lord: Your Lordship may be assured that I am doing everything in my power to relieve you by a direct move, and I have reason to hope, from the assurances given me this day by Admiral Graves, that we may pas the bar by the 13th of October, if the winds permit, and no foreseen accident happens, this, however, is subject to disappointment wherefore if I hear from you, your wishes will of course direct me, and I shall persist in my idea of a direct move, even to the middle of November.*

General Washington sent the deciphered text to the admiral of the French fleet, Admiral de Grasse, who was stationed at the mouth of the Chesapeake Bay. With this information the French fleet was able to block supplies from Cornwallis, which resulted in his surrender.

Another less-used system consisted of the cipher values that were the reverse of the plain alphabet. For example, plain A equaled cipher Z in the first line and plain A equaled Y in the second line of the message. The cipher line changed with each subsequent line. When the cipher letter O equaled the plain A, the cipher line reverted to plain A equaling cipher Z. The simplicity of the system did not require the sender to carry incriminating documents on their person—a plus from the security aspect.

The Loyalists in the Colonies developed their own system to encipher their correspondence, not only for use among themselves and their friends abroad, but also to communicate to the British authorities as well.

A	✳	N	○
B	♯	O	⊏
C	✝	P	✕
D	±	Q	z
E	⌐	R	ʊ
F	⋋	S	ν
G	⊬	T	8
H	≠	U	E
I	/	V	9
J	∧	W	✕
K	∨	X	Δ
L	⊬⊦	Y	˅
M	4	Z	α
		&	=

LOYALIST CIPHER VALUE CHART

American

The American substitution system can best be shown from a chart developed by Washington written in his own hand:

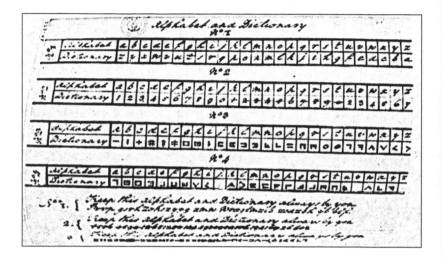

Four separate substitution systems are described in the chart. The first (shown as number 1) merely reverses the alphabet for the cipher. A becomes Z and Z becomes A. The second system uses the numbers 1 through 10 for the first 10 letters, then the numbers 1 through 10 with a line through the number for the second 10 letters, and then the numbers 2 through 7 for the six final letters. The third system is composed of 26 symbols representing the letters. The fourth system, which came to be known as the "pigpen cipher," is once again symbols, but not randomly chosen as those of the third system. The letters are placed in specialized matrices and extracted using only the cell representing the letter as the cipher. An example follows:

It is important to note how Washington instructed his staff to use the systems as shown in the writing below the ciphers. He explains very carefully that the cipher stream shouldn't have any spaces or breaks, so the word lengths within the message would be disguised, making it more difficult to decipher.

LOVELL CIPHER SYSTEM

Early in the war period, James Lovell, a member of the Committee for Foreign Affairs developed a cipher for the use of American representatives abroad. The Lovell cipher system is a modified substitution system. The system is based on the first two or three letters of a keyword. The letters are listed under the keyword letters. For example using "CRETE" as the keyword, C, R, and E would become the initial letters for the three cipher columns, and the alphabetic sequence follows, as shown at right:

Thus the first E in the message would be "02" for the E in column 1; the second E would be "14" for the E in column 2; the third E would be "01" for the E in column 3; the fourth E would revert to column one. The system was given to John Adams in November 1777, but Adams found it to be clumsy and awkward and did not use the system. He complained bitterly about it to his wife Abigail, since he had no easy way to secure his letters.

BEN FRANKLIN'S SUBSTITUTION

Charles Dumas, a German scholar living in the Netherlands, invented a new cipher system for his correspondence with the

	C	R	E
1	D	S	F
2	E	T	G
3	F	U	H
4	G	V	I
5	H	W	J
6	I	X	K
7	J	Y	L
8	K	Z	M
9	L	&	N
10	M	A	O
11	N	B	P
12	O	C	Q
13	P	D	R
14	Q	E	S
15	R	F	T
16	S	G	U
17	T	H	V
18	U	I	W
19	V	J	X
20	W	K	Y
21	X	L	Z
22	Y	M	&
23	Z	N	A
24	&	O	B
25	A	P	C
26	B	Q	D
27	C	R	E

Continental Congress and Benjamin Franklin. Dumas took a lengthy portion of French prose consisting of 682 letters, numbered each letter successively and used that as substitution for the plain text letter. By using French there were many possibilities for the letter "e," the most common letter in English.

CODES

Unlike ciphers, codes replace an entire word or phrase with another word or digital representation. Both parties hold identical code books, which contain the code values, normally in two parts: alphabetical for the plain language and another in either alphabetical or numerical order for the code word values. For example, New York = SHASTA and SHASTA= New York, or a digital form like "245."

Evidence doesn't reveal that the British ever had a complete code system during the American Revolution, but they did employ code groups for important people, places, and other sensitive words. The code words would be interspersed in a message, replacing the plain text word it represented. For example:

George Washington = James
Fort Pitt = Gomorrha
Congress = Synagogue

The system was developed by Major John André at the request of General Clinton.

In 1778, Major Benjamin Tallmadge formed a spy ring in New York City with the cover name of "Culper, Jr." In an effort to secure communications, Tallmadge developed a code system that was used for the duration of the war. Only three copies of the original codebook were created: one for Tallmadge, one for Robert Townsend disguised as Culper, Jr., and one for George Washington. The system consisted of code groups numbering from 1 to 710 with word values arranged in alphabetical order from Entick's Spelling Dictionary. There were an additional fifty-three code values from 710 to 763 for personages and locations. Examples of basic word values and specific word values are:

Code Group	Plain Text
350	lot
351	lord
352	light
355	lady
711	George Washington
712	General Clinton

Code group "355" is of special interest as there was a lady spy working in the Culper Ring who was only identified as "355" for "lady." The lady was captured by the British late in 1780, and kept as a prisoner on the prison ship *Jersey* where she ultimately died during childbirth. The true identify of code group "355" has never been established.

Another American original code system was developed and used by Isaac Barker in Rhode Island, which Barker referred to as a "Stake & Crutch & Stone Wall" system used to send intelligence across the Sakonnet River to an American Rebel encampment. Lieutenant Seth Chapman would receive the intelligence via a telescope at a camp in Little Compton across the river. No one is certain how the system worked, but some basic facts can be surmised. Presumably, the stake was a long stick and the crutch was the fork of a tree that stood halfway between two sections of the stone wall. Two gates were in the wall, which were either opened or closed to indicate which half of the wall contained the message. The position of the stake on the wall, seen with a spy glass, revealed a specific rock that had an encoded meaning. Barker speaks of about fifty to sixty different encoded meanings that could be sent depending on the rock's placement. If a message was too long, the code group merely told Lieutenant Chapman to cross the river and pick up the message at a designated spot. Hezekiah Barker was the pilot of such a boat and stated:

> *Entered the Continental Service of the United States at Little Compton & ... served on board of a Boat as Pilot with seven men & a Lieutenant's waiter, making a whale boats Crew. The duty of this boat Crew was to serve as a guard, and convey intelligence and information of the Conduct, doings and movements of the British who were then on Rhode Island, to Little Compton on the mainland, and this Declarant was the Pilot of said Boat.*

The system lasted for six months before the British realized that their actions and plans were being reported. At that point Barker went to a new system that he called his "Post Office," which was located on Great Rock. When Barker had a message to send, he would hide it at a specific spot on Great Rock and then open a window on Mr. Peleg Beckham's barn. The signal would alert Lieutenant Compton that he had a message at Great Rock. When the British evacuated from Aquidneck Island in October 1777, the system stopped. Isaac Barker's work was recognized by General Gates as being "highly significant" by keeping Gates alerted to the movement of the British troops.

Dictionary Codes

Both sides made use of what is called a dictionary or book code. To use a dictionary code both the sender and receiver of a message have the same dictionary in their possession. It produces both the cipher and plain text. Encoding is done by finding the plain text word in the dictionary and substituting the page number, column number, and line number of the word. For example, if the word appeared on page 32, column 1 and was the 22nd word, the coded word would become 32-1-22. Franklin further complicated the system by adding the number 7 to the value of the word placement in its column.

The book code system works similarly to the dictionary, except the coded value is created by the page number, line number, and number of the word within that line. For example, page 120, line 14, 5th word, would be 120-14-5. This system is more difficult to use, the word to be searched for had to be within the text of the book and finding it when compiling the message was time consuming at best.

Agents on both sides often created their own dictionaries to be used, or carried a book as agreed upon by the agents in the net. Some of the dictionaries used then are still in existence today.

Some code users in the American Revolution were:

BENEDICT ARNOLD AND JOHN ANDRÉ—Benedict Arnold used a dictionary code as well as his book code when communicating with John André prior to his defection to the British. Arnold and André used *Nathan Hailey's Dictionary* and the *Universal Etymological English Dictionary*, and for a book they used Volume 1 of *Blackstone's Commentaries on the Laws of England*. The preferred system was the dictionary due to its ease of use. Arnold and André encoded only the words they considered important. Upon arrival at the British headquarters, the messages would be decoded either by Jonathan Odell or Joseph Stansbury, both British Loyalists.

An example of Arnold's encoded correspondence follows from a letter written to André on July 12, 1780:

Encoded Text:
I 293.9.7 **to C t B**. 103.8.2 **the 7th** 152.9.17 **that, a F** 112.9.1 **and** 22.8.29 **were** 105.9.30 **to** 49.71 **in** 62.8.20 **with A** 163.8.19
(The bold words in the encoded message are plain language.)

Plain Text:
I wrote to Capt. B. on the 7th of June, that a fleet and army were expected to act in conjunction with the Army.

It should be noted that the second number is always an 8 or a 9. This is because Arnold and André decided to add the number 7 to the second number, hence 8 equals 1 and 9 equals 2.

THOMAS JEFFERSON—In 1764, twenty-year-old Virginian Thomas Jefferson employed a dictionary code to communicate with his close friend John Page. To secure his communications he used Thomas Shelton's *Tachygraphy, The Most Exact and Compendious Method of Sort and Swift Writing that Hath Ever Been Published*, published over a century earlier in London. Later in 1793, he again used a dictionary code to communicate with James Madison, this time using Thomas Nugent's *New Pocket Dictionary of the French Languages*. This later use of a dictionary code proved difficult for both correspondents to employ and it eventually fell into disuse.

JOHN JAY—When Colonist John Jay arrived in Spain as the Minister Plenipotentiary, he was well aware of the propensity of mail being intercepted and read. To avoid this practice Jay opted to use dictionary codes, individualizing the codes for specific users. When he corresponded with John Livingston, Jay used Abel Boyer's *French Dictionary, 13th Edition*. Jay instructed Livingston to add 7 to the numerical value of the placement of the word on the page. With Charles Thompson, Secretary of the Continental Congress, Jay used the same book, however, he had Thompson add 5 to the page number where the word was found. Jay used *Entick's Spelling Dictionary* with Robert Morris, a Philadelphia banker. He instructed Morris to number the pages in reverse order making the last page number first. Also using *Entick's*, Jay instructed William Bingham, the founder of the Bank of North America, to add 20 to the page number and 10 to the word placement.

ARTHUR LEE—Lee recommended a book code to be used between himself and the Committee on Foreign Correspondence. Though the books are not identified in his correspondence, his method to find out if his correspondent had the book or books is interesting. He states:

"You can write to Mrs. Lee on Tower Hill in a woman's hand. If you have both books say the children are well; if the first only, the eldest child is well, and if the second only, the youngest child is well. They will let this pass."

DELIVERING INTELLIGENCE
British

Sir Henry Clinton used two methods of secret writing during the Revolutionary War never discovered by the Colonials. Both of these methods did not require altering the plain text which remained in plain view.

The first method was called Clinton's mask. Most likely influenced by the Cardan Screen (or Grille), invented by the 16th-century cryptographer Girolamo Cardano, General Clinton is claimed to have used this invention throughout the Revolutionary War. Clinton's communication required two parts: a mask and letter. In order for the message to be read, the user would have to place the mask over a blank piece of paper and write the secret message within that area. Once the mask was removed, a false letter was written around the true letter. The tricky part of this method was to construct a clear letter around the true message. The beauty of the system was that if the letter fell into enemy hands there would be no chance of them deciphering the real text. Ideally the enemy, unaware of the imbedded letter, would read only the entire text which may, in fact, be total fabrication (as it was in the Clinton letter, as seen below).

In addition, the message was secure in that the screen or mask could be sent via one courier and the letter by another. The example below was written by General Clinton on August 10, 1777, and was addressed to General Burgoyne:

You will have heard, Dr Sir, I doubt not long before this can have reached you that Sir W Howe is gone from hence. The Rebels imagine that he is gone to the Eastward. By this time however he has filled Chesapeak bay with surprize and terror. Washington marched the greater part of the Rebels to Philadelphia in order to oppose Sir Wm's army. I hear he is now returned upon finding none of our troops landed but am not sure of this, great part of his troops are returned for certain. I am sure this countermarching must be ruin to them. I am left to command here, half of my force may, I am sure, defend everything here with much safety. I shall therefore send Sir W 4 or 5 Bat[tallio]ns. I have too small a force to invade the New England provinces; they are too weak to make any effectual efforts against me and you do not want any diversion in your favour. I can, therefore very well spare him 1500 men. I shall try some thing certainly towards the close of the year, not till then at any rate. It may be of use to inform you that report says all yields to you. I own to you that I think the business will quickly be over now. Sr W's move just at this time has been capital. Washingtons have been the worsthe could take in every respect. Sincerely give you much joy on your success and am with great Sincerity your HC.

The real message reads:

Sir W Howe is gone to the Chesapeak bay with the greatest part of the army. I hear he is landed but am not certain. I am left to command here with too small a force to make any effectual diversion in your favour, I shall try something at any rate. It may be of use to you, I own to you I think Sr W's move just at this time the worst he could take. Much joy on your success.

It is not known if the Colonist ever intercepted one of the letters, and there is no record of their ever deciphering the true contents of the letters.

General Clinton's second (and lesser-known) method was similar to the Cardan Screen (or mask) system. He would cut out areas of a piece of paper that when fitted over a pre-arranged reference the desired words of a message would appear in the cut out holes.

American—Continental Congress's Unique Use of Ciphers

The American systems described above were used either by the military or the diplomatic agents abroad. However, on February 8, 1782, an anomaly occurred when the Continental Congress issued a resolution in cipher, indicating the awareness of the Congress in maintaining secrecy for some actions. The text reads:

BY THE UNITED STATES IN CONGRESS ASSEMBLED
FEBY. 8ᵀᴴ 1782

The Secretary for Foreign Affairs having stated to Congress a verbal communication made to him by the Minister of France from letters lately received from the Comte de Vergennes which contain among other things an opinion that His Catholic Majesty will not have it in his power to advance any money to the United States and expressing, in strong terms his hope that the United States will not imagine that France should make up the sums they expected from Spain, after the assistance they have already derived from France.

Resolved, *That Congress are fully sensible of the frequent, friendly and generous interposition of his most Christian Majesty in their behalf and, are led from thence to hope a continuation of his assistance, since nothing has been wanting on their part so to apply the aid he generously affords as to distress the common enemy, and lead to the great object of their alliance, a safe and honourable peace.*

Resolved, *That Congress cannot, without injustice to themselves and their ally, withhold from him a knowledge of their present circumstances, or neglect to mention the ruinous consequences that may attend a refusal of those aids, which as well the friendly disposition, of his most Christian Majesty, as the success that hath attended his interposition in their behalf, gave them reason to hope would be continued till the states, which have lately been ravaged by the enemy, had so far recovered their commerce and agriculture as to be able more effectually to contribute to the general expense; and that his Majesty may be assured that their applications for this purpose shall not exceed what may be absolutely necessary for the support of the common cause.*

Resolved, *That the Secretary for Foreign Affairs consulting with the Superintendent of Finance, explain to the of the United States at the Court of Versailles the extensive advantages which have resulted from monies supplied by his most Christian Majesty to these United States, and the engagements which have been entered into with a view to render the next campaign decisive, the consequence of failing in those engagements, and the little prospect there is of fulfilling them without an additional loan or subsidy, for the year 1782, of at least twelve millions of livres tournois, in order that said minister may present a memorial on this subject to his most Christian Majesty, and at the same time lay before him the several resolutions lately passed by the United States Congress assembled, which evidence their unalterable resolution to make every exertion for a vigorous campaign which their present situation will allow.*

Resolved, *That the Minister Plenipotentiary of the United States of America at the Court of Versailles be and he is hereby instructed and empowered to borrow, on account of these United States, the sum of twelve millions of livres tournois, and enter into engagement on the part of the United States for the repayment of the same, together with the interest which is not to exceed the terms allowed or given on national security in Europe.*

> *Extract from the minutes*

> Signed
>
> *Chas. Thomson*
>
> *Secretary*

The French Minister usually relayed information from France to a closed session of the Congress in order to maintain secrecy and this resolution indicates the Congress' actions to maintain the secrecy. The resolution is one of only four enciphered resolutions ever passed by Congress.

CODE BREAKERS

Although there are no firm identifications of British code breakers within the British Army, the Americans did have a select few who contributed to the intelligence efforts. Probably the earliest Colonial code breakers were three amateurs who were key figures in the arrest of Dr. Benjamin Church for treason in 1775. They were Elbridge Gerry, the future fifth vice-president of the U.S., Colonel Elisha Porter, and Reverend Samuel West.

When General Washington received the enciphered letter that Dr. Church had written, Gerry, Porter, and West were recommended to him as potential code breakers, and each was given a copy of Church's letter. Within days General Washington received two decipherments of the Church letter, both independently deciphered. The text of the two decipherments agreed, verifying the authenticity of the decipherments.

When the American Revolution began in 1775, James Lovell was a teacher in his father's school in Boston. After the revolution broke out, he was selected as a member of the Continental Congress and soon became a member of the Committee of Foreign Affairs. Lovell's talent for codes and ciphers made him the central figure for cryptologic matters in the Continental Congress and Continental Army. Not only was he able to decipher the British substitution system, but he was also able to learn their dictionary codes. His successes were well known to General Washington with whom he had a steady correspondence. Lovell predominantly served as a code breaker, but he also developed various systems that aided American diplomats abroad.

SUMMARY

In the final analysis, just how important was code making and code breaking in the Revolutionary War? All systems used by either side are simple systems that today represent little challenge for the modern cryptanalyst. But there were no trained cryptanalysts—American or British—in the Colonies at that time. The Colonists fortunately had men such as James Lovell, who had a natural talent for creating codes and ciphers as well as deciphering them which proved to be highly effective during the war years.

The British Army was inadequately trained when it came to ciphers. Their army arrived in this country without any covert system for communications and without the ability to decipher enemy communications. Believing that the Colonials would not be sophisticated enough to make or break enciphered communications, it's not difficult to see why the war resulted in a British loss. One only has to look at the surrender of Lord Cornwallis and the events leading up to that event to see how wrong the British were.

The Colonials on the other hand, thanks to men like George Washington and James Lovell, made great use of the art of both code making and code breaking. The code-making efforts were limited as it was difficult to train people, especially diplomats abroad who had to learn the system by written text rather than hands-on training. It didn't help that most systems were too complicated to effectively learn simply from text. But in the case of code breaking, it's quite the opposite; American code breaking significantly affected the results of the American Revolution.

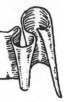

a person of interest
in codes and ciphers

JAMES LOVELL

JAMES LOVELL WAS BORN IN BOSTON ON OCTOBER 31, 1737. HIS education began at the Boston Latin School, where his father was the headmaster. In 1756, he studied at Harvard where he obtained a Bachelor's degree. In 1759, while teaching at the Latin School, he received a Master's degree. John Hancock and Samuel Adams were two of his students. In April 1775, the school was forced to close due to the siege of Boston.

Revolutionary activity in the Boston area impacted James and his father in distinctly different ways. The senior Lovell espoused the Loyalist philosophy while his son became a vocal supporter of the Revolution. Following the battle of Bunker Hill, James's activities were noticed by the British and he was arrested and sent to a prison in Halifax, Nova Scotia. One year later his father, a Loyalist refugee, arrived in Nova Scotia. It is not known if father and son reunited.

In November 1776, James Lovell was exchanged by the British and he returned to the Boston area. In 1777, he was elected as a delegate to the Continental Congress where he served until 1782. Lovell took his responsibilities so seriously that he did not return to Boston and his family from 1777 to 1782. Having an interest in codes and ciphers, he soon found himself as a member of the Committee of Foreign Correspondence as well as the Committee of Secret Correspondence. Lovell had always been fascinated by codes and ciphers, and quickly found himself devising codes and ciphers for the Colonial delegates abroad. Unfortunately, the delegates had great difficulty in using the Lovell codes and generally ignored them.

When the British forces arrived in America, they brought their own cipher system with them. They used the same system for the entire war period and for the majority of that time, James Lovell was able to read all of the British correspondence that fell into Patriot hands—a real coup for the Americans. However, since Lovell was in Philadelphia, the intercepted correspondence had to be sent to Philadelphia for Lovell to work his magic. The value of Lovell's work is shown in an October 1781 report of Elias Boudinot which stated the following:

Before the capture & at the first preparation for the siege before Count de Grasse arrived, General Clinton sent a row boat well manned with a confidential officer along the coast, to get into Yorktown with a letter to Lord Cornwallis, setting forth his situation and the impossibility of his relieving him with a fleet till a certain day and encouraging him to hold out till that period.

The boat was driven on shore somewhere near Egg Harbor & the crew taken & brought to Philadelphia. One of the men discovered in private, where they were bound & that the confidential letter had been hidden under a certain large stone on the shore by the officers. A person was sent to the Place & brought it to Congress.

It was in cipher and after some trouble it was discovered to be in three different ciphers. However, it was deciphered by a Mr. Lovell, a Member of Congress from Boston, after about two days' labor.

The original letter was carefully returned to the stone or some means used so that it finally got to Lord Cornwallis, but not before Count de Grasse's arrival and having the copy fairly translated. By this means W[ashington] was enabled to counteract all their intended measures.

Almost simultaneously, Lovell discovered that the British were using the same system for enciphering their correspondence throughout the Colonies. He advised General Washington of this fact and suggested that personnel in the various departments be trained to decipher the British correspondence in order to shorten the time between interception and decipherment. Ciphered messages would no longer have to come to Philadelphia to be read. Later, General Greene reported to Washington that they had successfully deciphered a British message on their own on a timely basis. They could react immediately if required. His sense of security and the necessity of timeliness can be seen in the following letter:

Sir:

It is not improbable that the Enemy have a plan of cyphering their letters which is pretty general among their Chiefs. If so, your Excellency, will perhaps reap some benefit from making your Secretary take a copy of the Keys and observations which I send to General Greene, through your care.

James Lovell

Instead of an intercepted message having to be sent to Philadelphia to be deciphered and the plain letter returned, it would then be possible for the Command to decipher the message in the field, thus saving critical time. And the system worked:

My Secretary has taken a copy of the Cyphers, and by help of one of the Alphabets has been able to decypher one paragraph of a letter lately intercepted going from Lord Cornwallis to Sir H'y Clinton.

Lovell was very aware of maintaining security as it pertained to his work as shown in the following letter to General Washington:

Philadelphia, Sept. 21, 1781
Sir:

You once sent some papers to Congress which no one about you could decipher. Should such be the case with some you have lately forwarded, I presume that the results of my pains, herein sent, will be useful to you. I took the papers out of Congress, and I do not think it necessary to let it be known here what my success has been in the attempt. For, it appears to me that the enemy make only such changes in their Cypher, when they meet with misfortunes, as makes difference of position only to the same Alphabet and therefore, if no talk of discovery is made by us here or by your Family, you may be in chance to draw benefit this Campaign from my last Night's Watching.

I am Sir with much respect.
Your Friend
James Lovell

A very astute observation, as relevant today as it was during the American Revolutionary War.

Lovell remained in Philadelphia until 1782, when he returned to his family after a six-year absence. Acting as a one-man National Security Agency, his work in the realm of codes and ciphers was well recognized by General Washington and General Greene, among others. His unique ability to decipher the encrypted British messages, when acquired, gave Washington a major tactical advantage, particularly at Yorktown.

EPILOGUE

―――・―――

WHEN THE NEWS OF CORNWALLIS'S SURRENDER AT YORKTOWN reached London in November 1781, the impact was immediate. The current government fell and King George III very quickly asked for negotiations to end the Revolutionary War.

However, until the Treaty of Paris was signed on September 3, 1783, America was still technically at war with the British. Hence, Washington insisted that the Continental Army be maintained—not a popular move for the citizens for financial reasons. This meant that the military departments were also maintained along with their intelligence activities. There were Loyalists who remained in America and Washington saw the importance of keeping an eye on their activities.

The Continental Army and the military departments were abolished shortly after the Treaty of Paris was signed. This move returned the responsibility of protecting the citizens of a state to the local militia. Realizing this, Washington wrote a treatise titled "Military of the Continent" to be distributed to all the governments of the Colonial states.

On the other hand, the committee system of governing, established by the first Continental Congress continued to exist until the U.S. Constitution went into effect on March 4, 1789. Soon thereafter President Washington created four Cabinet posts: Secretary of State, Secretary of the Treasury, Secretary of War, and Attorney General and the committee structure was abolished.

The abolishment of the Continental Army along with the ending of the committee system of governing in essence ended any intelligence activities in the new government. However, even though intelligence was no longer of interest to the government, many of the intelligence techniques employed by George Washington were not forgotten and can be seen still in use centuries later.

For example, his system now known as "stay behind teams" is a capability that most governments to this day practice and have contingency plans to deploy in case of occupation. In addition one only has to look at the deception plan employed by the Allies prior to D-Day to see that Washington's deception skills are still practiced. Washington's practice of having aide-de-camps on his staff focus on one specific geographic area in order to keep him informed of happenings in that area is still in effect in the Department of State. They are now called Country Desk Officers.

At the time of the Revolution, the population in general was not aware of the intelligence activities in support of the war. They tended to be alert only for British spies. Individuals on their own initiative came forward with information of use to the army. Washington did recruit agents from the military ranks and these agents paid a heavy price for their duty. Typically these individuals were asked to desert and go over to the British to gather information and then return. This meant that overtly their families and townspeople would think of them as deserters, bringing shame to all. After the war they tended to settle in the western area where their past would not haunt them. That is definitely not true today, where we have a professional service of agents and the art of espionage has become an honored profession.

Intelligence gathering in this country fell into disuse after the Revolutionary War. With an ocean on both sides it was thought that would protect them from enemies. It was not until the onset of the Civil War that code breaking and spying once again became part of the government structure. In February 1863, Colonel George Sharpe became the commanding officer of the Bureau of Military Information (BMI), the first U.S. Army unit formed specifically for intelligence work.

One of the reasons for the renewed interest in intelligence and spying was the invention of the Morse telegraph that was first displayed to Congress on May 1, 1844, just 45 years after the death of George Washington. Now the government elements had a way to transmit information quickly and securely. Washington would have been shocked to see how quickly data could now be moved. In 1850, cipher systems began to appear on the telegraph that caused a new interest in codes and ciphers and the breaking thereof.

However, after the end of the Civil War, the BMI was disbanded and once again, the government and the services were without intelligence support. They seemed to have forgotten Washington's warning about the need of good intelligence to a government. Finally in 1885, the U.S. entered into the international intelligence arena when the first U.S. military attachès were sent abroad. The move was in response to the fact that Europe was becoming the main producer of military armaments.

Post-Civil War code making and code breaking became the responsibility of the State Department where it remained until the post-World War I period. However, in 1929 when Secretary of State Stimson learned of what his Cipher Bureau was doing (the reading of other country's coded messages) he closed the Bureau saying "gentlemen do not read other gentlemen's mail." Intelligence had become a bad word, and that attitude remained well into World War II. Today, the U.S. government intelligence bureaucracy has become a large organized complex.

It is no longer manned by untrained volunteers who just want to help the cause. It is now a recognized and respected profession.

There is no doubt that George Washington, "The Fox," was a master craftsman in the world of intelligence. However, it is important to remember that many of the participants in the world of intelligence in support of the American Revolution, while untrained, made considerable contributions to the cause. The Fox was proud of what they did and would be amazed to see how intelligence gathering is done today.

SYNOPSIS

So can we conclude that the answer to the question "Did the intelligence activities of the Revolutionary War actually contribute to the winning of the war?" is a definite "yes"? The best method of verifying the point is to look at each military department for events where the impact of intelligence is readily apparent.

New England Department

APRIL 1775—The ride of Paul Revere to warn the inhabitants of Lexington and Concord. With his warning the citizens had time to relocate their supplies and prepare for the attack.
MARCH 1776—The deception efforts to fortify Dorchester Heights forced the retreat of the British from Boston.

Canadian Department

SEPTEMBER 1775—Not all the intelligence events proved beneficial to the Colonists. For example, the map Benedict Arnold used to move his troops toward Montreal was without distances or place names and probably bogus. It caused a critical delay of the arrival of his troops in the Montreal area.
JUNE 1776—General Sullivan wanted to move his troops against Trois Rivieres He hired guides to lead the way. The guides were actually British and they led his two columns into swamps and had them facing one another.

Benjamin Franklin's plan of using propaganda to convince the Canadians to join the Colonies in their war with England received little response from the Canadians.

New York Department

AUGUST 1776—Using deceptive tactics Washington withdrew his army from Long Island at night. The British were totally unaware of the move.
SEPTEMBER 1776—Nathan Hale was captured and hanged as an American spy. This event made Washington much more cautious in his recruitment of spies.

Middle Department

DECEMBER 1776—Using deception, Washington was able to move his army away from General Clinton's British Army and avoid contact.

DECEMBER 1776—Washington was informed of the Hessian tradition of celebrating Christmas in a heavy drinking manner. This information provided the impetus for the attack on the Hessian camp conducted on Christmas Day 1776. The attack was a major victory for Washington.

JANUARY 1777—Receipt by Washington of a drawn plan of the fortifications in the town of Princeton provided him with a much-needed victory.

Highlands Department

FEBRUARY 1777—The receipt of the British plan to enter New York from Canada with the goal of joining the troops from New York and thereby splitting the Colonies in two was received by Washington 15 days before it was received by King George III. This provided adequate time for Washington to prepare his defensive moves.

SEPTEMBER 1780—Washington's intelligence sources failed to uncover Benedict Arnold's plan to defect to the British. However with the capture of John Andrè the full extent of the plot was revealed.

SEPTEMBER 1780—A volunteer is sent into New York to kidnap Benedict Arnold and return him to the Colonists for trial. The mission failed.

Northern Department

SEPTEMBER 1777—An innkeeper in Saratoga Springs is recruited to enter the British camp to gather intelligence on an impending British attack. He succeeded in his mission and reported to General Gates what he had learned. With this intelligence Gates was able to position his forces appropriately and win the battle of Saratoga.

Eastern Department

SEPTEMBER 1778—Washington is kept abreast of efforts of the French to land troops at Newport, Rhode Island. The attempted landings failed and the troops returned to France.

SEPTEMBER 1778—General Clinton also is advised of the failed French attempt and the intelligence allows him to withdraw troops from Rhode Island for more important duties.

Western Department

FEBRUARY 1779—Friendly Indians meeting George Roger Clark's expedition informed him of routes to take to avoid the British patrols in the area. Clark is able to surprise the fort at Vincennes.

Southern Department

SEPTEMBER 1780—A young rider rode over 100 miles from southern Virginia to Tennessee alerting local militias to move to the area of King's Mountain to counter a British intrusion. The battle of King's Mountain was a draw but it did blunt British efforts to control the area.

JANUARY 1781—A female colonial spy passed on to Colonel Daniel Morgan intelligence regarding British forces in his pursuit. The intelligence allowed Morgan to take up an advantageous position and subsequently defeat the British in the battle of Cowpens.

SEPTEMBER 1781—An American code breaker deciphered a British cipher message from Admiral Graves stating he could not re-supply Cornwallis as long as the French blockade remained in place.

These examples are by no means the only events in which one can point to an intelligence impact on a battle or event. They do, however, serve to indicate how successful intelligence operations under George Washington did, in fact, impact on the Revolutionary War. The concept of decentralized intelligence operations rudimentary at the time, did serve its purpose and as all intelligence operations it had its failures as well as its successes.

IMAGE CREDITS

BOSTON PUBLIC LIBRARY
38

LIBRARY OF CONGRESS
65

NEW YORK PUBLIC LIBRARY, MAP DIVISION
80

NEW YORK STATE OFFICE OF PARKS, RECREATION AND HISTORIC PRESERVATION
77

PRIVATE COLLECTION
59, 69, 151, 167, 234

TENNESSEE STATE LIBRARY AND ARCHIVES
104

VIRGINIA HISTORICAL SOCIETY
138

WEST POINT MUSEUM COLLECTION, UNITED STATES MILITARY ACADEMY
25

WILLIAM L. CLEMENTS LIBRARY, UNIVERSITY OF MICHIGAN
173, 240

WINDSOR HISTORICAL SOCIETY, WINDSOR, CONNECTICUT
79

BIBLIOGRAPHY

Primary Source

George Rogers Clark papers, 1770–1781, edited by Alton J. James, Illinois State Historical Library, 1912

George Washington Presidential Papers, Series Microfilm, Library of Congress, Washington, D.C.

New York City Public Library, Map Division, New York, NY

Books

Allen, Thomas B., *George Washington, Spymaster*, National Geographic, Washington, D.C., 2004

Allman, C. B., *Lewis Wetzel, Indian Fighter: The Life and Times of a Frontier Hero*, The Devin-Adair Publishing Co., Old Greenwich, CT, 1961

Bakeless, John, *Turncoats, Traitors and Heroes, Espionage in the American Revolution*, Da Capo Press, Inc., New York, NY, 1998

Bakeless, Katherine & John, *Spies of the Revolution*, Scholastic Book Services, Lippincott, Philadelphia, PA, 1966

Brands, H.W., *The First American, The Life and Times of Benjamin Franklin*, Anchor Books, New York, NY, 2000

Burke, James, *American Connections: The Founding Fathers Networked*, Simon & Schuster Paperbacks, New York, NY, 2007

Burrows, Edwin G., *Forgotten Patriots: The Untold Story of American Prisoners During The Revolutionary War*, Basic Books, New York, NY, 2008

Carbone, Gerald M., *Nathaniel Greene, A Biography of the American Revolution*, Rhode Island Publications Society, Providence, RI, 2008

Caughey, John Walton, *McGillivray of the Creeks*, University South Carolina Press, Columbia, SC, 1939

Chartrand, Renè, *American Loyalist Troops 1775–84*, Osprey Publishing Ltd., New York, NY, 2008

Coleman, Kenneth, *American Revolution in Georgia 1763–1789*, University of Georgia Press, Athens, GA, 1958

Davis, Kenneth C., *America's Hidden History: Untold Tales of The First Pilgrims, Fighting Women, and Forgotten Founders Who Shaped A Nation*, Smithsonian Books, Washington, D.C., 2008

Ellis, Joseph J., *Founding Brothers, The Revolutionary Generation*, Knopf, New York, NY, 2001

_____, *His Excellency: George Washington*, Knopf, New York, NY, 2004

Ferris, Frederick L., *A History of Trenton 1679*, Princeton University Press, Princeton, NJ, 1929

Ferling, John E., *The First of Men: A Life of George Washington*, University of Tennessee, Knoxville, TN, 1988

_____, *Almost a Miracle, The American Victory in the War of Independence*, Oxford University Press, Oxford, UK, 2007

Fischer, David H., *Paul Revere's Ride,* Oxford University Press, Oxford, UK, 1994

Fitzpatrick, Alan, *Wilderness War on the Ohio*, Fort Henry Publications, Benwood, WV, 2003

Fleming, Thomas, *Liberty!: The American Revolution*, Viking Press, New York, NY, 1997

_____, *Washington's Secret War: The Hidden History of Valley Forge*, Smithsonian Books, Harper Collins, New York, NY, 2005

Flexner, James Thomas, *The Traitor and the Spy: Benedict Arnold and John André*, Syracuse University Press, Syracuse, NY, 1991

_____, *George Washington In The American Revolution*, Little, Brown, Boston, MA, 1968

Frantz, John B. & William Pencak (edited by), *Beyond Philadelphia: The American Revolution in the Pennsylvania Hinterland*, The Pennsylvania State University Press, University Park, PA 1998

French, Allen, *General Gage's Informers*, Scholar's Bookshelf, Cranbury, NJ, 1932

Garrison, Webb, *Great Stories of the American Revolution*, Rutledge Hill Press, Nashville, TN, 1990

Hallahan, William H., *The Day the American Revolution Began: 19 April 1775*, Harper Collins, New York, NY, 2000

_____., *The Day The Revolution Ended: 19 October 1781*, John Wiley & Sons, Inc., Hoboken, NJ, 2004

Hibbert, Christopher, *Redcoats and Rebels: The American Revolution Through British Eyes*, W.W. Norton & Co., New York, NY, 1990

Hogg, Ian V. & John H. Batchelor, *Armies of the American Revolution*, Prentice Hall Inc., Upper Saddle River, NJ, 1975

Kahn, David, *The Codebreakers*, Scribner, New York, NY, 1996

Ketchum, Richard M., *Victory at Yorktown: The Campaign That Won the Revolution*, Henry Holt & Co. LLC, New York, NY, 2004

Langguth, A. J., *Patriots: The Men Who Started the American Revolution*, Simon & Schuster, New York, NY, 1988

Lee, Henry (edited by Robert E. Lee), *The Revolutionary War Memoirs of General Henry Lee*, 1812, reprinted by Da Capo Press, Inc., New York, NY, 1998

Lefkowitz, Arthur S., *George Washington's Indispensable Men, The 32 Aides-de-Camp Who Helped Win American Independence*, Stackpole Books, Mechanicsburg, PA, 2003

Lossing, Benson J., *Pictorial Field-Book of the Revolution, Volume I and II*, Harper & Brothers, New York, NY, 1851

Lumpkin, Henry, *From Savannah to Yorktown, The American Revolution in the South*, University of South Carolina Press, Columbia, SC, 1981

McAllister, J. T., *Virginia Militia in the Revolutionary War*, McAllister Publishing Co., Hot Springs, VA, 1913

McCarthy, Pat, *The Thirteen Colonies From Founding To Revolution, American History*, Enslow Publishers, Inc., Berkeley Heights, NJ, 2004

McCullough, David, *1776*, Simon & Schuster, New York, NY, 2007

McDougall, Walter A., *Freedom Just Around the Corner: A New American History 1585–1828*, Harper Collins, New York, NY, 2004

Messick, Hank, *King's Mountain*, Little, Brown and Company, Boston, MA, 1976

Morrissey, Brendan, *Boston 1775: The Shot Heard Around The World*, Praeger Publishers, Westport, CT, 2004

Nagy, John A., *Rebellion in The Ranks, Mutinies of the American Revolution*, Westholme Publishing, LLC, Yardley, PA, 2008

Olmstead, Earl P., *David Zeisberger, A Life Among the Indians*, Kent State University Press, Kent, OH, 1997

O'Toole, G.J.A., *The Encyclopedia of American Intelligence and Espionage: From the Revolutionary War to The Present*, Facts on File, New York, NY, 1988

Pennypacker, Morton, *General Washington's Spies on Long Island and in New York*, Scholar's Bookshelf, Cranbury, NJ, 1926

Potts, James M., *French Covert Action in The American Revolution*, University of Nebraska Press, Inc., Lincoln, NE, 2005

Puls, Mark, *Henry Knox: Visionary General of the American Revolution*, McMillan, New York, NY, 2008

Raphael, Ray, *Founding Myths: Stories That Hide our Patriotic Past*, New Press, New York, NY, 2004

Rose, Alexander, *Washington's Spies, The Story of America's First Spy Ring*, Bantam Dell, New York, NY, 2006

Sanders, Jenning B., *Evolution of Executive Departments of The Continental Congress, 1774–1789*, University of North Carolina Press, Chapel Hill, NC, 1935

Sargent, Winthrop, *The Life and Career of Major John André, Adjutant-General of the British Army in America*, D. Appleton & Co., New York, NY, 1861

Savas, Theodore P. & J. David Dameron, *A Guide to the Battles of the American Revolution*, Savas Beatie LLC, New York, NY, 2006

Schecter, Barnet, *The Battle for New York: The City at the Heart of the American Revolution*, Walker Publishing Co. Inc., New York, NY, 2002

Stephenson, Michael, *Patriot Battles: How the War of Independence Was Fought*, Harper Collins, New York, NY, 2007

Swisher, James K., *The Revolutionary War in the Southern Back Country*, Pelican Publishing Co. Inc., Gretna, LA, 2008

Taylor, Alan, *The Divided Ground: Indians, Settlers, and the Northern Borderland of the American Revolution*, Knopf, New York, NY, 2006

Van Doren, Carl, *Secret History of the American Revolution*, Viking Press, New York, NY, 1941

Weber, Ralph E., *Masked Dispatches: Cryptograms and Cryptology, American History, 1775-1900*, National Security Agency, Center for Cryptologic History, Fort Meade, MD, 1993

Wilson, David K., *The Southern Strategy, Britain's Conquest of South Carolina and Georgia, 1775-1780*, University of South Carolina Press, Columbia, SC, 2005

Wright, Robert K. Jr., *The Continental Army*, Center of Military History, US Army, Washington, D.C., 1983

Wrixon, Fred B., *Codes, Ciphers and Other Cryptic and Clandestine Communications*, Black Dog and Leventhal, New York, NY, 1998

Journals

The Quarterly Journal of Military History, Autumn 1995, Volume 8, Number 1, American Historical Publications, 1995

Newport History, Journal of the Newport Historical Society, "A Great Landscape in Miniature: Great Rock, Paradise Farm and The Barkers of Middletown," James L. Yarnall and Natalie N. Nicholson, pp. 97–115, Volume 70, Part 4, Number 245, 2000

Bulletin of the New York Public Library, "The Use Of Invisible Ink For Secret Writing During the American Revolution," Volume 35, May 1935

Signals Security Agency, *Secret Writing in the Revolutionary War*, Chief Signals Officer, 21 Jul 1945

Magazines

American History, "The Badge of Merit," James Wensyel, pp. 26–46, May 1982

American History, "Founding Fury, The Maelstrom Unleashed by the Spirit of 1776," pp. 25–31, October 2007

Military History, "Negroes in Revolutionary War," John Swan, pp. 37–41, Volume 13, Number 1, November 2000

Military History, "Spymaster in Chief," Edward G. Lengel, pp. 26–34, June/July 2009

Smithsonian Magazine, "Myths About the American Revolution," John Ferling, pp. 48–55, Jan 2002